KU-749-794

The Economist

POCKET WORLD IN FIGURES

The
Economist

=== POCKET ===
WORLD IN
FIGURES

THE ECONOMIST IN ASSOCIATION WITH
PROFILE BOOKS LTD

Published by Profile Books Ltd,
58A Hatton Garden, London EC1N 8LX

First published by The Economist Books Ltd 1991

This edition published by Profile Books in association with
The Economist, 2000

Material researched and compiled by
Robert Eves, Andrew Gilbert, Conrad Heine, Carol Howard,
Stella Jones, David McKelvey, Henrietta Nelder, Nic Wiseman,
Simon Wright

Typeset in Univers by MacGuru
info@macguru.org.uk

Printed in Italy by
LEGO S.p.a. – Vicenza – Italy

A CIP catalogue record for this book is available
from the British Library

ISBN 1 86197 146 X

Contents

CONTENTS

CONTENTS

Notes

This 2001 edition of the annual *Economist Pocket World in Figures* has been expanded to include sections on space and defence, and more country profiles. The country profiles now cover some 64 major countries, including Slovenia and Vietnam. The world rankings consider 171: all those with a population of at least 1m or a GDP of at least $1bn; they are listed on page 228. The extent and quality of the statistics available varies from country to country. Every care has been taken to specify the broad definitions on which the data are based and to indicate cases where data quality or technical difficulties are such that interpretation of the figures is likely to be seriously affected. Nevertheless, figures from individual countries will often differ from standard international statistical definitions.

In ex-Yugoslavia, Serbia and Montenegro now constitute the Federal Republic of Yugoslavia, and Macedonia is officially known as the Former Yugoslav Republic of Macedonia. Data for Cyprus normally refer to Greek Cyprus only. Data for China do not include Hong Kong. For other countries such as Morocco they exclude disputed areas. Congo refers to the Democratic Republic of Congo, formerly known as Zaire. Congo-Brazzaville refers to the other Congo. Data for the EU refer to its 15 members following the enlargement of the Union on January 1 1995. The euro area of 11 EU members came into being on January 1 1999.

Statistical basis

The all-important factor in a book of this kind is to be able to make reliable comparisons between countries. Although this is never quite possible for the reasons stated above, the best route, which this book takes, is to compare data for the same year or period and to use actual, not estimated, figures wherever possible. Where a country's data is excessively out of date, it is excluded. The research for this edition of *The Economist Pocket World in Figures* was carried out in 2000 using the latest available sources that present data on an internationally comparable basis. Data, therefore, unless otherwise indicated, refer to the year ending December 31 1998.

In the country profiles, life expectancy, crude birth, death and fertility rates are based on 1995–2000 averages; human development indices are for 1997 and energy data refer to 1996; household data are latest available and marriage and divorce data refer to the latest year with available figures, 1990–98. In a number of cases, data are shown for the latest year within a range.

Other definitions
Data shown on country profiles may not always be consistent with those shown on the world rankings because the definitions or years covered can differ. Data may also differ between two different rankings.

Most countries' national accounts are now compiled on a GDP basis so, for simplicity, the term GDP has been used interchangeably with GNP. GDP figures in this book come from the World Bank, mainly based on the World Bank's Atlas method.

Statistics for principal exports and principal imports are normally based on customs statistics. These are generally compiled on different definitions to the visible exports and imports figures shown in the balance of payments section.

Definitions of the statistics shown are given on the relevant page or in the glossary at the end of the book. Figures may not add exactly to totals, or percentages to 100, because of rounding or, in the case of GDP, statistical adjustment. Sums of money have generally been converted to US dollars at the official exchange rate ruling at the time to which the figures refer.

Energy consumption data are not always reliable, particularly for the major oil producing countries. Consumption per head data may therefore be higher than in reality. Energy exports can exceed production and imports can exceed consumption if transit operations distort trade data or oil is imported for refining and re-exported.

Abbreviations

bn	billion (one thousand million)	GNP	Gross national product
CIS	Commonwealth of Independent States	GRT	Gross tonnage
		m	million
EU	European Union	PPP	Purchasing power parity
kg	kilogram	trn	trillion (one thousand billion)
km	kilometre	...	not available
GDP	Gross domestic product		

Part I
WORLD RANKINGS

Countries: *natural facts*

Countries: *the largest[a]*
'000 sq km

1	Russia	17,075		31	Nigeria	924
2	Canada	9,971		32	Venezuela	912
3	China	9,561		33	Namibia	824
4	United States	9,373		34	Pakistan	804
5	Brazil	8,512		35	Mozambique	799
6	Australia	7,682		36	Turkey	779
7	India	3,287		37	Chile	757
8	Argentina	2,767		38	Zambia	753
9	Kazakhstan	2,717		39	Myanmar	677
10	Sudan	2,506		40	Afghanistan	652
11	Algeria	2,382		41	Somalia	638
12	Congo	2,345		42	Central African Rep	622
13	Saudi Arabia	2,200		43	Ukraine	604
14	Mexico	1,973		44	Madagascar	587
15	Indonesia[b]	1,904		45	Kenya	584
16	Libya	1,760		46	Botswana	581
17	Iran	1,648		47	France	544
18	Mongolia	1,565		48	Yemen	528
19	Peru	1,285		49	Thailand	513
20	Chad	1,284		50	Spain	505
21	Niger	1,267		51	Turkmenistan	488
22	Angola	1,247		52	Cameroon	475
23	Mali	1,240		53	Papua New Guinea	463
24	South Africa	1,226		54	Sweden	450
25	Colombia	1,142		55	Morocco	447
26	Ethiopia	1,134			Uzbekistan	447
27	Bolivia	1,099		57	Iraq	438
28	Mauritania	1,031		58	Paraguay	407
29	Egypt	1,000		59	Zimbabwe	391
30	Tanzania	945		60	Japan	378

Mountains: *the highest[c]*

	Name	Location	Height (m)
1	Everest	Nepal-China	8,848
2	K2 (Godwin Austen)	Pakistan	8,611
3	Kangchenjunga	Nepal-Sikkim	8,586
4	Lhotse	Nepal-China	8,516
5	Makalu	Nepal-China	8,463
6	Cho Oyu	Nepal-China	8,201
7	Dhaulagiri	Nepal	8,167
8	Manaslu	Nepal	8,163
9	Nanga Parbat	Pakistan	8,125
10	Annapurna I	Nepal	8,091
11	Gasherbrum I	Pakistan-China	8,068
12	Broad Peak	Pakistan-China	8,047
13	Xixabangma (Gosainthan)	China	8,046
14	Gasherbrum II	Pakistan-China	8,035

a Includes freshwater.
b Excludes East Timor, 14,874 sq km.
c Includes separate peaks which are part of the same massif.

Rivers: *the longest*

	Name	Location	Length (km)
1	Nile	Africa	6,695
2	Amazon	South America	6,516
3	Yangtze	Asia	6,380
4	Mississippi-Missouri	North America	6,019
5	Ob'-Irtysh	Asia	5,570
6	Yenisey-Angara	Asia	5,550
7	Hwang He (Yellow)	Asia	5,464
8	Congo	Africa	4,667
9	Parana	South America	4,500
10	Mekong	Asia	4,425
11	Amur	Asia	4,416
12	Lena	Asia	4,400
13	Mackenzie	North America	4,250
14	Niger	Africa	4,030
15	Missouri	North America	3,969
16	Mississippi	North America	3,779
17	Murray-Darling	Australia	3,750
18	Volga	Europe	3,688
19	Kolyma	Asia	3,513
20	Madeira	South America	3,200
21	Yukon	North America	3,185
22	Indus	Asia	3,180
23	Syrdar'ya	Asia	3,078
24	Salween	Asia	3,060
25	Sao Francisco	South America	2,900
26	Rio Grande	North America	2,870
27	Danube	Europe	2,850
28	Brahmaputra	Asia	2,840
29	Euphrates	Asia	2,815
30	Para-Tocantis	South America	2,750

Waterfalls: *the highest*

	Name	Location	Height (m)
1	Angel	Venezuela	979
2	Tugela	South Africa	948
3	Utigard	Norway	800
4	Mongefossen	Norway	774
5	Yosemite	California, USA	739
6	Mardalsfossen	Norway	656
7	Tyssestrengane	Norway	646
8	Cuquenan	Venezuela	609
9	Ribbon	California, USA	491
10	Della	Canada	440

Notes: Estimates of the lengths of different rivers vary widely according to the rules adopted concerning the selection of tributaries to be followed, the path to take through a delta, where different hydrological systems begin and end etc. The Nile is normally taken as the world's longest river but some estimates put the Amazon as longer if a southerly path through its delta leading to the River Para is followed. Likewise, difficulties in waterfall measurements exist depending on which breaks in the fall are counted. The more famous waterfalls, Niagara and Victoria, are surprisingly small, 50m and 108m respectively; their notoriety evolving from their width and accessibility.

Population: *explosions revealed*

Largest populations, 1998
Millions

1	China	1,255.7	31	Argentina	36.1
2	India	982.2	32	Tanzania	32.1
3	United States	274.0	33	Canada	30.6
4	Indonesia	206.3	34	Algeria	30.1
5	Brazil	165.9	35	Kenya	29.0
6	Pakistan	148.2	36	Sudan	28.3
7	Russia	147.4	37	Morocco	27.4
8	Japan	126.3	38	Peru	24.8
9	Bangladesh	124.8	39	Uzbekistan	23.6
10	Nigeria	106.4	40	North Korea	23.3
11	Mexico	95.8	41	Venezuela	23.2
12	Germany	82.1	42	Nepal	22.8
13	Vietnam	77.6	43	Romania	22.5
14	Philippines	72.9	44	Taiwan	21.9
15	Egypt	66.0	45	Iraq	21.8
16	Iran	65.8	46	Afghanistan	21.4
17	Turkey	64.5		Malaysia	21.4
18	Thailand	60.3	48	Uganda	20.6
19	Ethiopia	59.6	49	Saudi Arabia	20.2
20	France	58.7	50	Ghana	19.2
21	United Kingdom	58.6	51	Mozambique	18.9
22	Italy	57.4	52	Australia	18.5
23	Ukraine	50.9		Sri Lanka	18.5
24	Congo	49.1	54	Yemen	16.9
25	South Korea	46.1	55	Kazakhstan	16.3
26	Myanmar	44.5	56	Netherlands	15.7
27	Colombia	40.8	57	Syria	15.3
28	Spain	39.6	58	Madagascar	15.1
29	South Africa	39.4	59	Chile	14.8
30	Poland	38.7	60	Cameroon	14.3

Largest populations, 2015
Millions

1	China	1,417.7	16	Iran	83.1
2	India	1,211.7	17	Germany	81.5
3	United States	307.7	18	Congo	80.3
4	Indonesia	250.4		Turkey	80.3
5	Pakistan	222.6	20	Thailand	68.9
6	Brazil	200.7	21	France	61.1
7	Bangladesh	161.5	22	United Kingdom	59.6
8	Nigeria	153.3	23	Italy	54.4
9	Russia	142.9	24	Myanmar	53.5
10	Japan	126.1	25	Colombia	53.2
11	Mexico	119.2	26	South Korea	51.1
12	Philippines	96.7	27	Ukraine	47.9
13	Vietnam	96.6	28	Tanzania	47.2
14	Ethiopia	90.9	29	Argentina	43.5
15	Egypt	85.2	30	South Africa	43.4

Fastest growing populations, 1990–2000
Average annual growth, %

1	West Bank and Gaza	5.56	11	Madagascar	3.16
2	Yemen	4.47	12	Saudi Arabia	2.98
3	Afghanistan	4.32	13	Swaziland	2.92
4	Jordan	3.67	14	Ghana	2.90
5	Oman	3.54	15	Israel	2.88
6	Gambia, The	3.50	16	Chad	2.87
7	Angola	3.33		Eritrea	2.87
8	Niger	3.28	18	Honduras	2.85
9	Mozambique	3.27	19	Congo-Brazzaville	2.83
10	Congo	3.24	20	Nicaragua	2.82

Slowest growing populations, 1990–2000
Average annual growth, %

1	Latvia	-1.30	11	Ukraine	-0.28
2	Estonia	-1.18	12	Lithuania	-0.18
3	Georgia	-0.95	13	Croatia	-0.10
4	Kuwait	-0.84		Russia	-0.10
5	Bosnia	-0.81	15	Armenia	-0.07
6	Bulgaria	-0.59	16	Czech Republic	-0.06
7	Albania	-0.55	17	Belarus	-0.03
8	Romania	-0.39	18	Portugal	0.01
9	Hungary	-0.33	19	Moldova	0.04
10	Kazakhstan	-0.32	20	Italy	0.05

Fastest growing populations, 2000–2015
Average annual growth, %

1	West Bank and Gaza	3.82	11	Burkina Faso	2.78
2	Yemen	3.27	12	Saudi Arabia	2.75
3	Liberia	3.25	13	Congo-Brazzaville	2.70
4	Afghanistan	3.21	14	Jordan	2.64
	Somalia	3.21	15	Mali	2.63
6	Oman	3.19	16	Ghana	2.59
7	Uganda	3.06		Iraq	2.59
8	Congo	2.94	18	Benin	2.55
	Niger	2.94		Bhutan	2.55
10	Angola	2.83		Madagascar	2.55

Slowest growing populations, 2000–2015
Average annual growth, %

1	Estonia	-0.91	11	Czech Republic	-0.21
2	Latvia	-0.88	12	Spain	-0.20
3	Bulgaria	-0.59	13	Russia	-0.19
4	Hungary	-0.43	14	Croatia	-0.18
5	Romania	-0.39	15	Greece	-0.17
6	Ukraine	-0.35	16	Portugal	-0.15
7	Italy	-0.34	17	Belgium	-0.05
8	Lithuania	-0.28		Germany	-0.05
9	Belarus	-0.26	19	Japan	-0.03
10	Slovenia	-0.23	20	Denmark	0.02

Population density

Highest population density
Population per sq km, 2000

1	Macau	26,301	21	Haiti	296
2	Hong Kong	6,628	22	Israel	295
3	Singapore	5,771	23	Rwanda	294
4	West Bank and Gaza	2,964	24	Sri Lanka	287
5	Malta	1,230	25	Réunion	279
6	Bermuda	1,128	26	Netherlands Antilles	271
7	Bahrain	910	27	Guadeloupe	267
8	Bangladesh	897	28	Philippines	253
9	Barbados	629	29	Trinidad & Tobago	252
10	Taiwan	607	30	Burundi	241
11	Mauritius	568		United Kingdom	241
12	South Korea	473		Vietnam	241
13	Puerto Rico	435	33	Jamaica	235
14	Netherlands	386	34	Germany	230
15	Martinique	359	35	North Korea	199
16	Japan	335	36	Pakistan	197
17	Belgium	333	37	Italy	190
18	Lebanon	316	38	Switzerland	179
19	India	308	39	Dominican Republic	174
20	El Salvador	298	40	Nepal	170

Lowest population density
Population per sq km, 2000

1	Australia	2		Papua New Guinea	10
	Mongolia	2		Saudi Arabia	10
	Namibia	2	23	Oman	12
4	Botswana	3		Sudan	12
	Canada	3		Zambia	12
	Iceland	3	26	Algeria	13
	Libya	3		Argentina	13
	Mauritania	3	28	New Zealand	14
	Suriname	3		Norway	14
10	Gabon	5		Paraguay	14
11	Central African Rep	6	31	Finland	15
	Chad	6	32	Somalia	16
	Kazakhstan	6	33	Uruguay	19
14	Bolivia	8	34	Brazil	20
	Niger	8		Chile	20
16	Congo-Brazzaville	9		Peru	20
	Mali	9		Sweden	20
	Russia	9	38	Bahamas	22
	Turkmenistan	9		Congo	22
20	Angola	10	40	Laos	23

Note: Estimates of population density refer to the total land area of a country. In countries such as Japan and Canada, where much of the land area is virtually uninhabitable, the effective population densities of the habitable areas are much greater than the figures suggest.

City living

Highest quality of life index[a]

New York=100, November 1999

1	Vancouver	106.16
2	Zurich	106.03
3	Vienna	105.97
4	Bern	105.76
5	Sydney	105.73
6	Geneva	105.51
7	Auckland	105.41
8	Copenhagen	105.37
9	Helsinki	104.58
10	Amsterdam	104.44
11	Frankfurt	104.13
12	Munich	104.10
13	Melbourne	103.99
14	Honolulu	103.78
15	Dusseldorf	103.65

Lowest quality of life index[a]

New York=100, November 1999

1	Brazzaville	23.01
2	Pointe Noire	30.36
3	Khartoum	32.97
4	Baghdad	33.13
5	Bangui	33.64
6	Luanda	36.35
7	Ougadougou	36.65
8	Kinshasa	36.80
9	Bamako	36.96
10	Niamey	37.82
11	Addis-Ababa	38.57
12	Belgrade	38.87
13	Port Harcourt	39.63
14	Nouakchott	39.75
15	Sanaa	40.10

Biggest cities[b]

Population m, 2000

1	Tokyo	26.4		16	Metro Manila	10.9
2	Mexico city	18.1		17	Beijing	10.8
	Mumbai (Bombay)	18.1		18	Cairo	10.6
4	Sao Paulo	17.8			Rio de Janeiro	10.6
5	New York	16.6		20	Seoul	9.9
6	Lagos	13.4		21	Paris	9.6
7	Los Angeles	13.1		22	Istanbul	9.5
8	Calcutta	12.9		23	Moscow	9.3
	Shanghai	12.9		24	Tianjin	9.2
10	Buenos Aires	12.6		25	London	7.6
11	Dhaka	12.3		26	Lima	7.4
12	Karachi	11.8		27	Bangkok	7.3
13	Delhi	11.7		28	Tehran	7.2
14	Jakarta	11.0		29	Chicago	7.0
	Osaka	11.0		30	Hong Kong	6.9

Highest urban pop.

% pop. living in urban areas, 2000

1	Bermuda	100.0
	Hong Kong	100.0
	Singapore	100.0
4	Guadeloupe	99.7
5	Macau	98.8
6	Kuwait	97.6
7	Belgium	97.3
8	Martinique	94.9
9	West Bank and Gaza	94.6
10	Qatar	92.5

Lowest urban pop.

% pop. living in urban areas, 2000

1	Rwanda	6.2
2	Bhutan	7.1
3	Burundi	9.0
4	Nepal	11.9
5	Uganda	14.2
6	Cambodia	15.9
7	Papua New Guinea	17.4
8	Ethiopia	17.6
9	Burkina Faso	18.5
10	Eritrea	18.7

a Based on 42 factors as diverse as personal security and political stability.
b Urban agglomerations. Estimates of cities' populations vary according to where geographical boundaries are defined.

Population: *age and sex*

Youngest populations
% aged under 15, 2000

1	West Bank and Gaza	51.6	21	Senegal	44.7
2	Uganda	50.1	22	Madagascar	44.4
3	Congo	48.3	23	Eritrea	44.1
	Yemen	48.3		Oman	44.1
5	Niger	48.2		Sierra Leone	44.1
6	Somalia	48.0	26	Guinea	44.0
7	Angola	47.5	27	Laos	43.9
8	Burkina Faso	47.3	28	Afghanistan	43.8
9	Malawi	47.2	29	Guatemala	43.6
	Zambia	47.2	30	Cameroon	43.5
11	Burundi	46.3	31	Côte d'Ivoire	43.4
	Congo-Brazzaville	46.3		Mauritania	43.4
	Mali	46.3	33	Ghana	43.1
14	Ethiopia	46.2		Nigeria	43.1
15	Benin	45.9	35	Swaziland	43.0
16	Togo	45.8		Kenya	43.0
17	Chad	45.6	37	Nicaragua	42.7
18	Rwanda	45.4	38	Bhutan	42.6
	Tanzania	45.4	39	Central African Rep	42.5
20	Mozambique	44.9		Guinea-Bissau	42.5

Oldest populations
% aged over 65, 2000

1	Italy	18.2	21	Ukraine	14.1
2	Greece	17.9	22	Estonia	13.8
3	Sweden	17.4		Netherlands	13.8
4	Japan	17.1		Slovenia	13.8
5	Spain	17.0	25	Belarus	13.6
6	Belgium	16.7		Czech Republic	13.6
7	Germany	16.4	27	Lithuania	13.3
8	United Kingdom	16.0		Romania	13.3
9	Bulgaria	15.9		Serbia & Montenegro	13.3
	France	15.9	30	Uruguay	12.9
11	Portugal	15.7	31	Canada	12.8
12	Norway	15.4	32	Georgia	12.6
13	Denmark	15.2	33	Russia	12.5
14	Finland	14.9		United States	12.5
15	Croatia	14.8	35	Australia	12.1
16	Austria	14.7	36	Poland	12.0
	Hungary	14.7	37	Malta	11.8
	Switzerland	14.7	38	Cyprus	11.6
19	Luxembourg	14.4		New Zealand	11.6
20	Latvia	14.3	40	Iceland	11.5

Median age[a]
Years, 2000

1	Japan	41.2		Ukraine	37.6
2	Italy	40.6	22	Czech Republic	37.5
3	Germany	40.0		Estonia	37.5
4	Sweden	39.9	24	Norway	37.4
5	Finland	39.4	25	Portugal	37.3
5	Greece	39.4	26	Canada	36.8
7	Belgium	39.3	27	Russia	36.7
8	Denmark	39.0	28	Belarus	36.4
9	Bulgaria	38.8	29	Malta	36.1
	Croatia	38.8	30	Lithuania	36.0
11	Switzerland	38.3	31	Hong Kong	35.9
12	United Kingdom	38.2	32	United States	35.8
13	Hungary	38.1	33	Serbia & Montenegro	35.6
	Slovenia	38.1	34	Australia	35.3
15	Spain	37.9	35	Bosnia	35.1
16	Austria	37.8		Poland	35.1
	Luxembourg	37.8	37	Qatar	35.0
	Netherlands	37.8	38	Romania	34.9
19	Latvia	37.7	39	Singapore	34.4
20	France	37.6	40	Georgia	34.1

Most male populations
No. of men per 100 women[b], 2000

1	Qatar	186.6
2	United Arab Emirates	172.1
3	Bahrain	132.3
4	Saudi Arabia	123.3
5	Oman	112.6
6	Hong Kong	112.4
7	Kuwait	110.8
8	Brunei	109.6
9	Libya	107.4
10	Jordan	106.8
11	India	106.7
12	Pakistan	106.6
13	Papua New Guinea	106.3
14	China	105.9
15	Afghanistan	105.4
16	Taiwan	105.2
17	Bangladesh	104.9
18	Albania	104.6
19	Côte d'Ivoire	103.5
	Iraq	103.5

Most female populations
No. of men per 100 women, 2000

1	Latvia	83.0
2	Ukraine	87.2
3	Russia	87.8
4	Belarus	88.5
5	Estonia	88.7
6	Lithuania	89.4
7	Hungary	91.5
8	Georgia	91.6
9	Moldova	91.8
10	Portugal	92.7
11	Puerto Rico	93.0
12	Swaziland	93.1
13	Netherlands Antilles	93.2
14	Croatia	93.6
15	Barbados	93.8
16	Martinique	94.1
17	Uruguay	94.2
18	Cambodia	94.3
19	Italy	94.3
20	Poland	94.5

a Age at which there are an equal number of people above and below.
b Large numbers of immigrant workers, mostly men, result in the high male ratios of several Middle East countries.

Population: *matters of breeding*

Highest crude birth rates
No. of live births per 1,000 population, 1995–2000

1	Somalia	52.3	21	Guinea	42.1
2	Afghanistan	51.3	22	Guinea-Bissau	42.0
3	Uganda	51.1	23	Togo	41.6
4	Niger	48.7	24	Benin	41.4
5	Angola	48.4	25	Tanzania	41.1
6	Yemen	47.7	26	Eritrea	40.7
7	Malawi	47.6	27	Gambia, The	40.6
8	West Bank and Gaza	47.1	28	Mauritania	40.5
9	Mali	46.9	29	Madagascar	40.4
10	Sierra Leone	46.6	30	Senegal	40.0
11	Congo	46.2	31	Laos	39.6
12	Burkina Faso	46.0	32	Cameroon	39.4
13	Ethiopia	44.6	33	Nigeria	38.8
14	Liberia	44.2	34	Swaziland	38.0
15	Chad	44.0	35	Bhutan	37.7
16	Congo-Brazzaville	43.6		Central African Rep	37.7
17	Mozambique	43.5	37	Gabon	37.5
18	Rwanda	43.3	38	Ghana	37.4
19	Zambia	42.5	39	Côte d'Ivoire	37.3
20	Burundi	42.3	40	Guatemala	36.6

Lowest crude birth rates
Number of live births per 1,000 population, 1995–2000

1	Bulgaria	8.8		Portugal	10.6
	Latvia	8.8	23	Belgium	10.7
3	Czech Republic	8.9	24	Slovakia	10.8
	Estonia	8.9	25	Poland	11.0
5	Italy	9.0	26	Switzerland	11.1
6	Germany	9.2	27	Finland	11.4
	Romania	9.2	28	Canada	11.5
	Slovenia	9.2	29	Netherlands	11.6
	Spain	9.2	30	United Kingdom	11.9
10	Greece	9.3	31	Denmark	12.2
11	Russia	9.6		France	12.2
12	Ukraine	9.7	33	Luxembourg	12.3
13	Belarus	9.8	34	Barbados	12.8
14	Hungary	9.9	35	Malta	12.9
	Japan	9.9		Serbia & Montenegro	12.9
16	Sweden	10.2	37	Cuba	13.1
17	Austria	10.3	38	Norway	13.2
	Lithuania	10.3	39	Armenia	13.3
19	Hong Kong	10.4		Macau	13.3
20	Bosnia	10.5		Moldova	13.3
21	Croatia	10.6			

Notes: The crude birth rate is the number of live births in one year per 1,000 population. In addition to the fertility rate (see below) it depends on the population's age structure and will tend to be higher if there is a large proportion of women of childbearing age.

The fertility rate is the average number of children born to a woman who completes her childbearing years.

Highest fertility rates

Average number of children per woman, 1995–2000

1	Yemen	7.60
2	West Bank and Gaza	7.30
3	Somalia	7.25
4	Uganda	7.10
5	Afghanistan	6.90
6	Niger	6.84
7	Angola	6.80
8	Malawi	6.75
9	Mali	6.60
10	Burkina Faso	6.57
11	Congo	6.43
12	Liberia	6.31
13	Ethiopia	6.30
14	Burundi	6.28
15	Mozambique	6.25
16	Rwanda	6.20
17	Chad	6.07
18	Congo-Brazzaville	6.06
	Sierra Leone	6.06
20	Togo	6.05

Lowest fertility rates

Average number of children per woman, 1995–2000

1	Spain	1.15
2	Romania	1.17
3	Czech Republic	1.19
4	Italy	1.20
5	Bulgaria	1.23
6	Latvia	1.25
7	Slovenia	1.26
8	Greece	1.28
9	Estonia	1.29
10	Germany	1.30
11	Hong Kong	1.32
12	Bosnia	1.35
	Russia	1.35
14	Belarus	1.36
15	Hungary	1.37
	Portugal	1.37
17	Ukraine	1.38
18	Slovakia	1.39
19	Macau	1.40
20	Austria	1.41

Highest abortion rates

Abortions per 1,000 women aged 15–44, latest year

1	Vietnam[a]	83.3
2	Romania[a]	78.0
3	Cuba	77.7
4	Belarus	67.5
5	Russia	65.4
6	Ukraine[a]	57.2
7	Serbia & Montenegro[a]	54.6
8	Estonia	53.8
9	Bulgaria	51.3
10	Tajikistan[a]	49.1
11	Turkmenistan[a]	44.9
12	Latvia	44.1
13	Kazakhstan	43.9
14	Macedonia[a]	38.5
15	Armenia[a]	35.4
16	Hungary	34.7
17	Lithuania[a]	34.4
18	Albania[a]	27.2
19	China[a]	26.1
20	Mongolia[a]	25.9

Lowest abortion rates

Abortions per 1,000 women aged 15–44, latest year

1	Zambia[a]	0.4
2	India[a]	2.7
	South Africa[a]	2.7
4	Bangladesh[a]	3.8
5	Spain[a]	5.7
6	Ireland[a]	5.9
7	Netherlands	6.5
8	Belgium	6.8
9	Germany	7.6
10	Switzerland	8.4
11	Tunisia	8.6
12	Finland	10.0
13	Italy[a]	11.4
14	Uzbekistan[a]	11.8
15	France[a]	12.4
16	Croatia[a]	12.9
17	Japan[a]	13.4
18	Israel	14.3
19	Hong Kong[a]	15.1
20	Canada	15.5

a Statistics incomplete or of unknown completeness.

The world economy

Biggest economies
GDP, $bn

1	United States		7,903	26	Norway	152
2	Japan		4,089	27	Poland	151
3	Germany		2,180	28	Saudi Arabia	143
4	France[a]		1,465	29	South Africa	137
5	United Kingdom		1,264	30	Thailand	132
6	Italy		1,157	31	Indonesia	131
7	China		924	32	Finland	125
8	Brazil		768	33	Greece	123
9	Canada		581	34	Portugal	106
10	Spain		555	35	Iran	102
11	India		427	36	Colombia	101
12	South Korea		399	37	Israel	97
13	Netherlands		389	38	Singapore	96
14	Australia		387	39	Venezuela	82
15	Mexico		368	40	Malaysia	81
16	Russia		332	41	Egypt	79
17	Argentina		290		Philippines	79
18	Switzerland		284	43	Chile	74
19	Taiwan		262	44	Ireland	69
20	Belgium		259	45	Pakistan	62
21	Sweden		227	46	Peru	61
22	Austria		217	47	New Zealand	55
23	Turkey		201	48	Czech Republic	53
24	Denmark		175	49	Ukraine	49
25	Hong Kong		158		United Arab Emirates	49

Biggest economies by purchasing power
GDP PPP, $bn

1	United States		8,002	21	Netherlands	348
2	China		3,846	22	Thailand	334
3	Japan		2,940	23	Iran	317
4	India		2,035	24	Poland	295
5	Germany		1,819	25	Philippines	267
6	France		1,246	26	Colombia	245
7	United Kingdom		1,201	27	Belgium	237
8	Italy		1,185	28	Pakistan	226
9	Brazil		1,098	29	Saudi Arabia	211
10	Russia		948	30	Austria	187
11	Mexico		738		Egypt	187
12	Canada		715	32	Sweden	183
13	Spain		638	33	Switzerland	181
14	South Korea		625	34	Malaysia	180
15	Indonesia		540	35	Bangladesh	171
16	Argentina		434	36	Ukraine	161
17	Taiwan		427	37	Greece	147
18	Australia		421		Portugal	147
19	Turkey		408	39	Algeria	143
20	South Africa		351	40	Hong Kong	139

a Includes overseas departments.
For list of all countries with their GDP see pages 228–231.

Regional GDP

$bn, 1998			*% growth 1990–98*	
World	28,520		World	3.0
Advanced economies	22,800		Advanced economies	2.4
G7	18,640		G7	2.2
EU15	8,330		EU15	1.8
Asia[a]	1,940		Asia[a]	7.8
Latin America	1,880		Latin America	3.7
Eastern Europe[b]	840		Eastern Europe[b]	-4.9
Middle East and Europe[c]	640		Middle East and Europe[c]	3.6
Africa	420		Africa	2.3

Regional purchasing power

GDP in PPP, % of total			*$ per head*	
World	100.0		World	6,530
Advanced economies	57.4		Advanced economies	23,350
G7	45.8		G7	24,990
EU15	20.3		EU15	20,460
Asia[a]	21.2		Asia[a]	2,640
Latin America	8.4		Latin America	6,570
Eastern Europe[b]	5.8		Eastern Europe[b]	5,630
Middle East and Europe[c]	4.0		Middle East and Europe[c]	5,050
Africa	3.2		Africa	1,800

Regions by population

% of total			*No. of countries[d]*	
Advanced economies	15.5		Advanced economies	28
G7	11.6		G7	7
EU15	6.3		EU15	15
Asia[a]	52.1		Asia[a]	27
Latin America	8.5		Latin America	33
Eastern Europe[b]	6.8		Eastern Europe[b]	28
Middle East and Europe[c]	5.0		Middle East and Europe[c]	17
Africa	12.0		Africa	51

Regional international trade

Exports of goods and services, % of tot.			*Current account balances, $bn*	
Advanced economies	77.6		Advanced economies	43.1
G7	45.9		G7	-53.9
EU15	39.3		EU15	88.0
Asia[a]	8.3		Asia[a]	48.9
Latin America	4.5		Latin America	-88.6
Eastern Europe[b]	4.4		Eastern Europe[b]	-24.8
Middle East and Europe[c]	3.4		Middle East and Europe[c]	-30.3
Africa	1.8		Africa	-20.0

a Excludes Hong Kong, Japan, Singapore, South Korea and Taiwan.
b Includes Russia and other CIS.
c Includes Turkey.
d IMF definition.

Living standards

Highest GDP per head

$

1	Luxembourg	45,100	36	Netherlands Antilles[b]	11,270
2	Switzerland	39,980	37	Portugal	10,670
3	Bermuda	39,060	38	Malta	10,100
4	Norway	34,310	39	Slovenia	9,780
5	Denmark	33,040	40	Réunion	9,680
6	Japan	32,350	41	Puerto Rico	9,110
7	Singapore	30,170	42	South Korea	8,600
8	United States	29,240	43	Barbados	8,580
9	Iceland	27,830	44	Guadeloupe	8,350
10	Austria	26,830	45	Argentina	8,030
11	Germany	26,570	46	Bahrain	7,640
12	Sweden	25,580	47	Liberia[b]	7,390
13	Belgium	25,380	48	Libya[b]	7,120
14	Netherlands	24,780	49	Saudi Arabia	6,910
15	Finland	24,280	50	Uruguay	6,070
16	France	24,210	51	Oman	5,960
17	Hong Kong	23,660	52	Czech Republic	5,150
18	United Kingdom	21,410	53	Chile	4,990
19	Australia	20,640	54	Brazil	4,630
20	Italy	20,090	55	Croatia	4,620
21	Qatar[a]	19,520	56	Trinidad & Tobago	4,520
22	Canada	19,170	57	Hungary	4,510
23	Ireland	18,710	58	Gabon	4,170
24	United Arab Emirates	17,870	59	Poland	3,910
25	Brunei[a]	17,530	60	Mexico	3,840
26	Bahamas	16,550	61	Mauritius	3,730
27	Israel	16,180	62	Slovakia	3,700
28	Macau	14,810	63	Malaysia	3,670
29	New Zealand	14,600	64	Lebanon	3,560
30	Spain	14,100	65	Venezuela	3,530
31	Kuwait	13,910	66	Estonia	3,360
32	Taiwan	12,040	67	South Africa	3,310
33	Cyprus	11,920	68	Turkey	3,160
34	Martinique	11,830	69	Botswana	3,070
35	Greece	11,740	70	Panama	2,990

Lowest GDP per head

$

1	Ethiopia	100		Nepal	210
	Myanmar	100	12	Tanzania	220
3	Congo	110	13	Chad	230
4	Burundi	140		Rwanda	230
	Sierra Leone	140	15	Burkina Faso	240
6	Guinea-Bissau	160	16	Mali	250
7	Eritrea	200	17	Cambodia	260
	Niger	200		Madagascar	260
9	Malawi	210	19	Yemen	280
	Mozambique	210	20	Sudan	290

a 1997
b Estimate.

Highest purchasing power
GDP per head in PPP (USA = 100)

1	Luxembourg	125.5	36	Czech Republic	41.7
2	United States	100.0	37	Argentina	40.1
3	Switzerland	91.9	38	Bahrain	39.5
4	Norway	89.6	39	Saudi Arabia	35.9
5	Singapore	86.5	40	Hungary	33.6
6	Brunei	85.1	41	Slovakia	32.9
7	Iceland	84.7	42	Uruguay	29.2
8	Denmark	81.6	43	Chile	29.1
9	Belgium	80.8	44	South Africa	28.4
10	Japan	80.7	45	Mauritius	28.2
11	Bermuda	79.7	46	Malaysia	26.3
12	Austria	79.2	47	Estonia	25.9
13	Malta	78.3	48	Poland	25.8
14	Canada	78.0	49	Mexico	25.5
15	Netherlands	76.4	50	Trinidad & Tobago	24.7
16	Germany	75.3	51	Croatia	22.9
17	Australia	74.5	52	Turkey	22.6
18	France	72.6	53	Brazil	22.1
19	Hong Kong	71.0	54	Belarus	21.6
20	Finland	70.6	55	Lithuania	21.5
21	Italy	69.6	56	Russia	21.1
22	United Kingdom	69.5	57	Colombia	20.0
23	Sweden	67.9	58	Costa Rica	19.9
24	United Arab Emirates	64.5	59	Botswana	19.8
25	Taiwan[b]	61.6		Latvia	19.8
26	Ireland	61.5	61	Venezuela	19.5
27	Cyprus	60.2	62	Gabon	19.2
28	Israel	57.7	63	Romania	19.1
29	New Zealand	55.0	64	Thailand	18.9
30	Spain	54.6	65	Namibia	18.1
31	Portugal	49.8	66	Tunisia	17.7
32	Slovenia	49.2	67	Iran	17.5
33	Greece	47.9	68	Panama	16.8
34	Bahamas	47.8	69	Bulgaria	16.0
35	South Korea	45.4	70	Algeria	15.7

Lowest purchasing power
GDP per head in PPP (USA = 100)

1	Sierra Leone	1.5		Mozambique	2.5
2	Tanzania	1.7		Niger	2.5
3	Burundi	1.9		Nigeria	2.5
	Ethiopia	1.9	15	Benin	2.9
	Malawi	1.9		Chad	2.9
6	Guinea-Bissau	2.0		Congo-Brazzaville	2.9
7	Yemen	2.2	18	Burkina Faso	3.0
8	Mali	2.3	19	Kenya	3.3
	Zambia	2.3	20	Angola	3.4
10	Congo	2.5		Eritrea	3.4
	Madagascar	2.5			

Note: for definition of purchasing power parity see page 227.

The quality of life

Human development index

1	Canada	93.2		41	Slovakia	81.3
2	Norway	92.7		42	United Arab Emirates	81.2
	United States	92.7		43	Poland	80.2
4	Japan	92.4		44	Costa Rica	80.1
5	Belgium	92.3		45	Trinidad & Tobago	79.7
	Sweden	92.3		46	Hungary	79.5
7	Australia	92.2		47	Venezuela	79.2
8	Netherlands	92.1		48	Panama	79.1
9	Iceland	91.9		49	Mexico	78.6
10	France	91.8		50	Croatia	77.3
	United Kingdom	91.8			Estonia	77.3
12	Switzerland	91.4		52	Colombia	76.8
13	Finland	91.3			Malaysia	76.8
14	Germany	90.6		54	Cuba	76.5
15	Denmark	90.5		55	Mauritius	76.4
16	Austria	90.4		56	Belarus	76.3
17	Luxembourg	90.2			Fiji	76.3
18	New Zealand	90.1		58	Lithuania	76.1
19	Ireland	90.0		59	Bulgaria	75.8
	Italy	90.0		60	Suriname	75.7
21	Spain	89.4		61	Libya	75.6
22	Singapore	88.8		62	Thailand	75.3
23	Israel	88.3		63	Romania	75.2
24	Hong Kong	88.0		64	Lebanon	74.9
25	Brunei	87.8		65	Ecuador	74.7
26	Cyprus	87.0			Russia	74.7
27	Greece	86.7		67	Macedonia	74.6
28	Portugal	85.8		68	Latvia	74.4
29	Barbados	85.7		69	Kazakhstan	74.0
30	South Korea	85.2			Philippines	74.0
31	Bahamas	85.1			Saudi Arabia	74.0
32	Malta	85.0		72	Brazil	73.9
33	Slovenia	84.5			Peru	73.9
34	Chile	84.4		74	Jamaica	73.4
35	Czech Republic	83.3		75	Paraguay	73.0
	Kuwait	83.3		76	Georgia	72.9
37	Bahrain	83.2		77	Armenia	72.8
38	Argentina	82.7			Turkey	72.8
39	Uruguay	82.6		79	Dominican Republic	72.6
40	Qatar	81.4		80	Oman	72.5

Notes: GDP or GDP per head is often taken as a measure of how developed a country is but its usefulness is limited as it refers only to economic welfare. In 1990 the UN Development Programme published its first estimate of a Human Development Index, which combined statistics on two other indicators – adult literacy and life expectancy – with income levels to give a better, though still far from perfect, indicator of human development. In 1991 average years of schooling was combined with adult literacy to give a knowledge variable. The index is shown here scaled from 0 to 100; countries scoring over 80 are considered to have high human development, those scoring from 50 to 79 have medium human development and those under 50 have low human development.

Economic freedom index

1	Hong Kong	1.30
2	Singapore	1.45
3	New Zealand	1.70
4	Bahrain	1.80
	Luxembourg	1.80
	United States	1.80
7	Ireland	1.85
8	Australia	1.90
	Switzerland	1.90
	United Kingdom	1.90
11	Canada	2.00
	Chile	2.00
	El Salvador	2.00
	Taiwan	2.00
15	Austria	2.05
	Netherlands	2.05
17	Argentina	2.10
	Belgium	2.10
19	Iceland	2.15
	Japan	2.15
	United Arab Emirates	2.15
22	Bahamas	2.20
	Czech Republic	2.20
	Estonia	2.20
	Finland	2.20
	Germany	2.20
27	Denmark	2.25
28	Italy	2.30
	Norway	2.30
	Portugal	2.30
31	Sweden	2.35
	Trinidad & Tobago	2.35
33	Panama	2.40
	South Korea	2.40
	Spain	2.40
36	Peru	2.45
37	Barbados	2.50
	France	2.50
	Jamaica	2.50
	Kuwait	2.50
41	Cyprus	2.55
	Hungary	2.55
	Uruguay	2.55
44	Bolivia	2.65
	Latvia	2.65
46	Guatemala	2.70
	Malaysia	2.70
	Thailand	2.70
49	Greece	2.75
	Israel	2.75
	Morocco	2.75
	Turkey	2.75
53	Oman	2.80
	Paraguay	2.80
	Poland	2.80
56	Costa Rica	2.85
	Mauritius	2.85
	Philippines	2.85
59	Benin	2.90
	Colombia	2.90
	Dominican Republic	2.90
	Jordan	2.90
	Lithuania	2.90
	Mali	2.90
	Namibia	2.90
	South Africa	2.90
	Sri Lanka	2.90
	Zambia	2.90
69	Botswana	2.95
	Malta	2.95
	Saudi Arabia	2.95
72	Cambodia	3.00
	Mexico	3.00
	Slovakia	3.00
	Slovenia	3.00
	Swaziland	3.00
	Tunisia	3.00
	Uganda	3.00
79	Kenya	3.05
	Qatar	3.05
	Senegal	3.05
82	Armenia	3.10
	Ecuador	3.10
	Gabon	3.10
	Ghana	3.10

Notes: The index of economic freedom, published by the Heritage Foundation, ranks countries on the basis of ten indicators of how government intervention can restrict the economic relations between individuals. The economic indicators are trade policy, taxation, monetary policy, the banking system, foreign-investment rules, property rights, the amount of economic output consumed by the government, regulation policy, the size of the black market and the extent of wage and price controls. A country can score between 1 and 5 in each category, 1 being the most free and 5 being the least free.

Economic growth

Fastest economic growth, 1990–98
Average annual % increase in real GDP

1	China	11.2	27	El Salvador	5.2
2	Singapore	8.5		Eritrea	5.2
3	Vietnam	8.4		Mauritius	5.2
4	Sudan	8.0	30	Cambodia	5.1
5	Chile	7.9	31	Nepal	5.0
6	Ireland	7.7	32	Ethiopia	4.8
	Lebanon	7.7	33	Bangladesh	4.7
8	Malaysia	7.4		Papua New Guinea	4.7
9	Uganda	7.3	35	Benin	4.6
10	Lesotho	7.2		Poland	4.6
11	Laos	6.6	37	Hong Kong	4.4
12	Myanmar	6.3		Panama	4.4
	Taiwan	6.3		Tunisia	4.4
14	India	6.1	40	Botswana	4.3
	South Korea	6.1	41	Bolivia	4.2
16	Oman	5.9		Egypt	4.2
	Syria	5.9		Ghana	4.2
18	Indonesia	5.8		Guatemala	4.2
19	Mozambique	5.7		Guinea	4.2
	Peru	5.7		Mauritania	4.2
	Thailand	5.7		Pakistan	4.2
22	Argentina	5.6		Turkey	4.2
23	Dominican Republic	5.5	49	Uruguay	4.0
24	Israel	5.4	50	Colombia	3.9
	Jordan	5.4		Costa Rica	3.9
26	Sri Lanka	5.3		Norway	3.9

Slowest economic growth, 1990–98
Average annual % increase in real GDP

1	Georgia	-12.8	23	Croatia	-0.4
2	Moldova	-12.6	24	West Bank and Gaza	0.0
3	Ukraine	-11.9	25	Angola	0.1
4	Azerbaijan	-11.5	26	Jamaica	0.2
5	Tajikistan	-9.8		Mongolia	0.2
6	Turkmenistan	-8.7	28	Switzerland	0.4
7	Kirgizstan	-7.3	29	Hungary	0.5
8	Russia	-7.0	30	Cameroon	0.6
9	Kazakhstan	-6.9	31	Congo-Brazzaville	0.9
10	Latvia	-6.3		Czech Republic	0.9
11	Congo	-5.1	33	Zambia	1.0
12	Lithuania	-5.0	34	Guinea-Bissau	1.1
13	Armenia	-4.7	35	Algeria	1.2
	Sierra Leone	-4.7		Italy	1.2
15	Belarus	-4.3		Sweden	1.2
16	Burundi	-3.3	38	Madagascar	1.3
17	Rwanda	-3.2	39	Central African Rep	1.5
18	Bulgaria	-3.1		France	1.5
19	Estonia	-2.2		Germany	1.5
20	Uzbekistan	-2.0		Japan	1.5
21	Haiti	-1.7		Slovakia	1.5
22	Romania	-0.7			

Fastest economic growth, 1980–90
Average annual % increase in real GDP

1	Botswana	10.3		Indonesia	6.1
2	China	10.1	13	India	5.8
3	South Korea	9.4	14	Egypt	5.4
4	Oman	8.4		Mongolia	5.4
5	Taiwan	7.9		Turkey	5.4
6	Thailand	7.6	17	Malaysia	5.3
7	Hong Kong	6.9	18	Nepal	4.6
8	Singapore	6.7		Vietnam	4.6
9	Pakistan	6.3	20	Burundi	4.4
10	Mauritius	6.2		Lesotho	4.4
11	Chad	6.1	22	Bangladesh	4.3

Slowest economic growth, 1980–90
Average annual % increase in real GDP

1	Iraq	-6.8	12	Mauritania	0.0
2	Libya	-5.7		Saudi Arabia	0.0
3	United Arab Emirates	-2.1	14	El Salvador	0.2
4	Nicaragua	-1.9	15	Sierra Leone	0.3
5	Trinidad & Tobago	-0.8	16	Georgia	0.4
6	Argentina	-0.7		Sudan	0.4
7	Peru	-0.3		Uruguay	0.4
8	Bolivia	-0.2	19	Panama	0.5
	Haiti	-0.2		Romania	0.5
10	Mozambique	-0.1	21	Myanmar	0.6
	Niger	-0.1	22	Côte d'Ivoire	0.7

Highest industrial growth, 1990–98
Average annual % increase in real terms

1	China	15.4	6	Myanmar	10.1
2	Vietnam	13.0	7	Cambodia	9.6
3	Uganda	12.8	8	Malaysia	9.4
4	Laos	11.8	9	Lesotho	9.2
5	West Bank and Gaza	11.7	10	Mozambique	8.5

Highest services growth, 1990–98
Average annual % increase in real terms

1	Georgia	17.2	7	Uganda	8.3
2	Chile	9.4	8	Slovakia	8.0
	China	9.4	9	India	7.7
4	Zambia	8.9	10	Malaysia	7.6
5	Singapore	8.6		Taiwan	7.6
	Vietnam	8.6	12	Cambodia	6.9

Highest agricultural growth, 1990–98
Average annual % increase in real terms

1	Sudan	15.3		Peru	5.5
2	Malawi	8.9	7	Chad	5.4
3	Albania	6.2	8	Benin	5.3
4	Lesotho	6.0		Nicaragua	5.3
5	Georgia	5.5	10	Cameroon	5.0

Trading places

Biggest traders
% of total world exports (visible & invisible)

1	Euro area	17.29	22	Ireland	1.05
2	United States	15.30	23	Australia	1.01
3	Germany	9.01	24	Denmark	0.93
4	Japan	8.29	25	Thailand	0.89
5	United Kingdom	7.10	26	Brazil	0.82
6	France	5.77	27	Norway	0.79
7	Italy	4.64	28	Hong Kong	0.76
8	Netherlands	3.47	29	Indonesia	0.73
9	Canada	3.45		Turkey	0.73
10	Belgium & Luxembourg	3.29	31	Finland	0.70
11	China	2.74	32	Saudi Arabia	0.63
12	Spain	2.23	33	India	0.61
13	Switzerland	2.11	34	Poland	0.59
14	South Korea	2.05	35	Philippines	0.56
15	Mexico	1.73	36	Portugal	0.50
	Taiwan	1.73	37	Argentina	0.48
17	Sweden	1.54	38	South Africa	0.46
18	Austria	1.36	39	Czech Republic	0.45
19	Singapore	1.22		Israel	0.45
20	Russia	1.18	41	Puerto Rico	0.39
21	Malaysia	1.08		United Arab Emirates	0.39

Most trade dependent
Trade as % of GDP[a]

1	Panama	84.5
2	Angola[b]	77.6
	Malaysia	77.6
4	Ireland	77.0
5	Puerto Rico	75.0
6	Congo-Brazzaville[c]	67.0
7	Estonia	66.3
8	Swaziland	62.5
9	Singapore	62.0
10	Slovakia	59.8
11	Macedonia	58.3
12	United Arab Emirates	58.0
13	Costa Rica	57.8
14	Malta	55.8
15	Nicaragua	54.5
16	Belgium & Luxembourg	53.9
17	Bahrain	53.1
18	Czech Republic	52.2
19	Suriname[d]	51.8
20	Lithuania	50.2

Least trade dependent
Trade as % of GDP[a]

1	Somalia	6.4
2	Brazil	7.1
3	Japan	7.7
4	Rwanda	8.6
5	India	9.2
6	Argentina	9.6
7	United States	10.1
8	Chad[e]	10.2
9	Burundi[c]	10.3
10	Iraq[b]	10.4
11	Greece[c]	10.7
12	Burkina Faso[e]	10.8
13	Peru	11.5
14	Egypt	12.0
	Liberia	12.0
16	Euro area	12.2
17	Uganda	12.3
18	Uzbekistan	12.5
19	Central African Rep[e]	12.6
	Colombia	12.6

Notes: The figures are drawn from balance of payment statistics and, therefore, have differing technical definitions from trade statistics taken from customs or similar sources. The invisible trade figures do not show some countries, notably ex-Soviet republics, due to unavailable data. For Hong Kong and Singapore, domestic exports and retained imports only are used.

Biggest visible traders
% of world visible exports

1	Euro area	15.39	22	Australia	1.13
2	United States	15.32	23	Brazil	1.05
3	Germany	9.64	24	Ireland	1.03
4	Japan	6.03	25	Denmark	0.89
5	United Kingdom	5.57	26	Thailand	0.86
6	France	5.56	27	Indonesia	0.79
7	Italy	4.33	28	Norway	0.77
8	Canada	4.06	29	India	0.76
9	Netherlands	3.12	30	Poland	0.75
10	China	3.09	31	Turkey	0.74
11	Belgium & Luxembourg	2.89	32	Finland	0.72
12	Mexico	2.34	33	Saudi Arabia	0.64
13	Spain	2.30	34	Portugal	0.62
14	South Korea	2.15	35	Hong Kong	0.59
15	Taiwan	2.02	36	Philippines	0.57
16	Switzerland	1.80	37	Argentina	0.54
17	Sweden	1.47		South Africa	0.54
18	Russia	1.28		United Arab Emirates	0.54
19	Austria	1.25	40	Czech Republic	0.53
20	Malaysia	1.22	41	Puerto Rico	0.50
21	Singapore	1.14			

Biggest invisible traders
% of world invisible exports

1	United States	20.26	22	Australia	0.88
2	Euro area	18.79	23	Norway	0.80
3	United Kingdom	10.98	24	Russia	0.67
4	Japan	10.60	25	Mexico	0.66
5	Germany	6.34	26	Ireland	0.65
6	France	5.76	27	Thailand	0.64
7	Italy	4.63	28	Philippines	0.54
8	Belgium & Luxembourg	4.01	29	India	0.53
9	Netherlands	3.86	30	Poland	0.51
10	Switzerland	2.74		Portugal	0.51
11	Spain	2.48	32	Brazil	0.49
12	Canada	2.01	33	Malaysia	0.48
13	Austria	1.68	34	Israel	0.47
14	Hong Kong	1.34	35	Finland	0.42
	Sweden	1.34	36	Argentina	0.41
16	Singapore	1.25		Greece[c]	0.41
17	China	1.15	38	Egypt	0.40
18	South Korea	1.09	39	Saudi Arabia	0.39
19	Turkey	1.01	40	Czech Republic	0.35
20	Denmark	0.96		Kuwait	0.35
21	Taiwan	0.95			

a Average of imports and exports of goods as % of GDP.
b 1996
c 1997
d 1995
e 1994

Current account

Largest surpluses
$m

1	Japan	120,700		21	Russia	1,644
2	Euro area	67,550		22	Philippines	1,287
3	South Korea	40,558		23	Ireland	806
4	France	40,160		24	Hong Kong	800
5	China	29,325		25	Botswana	170
6	Switzerland	24,547		26	Bermuda[a]	167
7	Netherlands	24,056		27	Namibia	162
8	Italy	19,998		28	Libya[b]	151
9	Singapore	17,614		29	Ethiopia	134
10	Thailand	14,241		30	Gabon[b]	100
11	Belgium & Lux	12,094		31	Cameroon[b]	90
12	Malaysia	9,400		32	Netherlands Antilles[b]	87
13	Finland	7,432		33	Mauritania	77
14	Sweden	4,639		34	Suriname[b]	73
15	Indonesia	4,096		35	Syria	59
16	Taiwan	3,728		36	Mauritius	34
17	Algeria[a]	3,500		37	Burkina Faso[c]	15
18	United Arab Emirates	2,870		38	Jordan	14
19	Kuwait	2,527		39	Burundi[a]	4
20	Turkey	1,871				

Largest deficits
$m

1	United States	-220,560		21	Egypt	-2,566
2	Brazil	-33,829		22	Venezuela	-2,562
3	Australia	-18,137		23	Vietnam[d]	-2,431
4	Mexico	-15,960		24	Hungary	-2,304
5	Argentina	-14,528		25	Ecuador	-2,169
6	Saudi Arabia	-12,880		26	Norway	-2,161
7	Canada	-11,213		27	Slovakia	-2,126
8	Portugal	-7,250		28	Denmark	-2,053
9	India	-6,903		29	South Africa	-1,936
10	Poland	-6,901		30	Iran	-1,897
11	Colombia	-5,293		31	Pakistan[a]	-1,713
12	Greece	-4,860		32	Spain	-1,606
13	Austria	-4,609		33	Croatia	-1,552
14	Nigeria	-4,244		34	Czech Republic	-1,392
15	Chile	-4,139		35	Azerbaijan	-1,365
16	Peru	-3,800		36	Lithuania	-1,298
17	Germany	-3,440		37	Ukraine	-1,296
18	New Zealand	-3,217		38	Panama	-1,212
19	Oman	-2,970		39	Kazakhstan	-1,201
20	Romania	-2,918		40	Bosnia	-1,097

a 1997
b 1995
c 1994
d 1996

Largest surpluses as % of GDP
%

1	Singapore	18.4	21	France	2.7
2	Malaysia	11.6	22	Ethiopia	2.2
3	Thailand	10.8	23	Gabon[a]	2.0
4	Suriname[a]	10.7	24	Sweden	2.0
5	South Korea	10.2	25	Italy	1.7
6	Kuwait	10.0	26	Philippines	1.6
7	Switzerland	8.6	27	Taiwan	1.4
8	Algeria[b]	7.5	28	Ireland	1.2
9	Mauritania	7.3	29	Cameroon[a]	1.0
10	Bermuda[b]	6.8		Euro area	1.0
11	Netherlands	6.2	31	Turkey	0.9
12	Finland	5.9	32	Mauritius	0.8
	United Arab Emirates	5.9	33	Burkina Faso[c]	0.6
14	Namibia	5.1	34	Hong Kong	0.5
15	Belgium & Lux	4.3		Russia	0.5
16	Botswana	3.5	36	Burundi[b]	0.4
	Netherlands Antilles[a]	3.5		Libya[c]	0.4
18	China	3.2		Syria	0.4
19	Indonesia	3.1	39	Jordan	0.3
20	Japan	3.0			

Largest deficits as % of GDP
%

1	Turkmenistan	-45.8		Latvia	-12.1
2	Azerbaijan	-35.9	22	Bahrain	-11.8
3	Nicaragua	-33.7		Ecuador	-11.8
4	Bosnia	-26.8	24	Nigeria	-11.7
5	Lesotho	-23.4		Sudan	-11.7
6	Armenia	-23.0	26	Macedonia	-11.1
7	West Bank and Gaza[b]	-22.2		Trinidad & Tobago	-11.1
8	Oman	-20.9	28	Congo	-10.8
9	Kirgizstan	-20.6	29	Slovakia	-10.7
10	Malawi[c]	-20.4	30	Myanmar	-9.9
	Moldova	-20.4	31	Estonia	-9.8
12	Sierra Leone[a]	-18.1	32	Romania	-9.5
13	Guinea-Bissau[b]	-15.1	33	Laos	-9.4
14	Panama	-14.6		Qatar	-9.4
15	Lithuania	-13.8	35	Vietnam[d]	-9.2
16	Congo-Brazzaville[b]	-13.3	36	Saudi Arabia	-9.0
	Tanzania	-13.3	37	Bolivia	-8.4
18	Mongolia	-12.9	38	Madagascar	-8.1
19	Mozambique	-12.3	39	Georgia	-7.9
20	Bahamas	-12.1	40	Cambodia	-7.7

a 1995
b 1997
c 1994
d 1996

Inflation

Highest inflation, 1998–99
% consumer price inflation

1	Belarus	293.7		32	Costa Rica	10.0
2	Congo[a]	175.5		33	Madagascar	9.9
3	Laos	128.4		34	Lesotho[c]	9.3
4	Tajikistan[a]	87.8		35	Armenia[b]	8.7
5	Russia	85.7			Haiti	8.7
6	Turkmenistan[a]	84.0			Vietnam[b]	8.7
7	Angola[b]	74.7		38	Bhutan[b]	8.5
8	Uzbekistan[a]	72.0		39	Bangladesh[a]	8.3
9	Turkey	64.9		40	Kazakhstan	8.2
10	Ecuador	52.2		41	Nepal	8.0
11	Moldova	45.9		42	Tanzania	7.9
12	Romania	45.8		43	Mongolia	7.6
13	Malawi	44.9		44	Poland	7.3
14	Kirgizstan	35.9		45	Botswana	7.1
15	Sierra Leone	34.1			Suriname[a]	7.1
16	Zimbabwe[b]	31.8		47	Mauritius	6.9
17	Zambia[a]	24.8		48	Paraguay	6.8
18	Venezuela	23.6		49	Philippines	6.7
19	Iran	21.0		50	Nigeria	6.6
20	Indonesia	20.5			Slovenia	6.6
21	Myanmar	18.4		52	Guinea-Bissau[b]	6.5
22	Sudan[b]	17.1		53	Uganda	6.4
23	Mexico	16.6		54	Namibia[b]	6.2
24	Ukraine[a]	15.9		55	Swaziland	6.1
25	Papua New Guinea	14.9		56	Jamaica	6.0
26	Ghana[b]	14.6		57	Uruguay	5.7
27	Honduras	11.6		58	Trinidad & Tobago[b]	5.6
28	Colombia	11.2		59	Mozambique[a]	5.5
	Nicaragua	11.2		60	Israel	5.2
30	Slovakia	10.6			South Africa	5.2
31	Hungary	10.3				

Highest inflation, 1990–99
% average annual consumer price inflation

1	Congo[d]	1,710.5		16	Macedonia[e]	116.3
2	Turkmenistan[d]	668.4		17	Romania	113.9
3	Tajikistan[d]	467.6		18	Croatia	105.9
4	Ukraine[d]	431.3		19	Lithuania	105.1
5	Armenia[e]	405.4		20	Sudan[e]	85.8
6	Georgia[e]	395.6		21	Suriname[d]	84.8
7	Belarus	353.4		22	Estonia	80.3
8	Azerbaijan[d]	333.6		23	Turkey	78.7
9	Uzbekistan[d]	296.4		24	Zambia[d]	77.9
10	Brazil	236.3		25	Latvia	73.0
11	Kazakhstan	231.5		26	Nicaragua	63.2
12	Russia	190.8		27	Mongolia[f]	59.3
13	Moldova	151.8		28	Venezuela	46.7
14	Kirgizstan	131.3		29	Peru	42.5
15	Bulgaria	123.5		30	Guinea-Bissau[e]	41.3

Lowest inflation, 1998–99
% consumer price inflation

1	Chad	-6.8		26	El Salvador	0.5
2	Bulgaria	-5.5			France	0.5
3	Hong Kong	-4.0			Macedonia[b]	0.5
4	Ethiopia[a]	-3.7			Sweden	0.5
5	Rwanda	-2.4		30	Austria	0.6
6	Niger	-2.3			Germany	0.6
7	Central African Rep[b]	-1.9		32	Morocco	0.7
8	Saudi Arabia	-1.6		33	Côte d'Ivoire	0.8
9	China	-1.4			Lithuania	0.8
10	Argentina	-1.2			Senegal	0.8
	Mali	-1.2			South Korea	0.8
	Syria[b]	-1.2			Switzerland	0.8
13	Burkina Faso	-1.1		38	Luxembourg	1.0
14	Bahrain[b]	-0.4		39	Belgium	1.1
15	Japan	-0.3			Netherlands Antilles[b]	1.1
16	Congo-Brazzaville[c]	-0.2		41	Finland	1.2
17	New Zealand	-0.1		42	Bahamas	1.3
	Togo	-0.1			Panama	1.3
19	Cameroon[b]	0.1		44	Australia	1.5
20	Kuwait[b]	0.2		45	Barbados	1.6
	Taiwan	0.2			Ireland	1.6
22	Benin	0.3			United Kingdom	1.6
	Thailand	0.3		48	Canada	1.7
24	Albania	0.4			Cyprus	1.7
	Singapore	0.4			Italy	1.7

Lowest inflation, 1990–99
% average annual consumer price inflation

1	Bahrain[e]	1.0		16	Austria	2.3
	Japan	1.0			Kuwait [e]	2.3
3	Panama	1.2			Norway	2.3
	Saudi Arabia	1.2		19	Sweden	2.4
5	Finland	1.7		20	Germany	2.5
	France	1.7			Netherlands	2.5
	New Zealand	1.7			Netherlands Antilles[e]	2.5
8	Singapore	1.8		23	Bahamas	2.6
9	Canada	1.9		24	Taiwan	2.7
10	Australia	2.0			United States	2.7
	Belgium	2.0		26	Barbados	2.8
	Switzerland	2.0		27	Malta	2.9
13	Denmark	2.1		28	Iceland	3.0
	Luxembourg	2.1			Qatar[d]	3.0
15	Ireland	2.2		30	United Kingdom	3.1

a 1996–97   d 1990–97
b 1997–98   e 1990–98
c 1995–96   f 1992–99

Notes: Inflation is measured as the % increase in the consumer price index between two dates. The figures shown are based on the average level of the index during the relevant years.

Debt

Highest foreign debt[a]
$m

1	Brazil	232,004	24	South Africa	24,711
2	Russia	183,601	25	Syria	22,435
3	Mexico	159,959	26	Vietnam	22,359
4	China	154,599	27	Morocco	20,687
5	Indonesia	147,475	28	Sudan	16,843
6	Argentina	144,050	29	Bangladesh	16,376
7	South Korea	139,097	30	Ecuador	15,140
8	Turkey	102,074	31	Côte d'Ivoire	14,852
9	India	98,232	32	Iran	14,391
10	Thailand	86,172	33	Serbia & Montenegro	13,742
11	Philippines	47,817	34	Congo	12,929
12	Poland	47,708	35	Ukraine	12,718
13	Malaysia	44,773	36	Angola	12,173
14	Venezuela	37,003	37	Tunisia	11,078
15	Chile	36,302	38	Ethiopia	10,352
16	Colombia	33,263	39	Bulgaria	9,907
17	Peru	32,397	40	Slovakia	9,893
18	Pakistan	32,229	41	Cameroon	9,829
19	Egypt	31,964	42	Romania	9,513
20	Algeria	30,665	43	Sri Lanka	8,526
21	Nigeria	30,315	44	Jordan	8,484
22	Hungary	28,580	45	Croatia	8,297
23	Czech Republic	25,301	46	Mozambique	8,208

Highest debt service[b]
$m

1	Brazil	46,365	22	Iran	2,667
2	Mexico	25,663	23	Pakistan	2,436
3	Argentina	19,078	24	Romania	2,095
4	Indonesia	17,461	25	Slovakia	1,954
5	China	16,784	26	Peru	1,860
6	South Korea	14,645	27	Ukraine	1,759
7	Thailand	11,575	28	Egypt	1,586
8	Turkey	11,507	29	Ecuador	1,529
9	India	11,343	30	Angola	1,308
10	Russia	9,129	31	Côte d'Ivoire	1,285
11	Hungary	6,947		Tunisia	1,285
12	Malaysia	5,615	33	Nigeria	1,283
13	Venezuela	5,175	34	Bulgaria	1,045
14	Czech Republic	4,983	35	Uruguay	1,022
15	Philippines	4,751	36	Vietnam	962
16	Algeria	4,587	37	Zimbabwe	880
17	Poland	4,284	38	Jordan	835
18	Colombia	4,217	39	Croatia	783
19	Chile	4,039	40	Kazakhstan	747
20	South Africa	3,324	41	Panama	682
21	Morocco	2,794	42	Bangladesh	570

a Foreign debt is debt owed to non-residents and repayable in foreign currency; the figures shown include liabilities of government, public and private sectors. Developed countries have been excluded.

Highest foreign debt burden
Foreign debt as % of GDP

1	Guinea-Bissau	503.6	21	Yemen	104.8
2	Congo	306.9	22	Guinea	102.0
3	Angola	297.1	23	Togo	97.4
4	Mauritania	272.5	24	Honduras	96.9
5	Mozambique	223.0	25	Tanzania	94.3
6	Zambia	217.4	26	Macedonia	92.6
7	Congo	208.2	27	Ghana	91.8
8	Laos	199.1	28	Gabon	90.7
9	Sierra Leone	197.7	29	Central African Rep	88.8
10	Sudan	182.7	30	Turkmenistan	87.7
11	Indonesia	172.5	31	Senegal	83.1
12	Ethiopia	160.4	32	Bulgaria	83.0
13	Côte d'Ivoire	145.4	33	Ecuador	82.5
14	Malawi	137.5	34	Vietnam	82.3
15	Mali	120.4	35	Niger	82.1
16	Madagascar	119.5	36	Zimbabwe	79.8
17	Cameroon	119.4	37	Nigeria	78.8
18	Burundi	119.1	38	Cambodia	77.7
19	Gambia, The	116.7	39	Papua New Guinea	76.9
20	Jordan	116.0	40	Thailand	76.4

Highest debt service ratios[b]
%

1	Brazil	73.0	24	Bulgaria	22.1
2	Argentina	58.2	25	Cameroon	21.7
3	Burundi	49.1	26	Nicaragua	21.1
4	Algeria	46.0	27	Central African Rep	20.9
5	Turkmenistan	42.0		Pakistan	20.9
6	Zimbabwe	38.2	29	Tanzania	20.8
7	Angola	34.4	30	Iran	20.2
8	Indonesia	32.6	31	Mexico	20.0
9	Colombia	29.7	32	Morocco	19.7
10	Bolivia	29.0	33	Turkey	19.5
11	Ghana	27.9	34	Guinea	19.4
12	Mauritania	27.6	35	Thailand	19.2
13	Venezuela	27.4	36	Kenya	18.8
14	Hungary	27.2	37	Lebanon	18.7
15	Peru	27.1	38	Moldova	18.5
16	Côte d'Ivoire	26.1	39	Niger	18.4
17	Guinea-Bissau	25.6	40	Sierra Leone	18.2
18	Ecuador	25.2	41	Mozambique	18.0
19	Uganda	23.6	42	India	17.7
20	Romania	23.5		Zambia	17.7
	Uruguay	23.5	44	Honduras	17.3
22	Senegal	23.2	45	Rwanda	16.6
23	Chile	22.3	46	Slovakia	15.9

b Debt service is the sum of interest and principal repayments (amortization) due on outstanding foreign debt. The debt service ratio is debt service expressed as a percentage of the country's exports of goods and services.

Aid

Largest bilateral and multilateral donors
$m

1	Japan	10,640	13	Australia	960
2	United States	8,786	14	Switzerland	898
3	France	5,742	15	Belgium	883
4	Germany	5,581	16	Austria	456
5	United Kingdom	3,864	17	Finland	396
6	Netherlands	3,042	18	Saudi Arabia	288
7	Italy	2,278	19	Kuwait	278
8	Denmark	1,704	20	Portugal	259
9	Canada	1,691	21	Ireland	199
10	Sweden	1,573	22	South Korea	183
11	Spain	1,376	23	Greece	179
12	Norway	1,321	24	New Zealand	130

Largest recipients of bilateral and multilateral aid
$m

1	China	2,359	36	Guinea	359
2	Egypt	1,915	37	Rwanda	350
3	India	1,595	38	Mali	349
4	Indonesia	1,258		Zambia	349
5	Bangladesh	1,251	40	Cambodia	337
6	Vietnam	1,163	41	Angola	335
7	Israel	1,066	42	Brazil	329
8	Pakistan	1,050	43	Honduras	318
9	Mozambique	1,039		Jamaica	318
10	Tanzania	998	45	Yemen	310
11	Bosnia	876	46	Niger	291
12	Côte d'Ivoire	798	47	Laos	281
13	Ghana	701	48	Zimbabwe	280
14	Thailand	690	49	Albania	242
15	Ethiopia	648	50	Lebanon	236
16	Bolivia	628	51	Guatemala	233
17	Philippines	607	52	Kirgizstan	216
18	West Bank and Gaza	598	53	Benin	210
19	Nicaragua	562	54	Sudan	209
20	Morocco	528	55	Kazakhstan	207
21	South Africa	512	56	Nigeria	204
22	Senegal	502	57	Mongolia	203
23	Peru	501	58	Malaysia	202
24	Madagascar	494	59	Namibia	180
25	Sri Lanka	490	60	Mauritania	171
26	Kenya	474	61	Chad	167
27	Uganda	471	62	Colombia	166
28	Malawi	434	63	Iran	164
29	Cameroon	424	64	Georgia	162
30	Jordan	408	65	Eritrea	158
31	Haiti	407	66	Syria	156
32	Nepal	404	67	Afghanistan	154
33	Burkina Faso	397	68	Tunisia	148
34	Algeria	389	69	Uzbekistan	144
35	Papua New Guinea	361	70	Armenia	138

Largest bilateral and multilateral donors
% of GDP

1	Denmark	0.99		New Zealand	0.27
2	Norway	0.91		United Kingdom	0.27
3	Netherlands	0.80	15	Germany	0.26
4	Sweden	0.72	16	Spain	0.24
5	France	0.40		Portugal	0.24
6	Belgium	0.35	18	Austria	0.22
7	Finland	0.32	19	Italy	0.20
	Switzerland	0.32		Saudi Arabia	0.20
9	Ireland	0.30	21	Greece	0.14
10	Canada	0.29	22	Kuwait	0.10
11	Japan	0.28		United States	0.10
12	Australia	0.27	24	South Korea	0.04

Largest recipients of bilateral and multilateral aid
$ per head

1	Netherlands Antilles	606		Gabon	39
2	West Bank and Gaza	577	37	Ghana	37
3	Israel	178	38	Benin	36
4	Bosnia	238	39	Burkina Faso	35
5	Suriname	143		Mauritius	35
6	Jamaica	125	41	Central African Rep	34
7	Nicaragua	117	42	Madagascar	33
8	Namibia	108		Mali	33
9	Guinea-Bissau	83	44	Georgia	32
10	Bolivia	79		Lesotho	32
	Mongolia	79	46	Cambodia	31
12	Albania	78		Gambia, The	31
	Papua New Guinea	78		Tanzania	31
14	Lebanon	74	49	Cameroon	30
15	Bahrain	69	50	Egypt	29
16	Botswana	68		Niger	29
	Mauritania	68		Togo	29
18	Jordan	65	53	Angola	28
19	Barbados	60		Bhutan	28
20	Malta	57	55	Liberia	27
21	Côte d'Ivoire	56		Sri Lanka	27
	Senegal	56	57	Zimbabwe	25
23	Mozambique	55	58	Chad	23
24	Laos	54		Congo-Brazzaville	23
25	Rwanda	53		Sierra Leone	23
26	Honduras	52		Uganda	23
27	Haiti	51	62	Guatemala	22
28	Guinea	49	63	Peru	20
29	Kirgizstan	47		Slovenia	20
30	Macedonia	46	65	Morocco	19
31	Fiji	45	66	Nepal	18
32	Eritrea	44		Yemen	18
33	Malawi	42	68	Tajikistan	17
34	Zambia	40	69	Kenya	16
35	Armenia	39		Tunisia	16

Industry and services

Largest industrial output
$bn

1	United States	2,055	26	Turkey	50
2	Japan	1,513	27	Norway	49
3	Germany	695	28	Poland	48
4	China	453	29	Denmark[b]	47
5	United Kingdom	392	30	South Africa	44
6	France	381	31	Finland	43
7	Italy	359	32	Iran	38
8	Brazil	223	33	Portugal	37
9	Spain	178	34	Greece	36
10	Canada	177		Israel	36
11	South Korea	171		Malaysia	36
12	Russia	116	37	Singapore	33
13	India	107	38	Venezuela	28
14	Netherlands	104	39	Ireland	27
15	Australia	101	40	Colombia	25
16	Mexico	99		Egypt	25
17	Switzerland[a]	91		Philippines	25
18	Taiwan	89	43	Hong Kong	24
19	Argentina	84	44	Algeria	22
20	Belgium	73		Chile	22
21	Saudi Arabia	69		Peru	22
22	Sweden	68	47	Czech Republic	21
23	Austria	65	48	Ukraine	17
24	Indonesia	59	49	Hungary	16
25	Thailand	54	50	Pakistan	15

Highest growth in industrial output
Average annual real % growth, 1990–98

1	China	15.4	11	Singapore	8.4
2	Vietnam	13.0	12	Papua New Guinea	7.9
3	Uganda	12.8	13	Indonesia	7.8
4	Laos	11.8	14	Mali	7.6
5	West Bank and Gaza	11.7		Nepal	7.6
6	Myanmar	10.1	16	Sri Lanka	7.4
7	Cambodia	9.6	17	Jordan	7.1
8	Malaysia	9.4	18	Peru	6.9
9	Lesotho	9.2		Thailand	6.9
10	Mozambique	8.5			

Lowest growth in industrial output
Average annual real % growth, 1990–98

1	Tajikistan	-17.2	11	Burundi	-7.8
2	Ukraine	-15.5	12	Estonia	-6.1
3	Latvia	-12.8	13	Belarus	-5.6
	Moldova	-12.8	14	Uzbekistan	-5.1
5	Kirgizstan	-12.0	15	Bulgaria	-4.9
6	Congo	-11.7		Slovakia	-4.9
7	Russia	-11.1	17	Croatia	-4.8
8	Kazakhstan	-10.1	18	Sierra Leone	-4.7
9	Lithuania	-9.9		Zambia	-4.7
10	Armenia	-9.0	20	Albania	-4.6

Largest manufacturing output
$bn

1	United States	1,423	22	Austria	43
2	Japan	981	23	Thailand	42
3	Germany	523	24	Indonesia	33
4	China	360	25	Turkey	32
5	France	278	26	Finland	31
6	United Kingdom	266	27	Poland	29
7	Italy	231	28	Denmark	28
8	Brazil	177	29	Portugal[b]	26
9	Russia[b]	132		South Africa	26
10	South Korea	124	31	Ireland[b]	25
11	Spain	100	32	Malaysia	24
12	Canada	96	33	Singapore	22
13	Mexico	74	34	Egypt	21
14	Taiwan	71	35	Norway	17
15	India	68		Philippines	17
16	Netherlands	67	37	Israel[b]	16
17	Switzerland	63	38	Iran	15
18	Argentina	55	39	Peru	14
19	Australia	54		Saudi Arabia	14
20	Belgium	47		Ukraine	14
21	Sweden	46	42	Colombia	13

Largest services output
$bn

1	United States	5,690	25	Turkey	114
2	Japan	2,494	26	Norway	100
3	France	1,055	27	Poland	94
4	Germany	959	28	South Africa	88
5	United Kingdom	847	29	Finland	78
6	Italy	775	30	Israel	76
7	Brazil	484	31	Greece	68
8	Canada	390	32	Portugal	65
9	China	305		Saudi Arabia	65
10	Australia	275	34	Thailand	63
11	Netherlands	272	35	Singapore	62
12	Mexico	250	36	Colombia	61
13	South Korea	207	37	Venezuela	50
14	India	197	38	Chile	46
15	Switzerland	196		Indonesia	46
16	Argentina	192	40	Egypt	40
17	Russia	189		Ireland	40
18	Belgium	184		Philippines	40
19	Taiwan	165	43	Iran	39
20	Sweden	158	44	New Zealand	38
21	Austria	147	45	Malaysia	35
22	Spain	139	46	Peru	34
23	Hong Kong	134	47	Czech Republic	30
24	Denmark	122		Pakistan	30

a 1994
b 1997

Agriculture

Most economically dependent on agriculture
% of GDP from agriculture

1	Guinea-Bissau	62	24	Mozambique	34
2	Congo	58		Nicaragua	34
3	Albania	54	26	Armenia	33
	Burundi	54		Burkina Faso	33
5	Central African Rep	53		Mongolia	33
	Laos	53	29	Côte d'Ivoire	32
	Myanmar	53		Nigeria	32
8	Cambodia	51	31	Madagascar	31
9	Ethiopia	50		Uzbekistan	31
10	Mali	47	33	Bangladesh	30
	Rwanda	47		Haiti	30
12	Kirgizstan	46	35	Moldova	29
	Tanzania	46	36	Gambia, The	27
14	Uganda	45		India	27
15	Sierra Leone	44	38	Georgia	26
16	Cameroon	42		Kenya	26
	Togo	42		Pakistan	26
18	Niger	41	41	Mauritania	25
19	Chad	40		Paraguay	25
	Nepal	40		Turkmenistan	25
21	Benin	39	44	Iran	24
	Sudan	39		Papua New Guinea	24
23	Malawi	36		Vietnam	24

Least economically dependent on agriculture
% of GDP from agriculture

1	Hong Kong	0		Israel	4
	Singapore	0		Netherlands	4
3	Austria	1		Portugal	4
	Belgium	1		Slovenia	4
	Germany	1		South Africa	4
6	Canada	2		Spain	4
	Iceland	2	30	Ireland	5
	Japan	2		Latvia	5
	Norway	2		Poland	5
	Sweden	2		Slovakia	5
	Trinidad & Tobago	2		South Korea	5
	United Kingdom	2		Venezuela	5
	United States	2	36	Estonia	6
14	Australia	3		Hungary	6
	France	3		Iraq	6
	Italy	3		Mexico	6
	Jordan	3		Tajikistan	6
	Switzerland	3	41	Argentina	7
	Taiwan	3		Gabon	7
20	Botswana	4		Russia	7
	Czech Republic	4		Saudi Arabia	7
	Denmark	4		West Bank and Gaza	7
	Finland	4			

a 1996

Fastest growth
Average annual real % growth, 1990–98[a]

1	Sudan	15.3		Nicaragua	5.3
2	Malawi	8.9	10	Cameroon	5.0
3	Albania	6.2	11	Myanmar	4.9
4	Lesotho	6.0		Vietnam	4.9
5	Georgia	5.5	13	Mauritania	4.8
	Peru	5.5		Mozambique	4.8
7	Chad	5.4	15	Laos	4.6
8	Benin	5.3			

Slowest growth
Average annual real % growth, 1990–98[a]

1	West Bank and Gaza	-15.4	10	Zambia	-4.9
2	Kazakhstan	-13.4	11	Haiti	-4.3
3	Tajikistan	-12.2	12	Estonia	-4.2
4	Latvia	-8.9	13	Angola	-4.1
5	Russia	-6.9	14	Croatia	-3.3
6	Moldova	-6.3	15	Hungary	-3.2
7	Ukraine	-5.8	16	Jordan	-3.1
8	Belarus	-5.4	17	Colombia	-3.0
9	Rwanda	-5.1	18	Spain	-2.5

Biggest producers
'000 tonnes

Cereals

1	China	458,395	6	Canada	50,851
2	United States	349,631	7	Russia	46,969
3	India	224,027	8	Germany	44,575
4	France	68,446	9	Brazil	40,625
5	Indonesia	59,406	10	Argentina	36,733

Meat

1	China	58,827	6	Russia	4,677
2	United States	35,965	7	India	4,609
3	Brazil	12,223	8	Spain	4,600
4	France	6,522	9	Mexico	4,127
5	Germany	6,139	10	Italy	4,047

Fruit

1	China	55,037	6	Spain	13,746
2	India	37,815	7	Mexico	11,495
3	Brazil	35,000	8	Iran	11,172
4	United States	31,466	9	Turkey	10,389
5	Italy	17,760	10	France	10,202

Vegetables

1	China	243,588	6	Iran	14,194
2	India	55,774	7	Japan	13,565
3	United States	34,475	8	Egypt	11,868
4	Turkey	21,777	9	Spain	11,681
5	Italy	14,722	10	Russia	10,884

a Or nearest available years.

Commodities

Wheat

Top 10 producers '000 tonnes		Top 10 consumers '000 tonnes	
1 China	109,700	1 China	116,500
2 EU15	103,800	2 EU15	85,200
3 United States	69,400	3 India	66,700
4 India	65,900	4 United States	37,700
5 Russia	27,000	5 Russia	37,200
6 Canada	24,100	6 Pakistan	21,100
7 Australia	22,100	7 Turkey	16,800
8 Pakistan	18,700	8 Ukraine	14,500
9 Turkey	18,500	9 Iran	13,700
10 Ukraine	14,900	10 Egypt	13,200

Rice

Top 10 producers[a] '000 tonnes		Top 10 consumers[b] '000 tonnes	
1 China	198,714	1 China	136,750
2 India	129,013	2 India	81,160
3 Indonesia	50,791	3 Indonesia	35,504
4 Vietnam	30,467	4 Bangladesh	21,954
5 Bangladesh	29,784	5 Vietnam	15,613
6 Thailand	23,000	6 Myanmar	9,276
7 Myanmar	16,034	7 Japan	9,100
8 Brazil	11,375	8 Thailand	8,900
9 Japan	11,201	9 Brazil	8,180
10 Philippines	10,268	10 Philippines	7,850

Sugar[c]

Top 10 producers '000 tonnes		Top 10 consumers '000 tonnes	
1 Brazil	19,168	1 India	14,602
2 EU15	17,939	2 EU15	14,550
3 India	14,281	3 Brazil	9,150
4 China	8,904	4 United States	9,049
5 United States	7,159	5 China	8,300
6 Mexico	5,287	6 Russia	5,450
7 Australia	5,085	7 Mexico	4,293
8 Thailand	4,143	8 Pakistan	3,139
9 Pakistan	3,909	9 Indonesia	2,736
10 Cuba	3,291	10 Japan	2,427

Coarse grains[d]

Top 5 producers '000 tonnes		Top 5 consumers '000 tonnes	
1 United States	271,500	1 United States	205,000
2 China	143,800	2 China	132,000
3 EU15	107,000	3 EU15	92,100
4 Brazil	33,000	4 Brazil	34,500
5 India	32,900	5 India	33,400

Tea

Top 10 producers '000 tonnes		*Top 10 consumers* '000 tonnes	
1 India	870	1 India	645
2 China	665	2 China	449
3 Kenya	294	3 Turkey	160
4 Sri Lanka	281	4 United Kingdom	146
5 Turkey	178	5 Russia	141
6 Indonesia	166	6 Japan	127
7 Japan	83	7 Pakistan	112
8 Iran	60	8 United States	97
9 Bangladesh	56	9 Iran	92
10 Argentina	50	10 Egypt	65

Coffee

Top 10 producers '000 tonnes		*Top 10 consumers* '000 tonnes	
1 Brazil	2,073	1 United States	1,143
2 Colombia	630	2 Brazil	892
3 Indonesia	502	3 Germany	638
4 Vietnam	416	4 Japan	376
5 Mexico	303	5 France	319
6 India	262	6 Italy	299
7 Guatemala	204	7 Spain	201
8 Uganda	198	8 Britain	142
9 Ethiopia	165	9 Indonesia	120
10 Côte d'Ivoire	164	10 Netherlands	114

Cocoa

Top 10 producers '000 tonnes		*Top 10 consumers* '000 tonnes	
1 Côte d'Ivoire	1,113	1 United States	654
2 Ghana	409	2 Germany	289
3 Indonesia	331	3 United Kingdom	202
4 Brazil	170	4 France	177
5 Nigeria	165	5 Japan	124
6 Cameroon	115	6 Brazil	120
7 Malaysia	65	Russia	120
8 Dominican Republic	60	8 Italy	92
9 Colombia	45	9 Canada	78
10 Mexico	35	10 Spain	70

a Paddy (unmilled rice, in the husk).
b Milled rice.
c Raw.
d Includes: maize (corn), barley, sorghum, rye, oats and millet.

Copper

Top 10 producers[a] '000 tonnes		*Top 10 consumers[b]* '000 tonnes	
1 Chile	3,687	1 United States	2,883
2 United States	1,860	2 China	1,397
3 Indonesia	809	3 Japan	1,255
4 Canada	706	4 Germany	1,138
5 Australia	607	5 Italy	590
6 Russia	518	6 Taiwan	584
7 China	487	7 France	583
8 Peru	483	8 South Korea	560
9 Poland	436	9 United Kingdom	374
10 Mexico	379	10 Mexico	341

Lead

Top 10 producers[a] '000 tonnes		*Top 10 consumers[b]* '000 tonnes	
1 China	712	1 United States	1,618
2 Australia	617	2 China	530
3 United States	463	3 Germany	362
4 Peru	258	4 Japan	327
5 Canada	184	5 United Kingdom	276
6 Mexico	163	6 South Korea	260
7 Sweden	114	7 Italy	259
8 South Africa	84	8 France	208
9 Morocco	70	9 Mexico	185
10 Poland	54	10 Spain	173

Zinc

Top 10 producers[a] '000 tonnes		*Top 10 consumers[c]* '000 tonnes	
1 China	1,210	1 United States	1,293
2 Canada	1,065	2 China	1,128
3 Australia	1,059	3 Japan	659
4 Peru	864	4 Germany	573
5 United States	702	5 Italy	372
6 Mexico	385	6 France	302
7 Kazakhstan	224	South Korea	302
8 India	190	8 Belgium	265
9 Ireland	181	9 India	241
10 Sweden	165	10 Taiwan	240

Tin

Top 5 producers[a] '000 tonnes		*Top 5 consumers[b]* '000 tonnes	
1 China	70.1	1 United States	52.7
2 Indonesia	55.9	2 China	34.9
3 Peru	25.7	3 Japan	24.4
4 Brazil	14.6	4 Germany	20.3
5 Bolivia	10.5	5 United Kingdom	10.6

Nickel

Top 10 producers[a] '000 tonnes		Top 10 consumers[b] '000 tonnes	
1 Russia	270.0	1 Japan	150.7
2 Canada	208.2	2 United States	115.6
3 Australia	144.0	3 Germany	90.1
4 New Caledonia	125.3	4 Taiwan	80.4
5 Indonesia	74.5	5 South Korea	72.4
6 Cuba	67.7	6 France	54.9
7 China	48.7	7 Italy	53.3
8 South Africa	36.7	8 China	42.0
9 Colombia	28.1	9 Finland	37.1
10 Brazil	25.7	10 Russia	31.7

Aluminium

Top 10 producers[d] '000 tonnes		Top 10 consumers[e] '000 tonnes	
1 United States	3,713	1 United States	5,814
2 Russia	3,005	2 China	2,425
3 Canada	2,374	3 Japan	2,080
4 China	2,336	4 Germany	1,580
5 Australia	1,626	5 France	744
6 Brazil	1,208	6 Canada	734
7 Norway	996	7 Italy	674
8 South Africa	693	8 United Kingdom	668
9 Germany	612	9 India	567
10 Venezuela	584	10 Brazil	521

Precious metals

Gold[a] Top 10 producers tonnes		Silver[a] Top 10 producers tonnes	
1 South Africa	473.8	1 Mexico	2,672
2 United States	366.0	2 United States	2,060
3 Australia	309.3	3 Peru	2,004
4 Canada	165.6	4 Australia	1,474
5 China	158.2	5 Chile	1,337
6 Indonesia	124.0	6 Canada	1,196
7 Russia	113.1	7 Poland	1,097
8 Peru	93.8	8 China	918
9 Uzbekistan	82.0	9 Kazakhstan	536
10 Brazil	65.0	10 Bolivia	404

a Mine production.
b Refined consumption.
c Slab consumption.
d Primary refined production.
e Primary refined consumption.

Rubber (natural and synthetic)

Top 10 producers '000 tonnes		*Top 10 consumers* '000 tonnes	
1 United States	2,610	1 United States	3,512
2 Thailand	2,246	2 China	1,839
3 Indonesia	1,731	3 Japan	1,823
4 Japan	1,520	4 Germany	816
5 China	1,039	5 India	735
6 Malaysia	886	6 France	674
7 India	657	7 South Korea	559
8 Russia	621	8 Brazil	475
9 Germany	619	9 Italy	423
10 France	606	10 Malaysia	413

Raw wool

Top 10 producers[a] '000 tonnes		*Top 10 consumers[b]* '000 tonnes	
1 Australia	684	1 China	290
2 China	295	2 Italy	148
3 New Zealand	252	3 Turkey	69
4 Russia	142	4 Russia	66
5 Turkey	72	5 India	59
6 Argentina	70	6 Japan	53
7 United Kingdom	69	United Kingdom	53
8 Uruguay	63	8 United States	48
9 Pakistan	56	9 Germany	43
10 South Africa	55	10 Iran	28

Cotton

Top 10 producers '000 tonnes		*Top 10 consumers* '000 tonnes	
1 China	4,510	1 China	4,600
2 United States	3,030	2 India	2,770
3 India	2,710	3 United States	2,270
4 Pakistan	1,480	4 Pakistan	1,530
5 Uzbekistan	1,000	5 Turkey	1,000
6 Turkey	882	6 Brazil	820
7 Australia	726	7 Indonesia	490
8 Brazil	528	8 Mexico	484
9 Greece	390	9 Italy	357
10 Syria	335	10 South Korea	325

Major oil seeds[c]

Top 5 producers '000 tonnes		*Top 5 consumers* '000 tonnes	
1 United States	83,829	1 United States	57,612
2 China	39,653	2 China	45,293
3 Brazil	32,002	3 EU 15	34,312
4 Argentina	27,219	4 Argentina	24,822
5 India	22,170	5 Brazil	24,026

Oil[d]

Top 15 producers '000 barrels per day		*Top 15 consumers* '000 barrels per day	
1 Saudi Arabia[e]	9,230	1 United States	17,810
2 United States	7,995	2 Japan	5,550
3 Russia	6,170	3 China	4,110
4 Iran[e]	3,800	4 Germany	2,915
5 Mexico	3,500	5 Russia	2,455
6 Venezuela[e]	3,335	6 South Korea	2,020
7 Norway	3,215	7 France	2,010
8 China	3,205	8 Italy	1,975
9 United Kingdom	2,800	9 India	1,820
10 United Arab Emirates[e]	2,710	10 Canada	1,815
11 Canada	2,670	11 Brazil	1,800
12 Kuwait[e]	2,180	12 Mexico	1,780
13 Iraq[e]	2,165	13 United Kingdom	1,735
14 Nigeria[e]	2,155	14 Spain	1,380
15 Indonesia[e]	1,525	15 Iran	1,200

Natural gas

Top 10 producers Billion cubic metres		*Top 10 consumers* Billion cubic metres	
1 Russia	551.3	1 United States	612.4
2 United States	543.8	2 Russia	364.7
3 Canada	160.4	3 United Kingdom	88.7
4 United Kingdom	90.3	4 Germany	79.5
5 Algeria	72.8	5 Canada	70.3
6 Indonesia	68.4	6 Japan	69.5
7 Netherlands	63.6	7 Ukraine	68.8
8 Uzbekistan	51.1	8 Italy	57.2
9 Iran	50.0	9 Iran	51.7
10 Saudi Arabia	46.0	10 Uzbekistan	47.0

Coal

Top 10 producers Million tonnes oil equivalent		*Top 10 consumers* Million tonnes oil equivalent	
1 China	625.7	1 China	615.4
2 United States	589.6	2 United States	533.7
3 India	147.8	3 India	153.6
4 Australia	147.5	4 Russia	102.8
5 South Africa	118.3	5 Japan	88.4
6 Russia	104.6	6 South Africa	87.9
7 Poland	76.3	7 Germany	84.7
8 Germany	61.3	8 Poland	60.9
9 Canada	41.1	9 Australia	45.8
10 Ukraine	39.6	10 United Kingdom	40.7

a Greasy basis.
b Clean basis.
c Soybeans, sunflower seed, cottonseed, groundnuts and rapeseed.
d Includes crude oil, shale oil, oil sands and natural gas liquids.
e Opec members.

Energy

Largest producers
Million tonnnes coal equivalent, 1996

#	Country	Value	#	Country	Value
1	United States	2,494.3	16	Algeria	179.2
2	Russia	1,430.2	17	South Africa	174.9
3	China	1,276.6	18	France	171.2
4	Saudi Arabia	668.1	19	Kuwait	162.7
5	Canada	489.5	20	Nigeria	139.4
6	United Kingdom	382.5	21	Japan	137.4
7	India	340.4	22	Poland	135.7
8	Iran	321.4	23	Netherlands	114.3
9	Indonesia	299.9	24	Ukraine	111.3
10	Norway	296.3	25	Libya	106.7
11	Mexico	292.5	26	Kazakhstan	105.1
12	Venezuela	287.7	27	Brazil	102.0
13	Australia	267.6	28	Argentina	101.4
14	United Arab Emirates	207.7	29	Malaysia	97.9
15	Germany	197.9	30	North Korea	88.5

Largest consumers
Million tonnes coal equivalent, 1996

#	Country	Value	#	Country	Value
1	United States	3,095.2	16	Poland	144.3
2	China	1,225.5	17	Indonesia	131.8
3	Russia	896.2	18	Iran	127.3
4	Japan	655.2	19	Spain	127.0
5	Germany	478.1	20	Netherlands	125.1
6	India	400.1	21	Saudi Arabia	121.8
7	United Kingdom	328.0	22	South Africa	116.0
8	France	326.6	23	Venezuela	101.3
9	Canada	326.5	24	North Korea	96.8
10	Italy	230.3	25	Thailand	87.0
11	Ukraine	223.2	26	Turkey	78.6
12	South Korea	201.5	27	Kazakhstan	75.9
13	Mexico	187.1	28	Argentina	73.8
14	Brazil	154.3	29	Belgium	73.3
15	Australia	151.2	30	Romania	60.8

Energy efficiency

Most efficient		*Least efficient*	
GDP per kg of energy, 1996, $		*GDP per kg of energy, 1996, $*	
1 Hong Kong	12.0	1 Mozambique	0.3
Switzerland	12.0	Azerbaijan	0.3
3 Japan	10.5	Turkmenistan	0.3
4 Austria	8.7	Tanzania	0.3
5 Denmark	8.2	5 Nigeria	0.4
6 Germany	7.0	Ethiopia	0.4
7 Italy	6.8	7 Congo	0.5
8 Norway	6.7	Tajikistan	0.5
9 Uruguay	6.4	Kazakhstan	0.5
10 France	6.1	Ukraine	0.5
		Bulgaria	0.5
		Uzbekistan	0.5
		Russia	0.5

Largest exporters
Million tonnes coal equivalent, 1996

1	Russia	539.5	14	Netherlands	124.6
2	Saudi Arabia	493.9	15	Nigeria	124.5
3	Norway	263.7	16	Mexico	119.9
4	Canada	240.3	17	Libya	87.2
5	Iran	193.0	18	South Africa	71.8
6	Venezuela	189.1	19	China	65.6
7	United Arab Emirates	156.9	20	Oman	60.3
8	Australia	156.2	21	Singapore	60.1
9	United Kingdom	145.7	22	Malaysia	52.6
10	Indonesia	145.4	23	Colombia	51.7
11	Kuwait	133.5	24	Angola	47.5
12	United States	127.6	25	Kazakhstan	42.9
13	Algeria	125.9			

Largest importers
Million tonnes coal equivalent, 1996

1	United States	804.8	14	Brazil	72.3
2	Japan	573.7	15	Canada	67.6
3	Germany	327.6	16	China	59.7
4	South Korea	226.4	17	Thailand	59.6
5	Italy	219.5	18	Turkey	58.0
6	France	209.7	19	Sweden	43.9
7	Netherlands	143.2	20	Poland	39.4
8	Ukraine	118.7	21	Russia	39.2
9	Spain	113.6	22	Belarus	34.7
10	Singapore	106.8	23	Greece	33.3
11	United Kingdom	103.8	24	Australia	32.1
12	Belgium	98.7	25	Finland	30.9
13	India	87.0			

Largest consumption per head
Kg coal equivalent, 1996

1	Qatar	34,663	16	Belgium	7,215
2	United Arab Emirates	22,405	17	Sweden	6,826
3	Bahrain	17,729	18	Saudi Arabia	6,499
4	Kuwait	12,773	19	Netherlands Antilles	6,312
5	United States	11,487	20	Russia	6,050
6	Luxembourg	11,292	21	New Zealand	5,987
7	Brunei	11,047	22	Germany	5,836
8	Canada	11,001	23	Czech Republic	5,695
9	Trinidad & Tobago	9,275	24	United Kingdom	5,620
10	Singapore	8,834	25	France	5,597
11	Australia	8,371	26	Japan	5,227
12	Netherlands	8,035	27	Estonia	4,741
13	Finland	7,707	28	Switzerland	4,692
14	Iceland	7,438	29	Ireland	4,629
15	Norway	7,221	30	Denmark	4,583

Note: Consumption data for small countries, especially oil producers, can be unreliable, often leading to unrealistically high consumption per head rates.

Workers of the world

Highest % of population in labour force
1998 or latest

1	Kuwait	68.6	26	Cambodia	45.8
2	China	55.7	27	Austria	45.7
3	Singapore	53.8	28	Belarus	45.5
4	Iceland	53.6		Slovenia	45.5
5	Thailand	53.3	30	New Zealand	45.4
6	Burundi	52.9	31	Ukraine	45.2
7	Switzerland	52.7	32	Estonia	45.0
8	Luxembourg	52.0	33	Bangladesh	44.9
9	Japan	51.6	34	Sweden	44.8
10	Denmark	51.1	35	Bahrain	44.6
11	Bahamas	51.0	36	Brazil	44.1
12	Czech Republic	50.7	37	Macau	43.8
	Norway	50.7	38	Germany	43.7
14	Romania	48.3	39	Finland	43.6
15	Central African Rep	48.2	40	South Korea	43.2
16	Hong Kong	48.1	41	Lithuania	43.0
	Portugal	48.1	42	Indonesia	42.5
18	United States	48.0	43	Latvia	41.6
19	Burkina Faso	47.6	44	Ireland	40.6
20	Netherlands	47.2	45	Greece	40.5
21	Cyprus	47.0	46	Mexico	40.3
22	Canada	46.9		Slovakia	40.3
23	Rwanda	46.3	48	Malaysia	40.2
24	Australia	46.2	49	Italy	39.8
25	United Kingdom	45.9	50	Poland	39.7

Most male workforce
Highest % men in workforce

1	Iran	90.0
2	Algeria	87.0
3	Pakistan	86.7
4	Bahrain	82.0
	Syria	82.0
6	Guatemala	81.0
7	Egypt	78.0
8	Kuwait	76.8
9	Tunisia	76.4
10	Dominican Republic	75.1
11	Morocco	74.0
	Senegal	74.0
13	Malta	72.8
14	Mauritania	72.0
15	Argentina	72.0
16	India	71.4
17	Turkey	71.0
18	Nicaragua	70.5
19	Sudan	69.4
20	Costa Rica	68.3

Most female workforce
Highest % women in workforce

1	Belarus	53.5
2	Rwanda	53.0
3	Cambodia	52.9
4	Burundi	52.6
5	Ukraine	51.1
6	Malawi	51.0
7	Barbados	49.0
8	Burkina Faso	48.7
9	Lithuania	48.5
10	Bulgaria	48.4
11	Estonia	48.2
12	Zimbabwe	48.0
13	Chad	47.9
14	Sweden	47.8
15	Kenya	47.7
	Mongolia	47.7
17	Russia	47.3
18	Bahamas	47.0
	Latvia	47.0
20	Finland	46.6
	Iceland	46.6

Lowest % of population in labour force
1998 or latest

1	Colombia	13.9	26	Panama	32.6
2	Bolivia	17.8	27	Botswana	33.3
3	Suriname	21.8		Spain	33.3
4	Guatemala	22.9	29	Costa Rica	33.8
5	Mauritania	23.2	30	Uruguay	33.9
6	Pakistan	23.8	31	Senegal	34.0
7	Netherlands Antilles	25.4	32	Turkey	34.1
8	Ecuador	25.9	33	Croatia	34.5
9	Iran	26.0	34	Zimbabwe	34.6
10	Algeria	26.3	35	Honduras	34.7
11	Egypt	26.9		Israel	34.7
12	Peru	27.6	37	Fiji	35.2
13	Syria	27.8		Madagascar	35.2
14	Gambia, The	28.1	39	Chile	36.6
15	Sudan	28.2		Hungary	36.6
16	Tunisia	29.7	41	Kirgizstan	36.7
17	Puerto Rico	29.8	42	Bulgaria	37.3
18	Mongolia	30.7	43	Chad	37.4
19	Dominican Republic	31.1		El Salvador	37.4
	Nigeria	31.1	45	Malta	37.5
21	Nicaragua	31.4		Moldova	37.5
22	India	32.0		South Africa	37.5
23	Kenya	32.0	48	Jamaica	37.6
24	Sri Lanka	32.2	49	Armenia	38.2
25	Morocco	32.5	50	Azerbaijan	38.3

Highest rate of unemployment
% of labour force

1	Macedonia	38.8	21	Slovakia	11.9
2	Algeria	26.4	22	France	11.8
3	Botswana	21.5	23	Ecuador	11.5
4	Barbados	19.7	24	Croatia	11.4
5	Spain	18.8	25	Egypt	11.3
6	Morocco	17.8		Finland	11.3
7	Netherlands Antilles	16.7		Ukraine	11.3
8	Argentina	16.3	28	Suriname	11.0
9	Dominican Republic	15.9	29	Sri Lanka	10.6
10	Colombia	15.0	30	Poland	10.5
11	Bulgaria	14.2	31	Greece	10.3
	Trinidad & Tobago	14.2		Venezuela	10.3
13	Panama	13.9	33	Uruguay	10.1
14	Latvia	13.8	34	Mauritius	9.8
15	Kazakhstan	13.7	35	Germany	9.7
16	Lithuania	13.5	36	Estonia	9.6
17	Nicaragua	13.3		Philippines	9.6
	Puerto Rico	13.3	38	Armenia	9.3
	Russia	13.3	39	Belgium	9.1
20	Italy	12.3	40	Israel	8.6

The business world

Global competitiveness

Overall	Government	Internationalisation
1 United States	Singapore	United States
2 Singapore	Hong Kong	Singapore
3 Finland	Ireland	Luxembourg
4 Netherlands	Australia	Netherlands
5 Switzerland	Iceland	Germany
6 Luxembourg	Switzerland	United Kingdom
7 Ireland	Netherlands	Finland
8 Germany	Malaysia	Ireland
9 Sweden	Finland	Hong Kong
10 Iceland	United States	Belgium
11 Canada	New Zealand	France
12 Denmark	Luxembourg	Austria
13 Australia	Chile	Sweden
14 Hong Kong	Taiwan	Spain
15 United Kingdom	Canada	Denmark
16 Norway	China	Italy
17 Japan	United Kingdom	Malaysia
18 Austria	Spain	Switzerland
19 France	Norway	Chile
20 Belgium	Mexico	Canada
21 New Zealand	Denmark	Thailand
22 Taiwan	Japan	Portugal
23 Israel	Thailand	Iceland
24 Spain	South Africa	Israel
25 Malaysia	Austria	Hungary
26 Chile	South Korea	Czech Republic
27 Hungary	Brazil	Japan
28 South Korea	Germany	Norway
29 Portugal	India	Australia
30 Italy	Hungary	South Korea
31 China	Philippines	Greece
32 Greece	Israel	Brazil
33 Thailand	Sweden	Turkey
34 Brazil	Portugal	Taiwan
35 Slovenia	Argentina	China
36 Mexico	Indonesia	New Zealand
37 Czech Republic	Greece	Mexico
38 South Africa	Turkey	Argentina
39 Philippines	Colombia	Indonesia
40 Poland	Belgium	Poland
41 Argentina	France	Philippines
42 Turkey	Czech Republic	Colombia
43 India	Poland	India

Notes: Rankings reflect assessments for the ability of a country to achieve sustained high rates of GDP growth per head. Column 1 is based on 259 criteria covering: the openness of an economy, the role of the government, the development of financial markets, the quality of infrastructure, technology, business management and judicial and political institutions and labour-market flexibility. Column 2 looks at the extent to which government policies are conducive to competitiveness. Column 3 is based on the extent to which a country participates in international trade and investment flows.

The business environment

		2000 score	1999 score	1999 ranking
1	Netherlands	8.84	8.56	3
2	United Kingdom	8.80	8.62	2
3	United States	8.69	8.49	4
4	Canada	8.66	8.47	5
5	Singapore	8.55	8.43	6
6	Hong Kong	8.52	8.64	1
7	Ireland	8.42	8.03	8
	Switzerland	8.42	8.01	9
9	Denmark	8.41	7.91	10
10	Germany	8.32	7.88	12
11	Sweden	8.26	7.89	11
12	Finland	8.21	7.81	14
13	Belgium	8.17	7.53	17
	France	8.17	7.65	15
15	Australia	8.14	7.87	13
16	Taiwan	8.13	7.17	20
17	New Zealand	8.10	8.14	7
18	Spain	8.01	7.08	21
19	Norway	8.00	7.54	16
20	Austria	7.96	7.52	18
21	Chile	7.85	7.21	19
22	Italy	7.68	6.75	23
23	Israel	7.61	6.50	27
24	Portugal	7.59	6.74	24
25	Japan	7.43	6.63	25
26	South Korea	7.30	6.18	29
27	Thailand	7.27	6.28	28
28	Argentina	7.22	6.63	25
29	Poland	7.15	5.77	33
30	Hungary	7.09	6.17	30
31	Czech Republic	7.07	6.00	31
32	Malaysia	6.91	7.04	22
33	Greece	6.90	5.85	32
34	Mexico	6.78	5.75	34
35	Philippines	6.72	5.55	36
36	Brazil	6.37	5.19	44
37	Peru	6.36	5.46	39
38	South Africa	6.25	5.47	38
39	Slovakia	6.19	5.28	43
40	Indonesia	6.16	5.65	35
41	Colombia	6.13	5.44	40
42	Egypt	6.10	5.39	42
43	Turkey	6.06	5.52	37
44	Saudi Arabia	6.02	5.40	41
45	India	5.97	5.12	45
46	China	5.88	5.05	47
47	Sri Lanka	5.87	5.11	46

Note: Scores reflect the opportunities for, and hindrances to, the conduct of business, measured by countries' rankings in ten categories including market potential, tax and labour-market policies, infrastructure, skills and the political environment.

Businesses and banks

Largest businesses

By sales, \$bn

1	General Motors	United States	161.3
2	DaimlerChrysler	United States	154.6
3	Ford Motor	United States	144.4
4	Wal-Mart Stores	United States	139.2
5	Mitsui[a]	Japan	109.4
6	Itochu[a]	Japan	108.7
7	Mitsubishi[a]	Japan	107.2
8	Exxon	United States	100.7
9	General Electric	United States	100.5
10	Toyota Motor[a]	Japan	99.7
11	Royal Dutch/Shell Group	United Kingdom/Netherlands	93.7
12	Marubeni[a]	Japan	93.6
13	Sumitomo[a]	Japan	89.0
14	Intl. Business Machines	United States	81.7
15	AXA	France	78.7
16	Citigroup	United States	76.4
17	Volkswagen	Germany	76.3
18	Nippon Telegraph & Telephone[ab]	Japan	76.1
19	BP Amoco	United Kingdom	68.3
20	Nissho Iwai[a]	Japan	67.7
21	Nippon Life Insurance[a]	Japan	66.3
22	Siemens	Germany	66.0
23	Allianz	Germany	64.9
24	Hitachi[a]	Japan	62.4
25	U.S. Postal Service[b]	United States	60.1
26	Matsushita Electric Industrial[a]	Japan	59.8
27	Philip Morris	United States	57.8
28	ING Group	Netherlands	56.5
29	Boeing	United States	56.2
30	AT&T	United States	53.6
31	Sony[a]	Japan	53.2
32	Metro	Germany	52.1
33	Nissan Motor[a]	Japan	51.5
34	Fiat	Italy	51.0
35	Bank of America Corp.	United States	50.8
36	Nestlé	Switzerland	49.5
37	Credit Suisse	Switzerland	49.1
38	Honda Motor[a]	Japan	48.7
39	Assicurazioni Generali	Italy	48.5
40	Mobil	United States	47.7
41	Hewlett-Packard	United States	47.1
42	Deutsche Bank	Germany	45.2
43	Unilever	United Kingdom/Netherlands	44.9
44	State Farm Insurance Cos.	United States	44.6

a Year ended March 31, 1999.
b Government owned.

Notes: Industrial and service corporations. Figures refer to the year ended December 31, 1998, except where specified. They include sales of consolidated subsidiaries but exclude excise taxes, thus differing, in some instances, from figures published by the companies themselves.

Largest banks
By capital, $m

1	Citicorp	United States	41,889
2	BankAmerica Corp	United States	36,887
3	HSBC Holdings	United Kingdom	29,352
4	Crédit Agricole	France	25,930
5	Chase Manhattan Corp	United States	24,121
6	Industrial and Commercial Bank of China	China	22,213
7	Bank of Tokyo-Mitsubishi	Japan	22,074
8	UBS	Switzerland	20,525
9	Sakura Bank	Japan	19,899
10	Bank One Corp	United States	19,654
11	Fuji Bank	Japan	19,590
12	Deutsche Bank	Germany	18,680
13	Sanwa Bank	Japan	17,745
14	Credit Suisse Group	Switzerland	17,579
15	ABN-Amro Bank	Netherlands	17,471
16	Dai-Ichi Kangyo Bank	Japan	17,234
17	Sumitomo Bank	Japan	16,220
18	Bank of China	China	14,712
19	Rabobank Nederland	Netherlands	14,688
20	Industrial Bank of Japan	Japan	14,529
21	First Union Corp	United States	13,592
22	Barclays Bank	United Kingdom	13,495
23	National Westminster Bank	United Kingdom	13,389
24	Tokai Bank	Japan	13,274
25	Dresdner Bank	Germany	13,042
26	ING Bank Group	Netherlands	12,961
27	Banque Nationale de Paris	France	12,824
28	Norinchukin Bank	Japan	12,585
29	Société Générale	France	12,521
30	Wells Fargo & Co	United States	12,424
31	Lloyds TSB Group	United Kingdom	12,111
32	Hypo-Vereinsbank	Germany	11,853
33	Commerzbank	Germany	11,760
34	Halifax	United Kingdom	11,564
35	J.P. Morgan & Co	United States	11,242
36	Crédit Mutuel	France	10,737
37	Banco Santander	Spain	10,654
38	Asahi Bank	Japan	10,314
39	Groupe Caisse d'Epargne	France	10,124
40	Paribas	France	9,919
41	Fortis Banking Group	Belgium	9,867
42	Sanpaolo IMI	Italy	9,423
43	Westdeutsche Landesbank Girozentrale	Germany	9,204
44	Abbey National	United Kingdom	8,659
45	Unicredito Italiano	Italy	8,420

Notes: Capital is essentially equity and reserves.
Figures for Japanese banks refer to the year ended March 31, 1999. Figures for all
other countries refer to the year ended December 31, 1998.

Stockmarkets

Largest market capitalisation
$m, end 1998

1	United States	13,451,352		27	Greece	79,992
2	Japan	2,495,757		28	Portugal	62,954
3	United Kingdom	2,374,273		29	Norway	56,285
4	Germany	1,093,962		30	Chile	51,866
5	France	991,484		31	Argentina	45,332
6	Australia	874,283		32	Saudi Arabia	42,563
7	Switzerland	689,199		33	Israel	39,628
8	Netherlands	603,182		34	Luxembourg	35,403
9	Italy	569,731		35	Philippines	35,314
10	Canada	543,394		36	Thailand	34,903
11	Spain	402,180		37	Austria	34,106
12	Hong Kong	343,394		38	Turkey	33,646
13	Sweden	278,707		39	Ireland	29,956
14	Taiwan	260,015		40	Egypt	24,381
15	Belgium	245,657		41	Indonesia	22,104
16	China	231,322		42	Russia	20,598
17	South Africa	170,252		43	Poland	20,461
18	Brazil	160,887		44	Morocco	15,676
19	Finland	154,518		45	Iran	14,874
20	South Korea	114,593		46	Hungary	14,028
21	India	105,188		47	Colombia	13,357
22	Denmark	98,881		48	Czech Republic	12,045
23	Malaysia	98,557		49	Peru	11,645
24	Singapore	94,469		50	Venezuela	7,587
25	Mexico	91,746		51	Bahrain	6,770
26	New Zealand	89,373		52	Jordan	5,838

Highest growth in market capitalisation, $ terms
% increase, 1989–98

1	China	11,306		21	Lithuania[b]	584
2	Russia[a]	9,349		22	Paraguay[e]	578
3	Poland[a]	9,117		23	New Zealand	563
4	Morocco	2,424		24	Australia	520
5	Hungary[a]	2,396		25	Armenia[b]	500
6	Ghana[a]	1,548		26	Lebanon[b]	496
7	Bulgaria[b]	1,526		27	Portugal	493
8	Namibia[c]	1,432		28	Bolivia[b]	488
9	Egypt	1,325		29	Croatia[b]	449
10	Greece	1,155		30	Chile	441
11	Peru	1,151		31	Venezuela	415
12	Colombia	1,076		32	Finland	404
13	Argentina	973		33	Turkey	396
14	Romania[b]	916		34	Israel	382
15	Indonesia	881		35	Hong Kong	343
16	Trinidad & Tobago	854		36	Mexico	307
17	Mauritius[d]	768		37	Kenya	306
18	Barbados	755		38	Oman[c]	304
19	Panama[c]	699		39	Switzerland	303
20	Slovenia[b]	688		40	Sri Lanka	299

Highest growth in value traded, $ terms
% increase, 1989–98

1	Romania[b]	59,100	23	Russia[b]	1,363
2	Hungary[a]	42,361	24	Italy	1,122
3	Bangladesh	15,760	25	Ghana[c]	1,100
4	Morocco	8,556	26	Sweden	1,069
5	Turkey	8,502	27	Luxembourg	1,007
6	Greece	8,461	28	Switzerland[d]	826
7	Egypt	5,425	29	Australia	810
8	Poland[a]	5,242	30	Brazil	775
9	Pakistan	4,616	31	South Africa	724
10	Nigeria	3,925	32	Finland	719
11	Sri Lanka	3,914	33	Argentina	687
12	Peru	2,984	34	Cote d'Ivoire	680
13	Portugal	2,388	35	Cyprus[a]	620
14	Colombia	1,980	36	Belgium	618
15	Mauritius[d]	1,940		Kenya	618
16	Spain	1,721	38	United States	502
17	Oman[c]	1,699	39	Bolivia[b]	500
18	Indonesia	1,695		Lithuania[b]	500
19	New Zealand	1,569	41	Hong Kong	495
20	Venezuela	1,524	42	Tunisia[a]	488
21	Panama[c]	1,386	43	Kuwait	446
22	China[a]	1,384	44	Mexico	443

Highest growth in number of listed companies
% increase, 1989–98

1	Romania[b]	82,086	24	Honduras[a]	114
2	Slovakia[b]	4,550	25	Iceland[b]	107
3	Bulgaria[b]	3,738	26	Greece	105
4	China[a]	1,540		Iran[a]	105
5	Poland[a]	1,138	28	Bolivia[b]	100
6	Russia[a]	812		Mauritius[d]	100
7	Paraguay[e]	511	30	Colombia	99
8	Turkey	454	31	Norway	93
9	Indonesia	404	32	Sweden	91
10	Namibia[c]	275	33	Bangladesh	79
11	Malaysia	193	34	Pakistan	76
12	Oman	152	35	Slovenia[c]	75
13	Swaziland[d]	150	36	Croatia[e]	72
14	Israel	148	37	Egypt	69
15	Panama[c]	145	38	Nigeria	68
16	India	143	39	Finland	65
17	Taiwan	141	40	Philippines	53
18	Hungary[a]	139	41	Cote d'Ivoire	52
	Thailand	139	42	Italy	47
20	Singapore	136	43	Barbados[d]	43
21	Hong Kong	132	44	Jordan	42
22	Fiji[b]	125	45	Ghana[a]	40
23	Tunisia[c]	124		Malta[b]	40

a 1992–98 b 1995–98 c 1993–98
d 1991–98 e 1994–98

Transport: *roads and cars*

Longest road networks
Km, 1998 or latest

1	United States	6,348,227	21	Sweden	210,907
2	India	3,319,644	22	Bangladesh	201,182
3	Brazil	1,980,000	23	Philippines	199,950
4	China	1,526,389	24	Nigeria	193,394
5	Japan	1,152,207	25	Hungary	188,203
6	Australia	913,000	26	Ukraine	176,310
7	Canada	901,903	27	Iran	165,724
8	France	893,300	28	Congo	157,000
9	Germany	656,140	29	Romania	153,359
10	Italy	654,676	30	Saudi Arabia	146,524
11	Russia	570,719	31	Belgium	145,850
12	South Africa	534,131	32	Austria	133,361
13	Turkey	382,059	33	Czech Republic	127,693
14	Poland	381,046	34	Netherlands	125,575
15	United Kingdom	371,603	35	Kazakhstan	119,390
16	Spain	346,858	36	Greece	117,000
17	Indonesia	342,700	37	Colombia	115,564
18	Mexico	313,977	38	Algeria	104,000
19	Pakistan	247,811	39	Sri Lanka	99,200
20	Argentina	215,434	40	Venezuela	96,155

Densest road networks
Km of road per km² land area, 1998 or latest

1	Malta	6.33	21	Puerto Rico	1.58
2	Belgium	4.78	22	United Kingdom	1.53
3	Singapore	4.75	23	Sri Lanka	1.51
4	Bahrain	4.58	24	Bangladesh	1.40
5	Barbados	3.72	25	Ireland	1.32
6	Japan	3.05	26	Poland	1.22
7	Netherlands	3.02	27	Cyprus	1.15
8	Macao	2.94	28	Estonia	1.09
9	Italy	2.17		Lithuania	1.09
10	Hungary	2.02	30	India	1.01
11	Luxembourg	2.00	31	Slovenia	0.97
12	Germany	1.83	32	Taiwan	0.96
13	Jamaica	1.73	33	Mauritius	0.94
14	Switzerland	1.72	34	Latvia	0.93
15	Denmark	1.66	35	Greece	0.89
16	France	1.64	36	South Korea	0.88
	Hong Kong	1.64	37	Israel	0.77
18	Czech Republic	1.62		Portugal	0.77
	Trinidad & Tobago	1.62	39	Costa Rica	0.73
20	Austria	1.59	40	Spain	0.69

Most crowded road networks
Number of vehicles per km of road network, 1998 or latest

1	Macau	1,048	26	Luxembourg	51
2	Hong Kong	296	27	Portugal	50
3	United Arab	232	28	Libya	48
4	Lebanon	219	29	Uzbekistan	45
5	Singapore	170	30	Jordan	44
6	Kuwait	156		Malaysia	44
7	Qatar	154		Mexico	44
8	Taiwan	149		Slovenia	44
9	South Korea	120	34	Serbia & Montenegro	42
10	Malta	109	35	Croatia	40
11	Israel	100		Barbados	40
12	Thailand	97	37	Russia	39
13	Slovakia	77	38	El Salvador	36
14	Puerto Rico	74	39	France	35
15	United Kingdom	67		Macedonia	35
16	Germany	66		Serbia	35
17	Brunei	63	42	Belgium	34
18	Bahrain	62		Cyprus	34
19	Japan	61	44	Austria	32
20	Netherlands	58		Czech Republic	32
21	Mauritius	57		United States	32
22	Bulgaria	56	47	Denmark	31
23	Spain	53		Greece	31
24	Italy	52	49	Dominican Republic	30
	Switzerland	52		Finland	30

Most used road networks
'000 vehicle-km per year per km of road network, 1998 or latest

1	Indonesia	8,134.1	16	Saudi Arabia	642.5
2	Hong Kong	6,071.0	17	Denmark	616.7
3	Bahrain	2,807.8	18	Finland	575.1
4	Mongolia	2,168.7	19	France	550.0
5	Israel	2,095.6	20	Slovakia	543.9
6	Thailand	1,546.4	21	Spain	514.6
7	Portugal	1,296.8	22	Macedonia	489.1
8	United Kingdom	1,088.5	23	Croatia	471.4
9	Belgium	1,073.9	24	El Salvador	423.2
10	Germany	888.7	25	Poland	401.7
11	Netherlands	868.2	26	Zimbabwe	399.7
12	South Korea	773.3	27	United States	399.6
13	Luxembourg	742.4	28	Oman	391.2
14	Switzerland	705.2	29	Slovenia	382.0
15	Japan	646.0	30	Italy	349.8

Highest car ownership
Number of cars per 1,000 people, 1998 or latest

1	Lebanon	732	26	Kuwait	359
2	Brunei	576	27	Czech Republic	358
	Luxembourg	576	28	Denmark	355
4	Italy	539	29	Estonia	312
5	Iceland	510	30	Portugal	309
6	Germany	506	31	Ireland	279
7	Australia	488	32	Bahrain	245
8	United States	486	33	Greece	238
9	Austria	481	34	Poland	230
10	Switzerland	477		Puerto Rico	230
11	New Zealand	470	36	Hungary	229
12	Malta	462	37	Slovakia	222
13	Canada	455	38	Bulgaria	220
14	France	442	39	Croatia	219
15	Belgium	435		Qatar	219
16	Sweden	428	41	Israel	215
17	Slovenia	403	42	Taiwan	207
18	Norway	402	43	Latvia	198
19	Japan	394	44	South Korea	163
20	Finland	392	45	Bahamas	161
	United Kingdom	392	46	Libya	154
22	Spain	385		Uruguay	154
23	Netherlands	379	48	Malaysia	145
24	Cyprus	375		Serbia & Montenegro	145
25	Lithuania	365	50	Macedonia	142

Lowest car ownership
Number of cars per 1,000 people, 1998 or latest

1	Central African Rep	0.1	16	Liberia	2.6
	Somalia	0.1	17	Burundi	2.8
	Tajikistan	0.1	18	Mali	2.9
4	Armenia	0.3	19	Chad	3.2
	Mozambique	0.3		China	3.2
6	Bangladesh	0.5	21	Laos	3.4
7	Myanmar	0.6	22	Burkina Faso	3.6
8	Tanzania	0.8	23	Niger	3.8
9	Ethiopia	0.9	24	Sierra Leone	3.9
10	Afghanistan	1.4	25	Madagascar	4.1
	Rwanda	1.4	26	Haiti	4.4
12	Eritrea	1.5	27	India	4.5
13	Uganda	1.8	28	Ghana	4.7
14	Guinea	2.0		Honduras	4.7
15	Malawi	2.3	30	Cambodia	4.8

Most accidents
Number of people injured per 100m vehicle-km, 1998 or latest

1	Malawi	2,730		Macedonia	81
2	Rwanda	1,764		Mongolia	81
3	South Korea	510	28	Spain	78
4	Costa Rica	406	29	Slovakia	76
5	Kenya	363		United States	76
6	India	333	31	United Kingdom	72
7	Honduras	317	32	Iceland	70
8	Turkey	231	33	Mexico	66
9	Egypt	222	34	Yemen	59
10	Sri Lanka	205	35	Hungary	58
11	Portugal	194	36	Senegal	56
12	Morocco	163	37	New Zealand	54
13	Hong Kong	162		Slovenia	54
14	Israel	145	39	Colombia	53
15	Kirgizstan	134		Iran	53
16	Japan	129		Oman	53
	South Africa	129		Switzerland	53
18	Canada	126	43	Thailand	40
19	Latvia	125	44	Ireland	38
20	Italy	122		Norway	38
21	Czech Republic	113	46	Bahrain	34
22	Belgium	108	47	France	32
23	Saudi Arabia	89		Mauritius	32
24	Philippines	86		Sweden	32
25	Germany	81		Zimbabwe	32

Most deaths
Number of people killed per 100m vehicle-km, 1998 or latest

1	Malawi	1,117		Yemen	11
2	India	65	17	Mexico	10
3	Egypt	44		South Africa	10
4	Kenya	41		Turkey	10
5	Latvia	25	20	Albania	8
6	Kirgizstan	24	21	Portugal	6
7	Sri Lanka	23		Slovakia	6
8	South Korea	17	23	Colombia	5
9	Honduras	16		Czech Republic	5
	Morocco	16		Ecuador	5
11	Mongolia	14		Iran	5
	Philippines	14		Romania	5
13	Thailand	13	28	Macedonia	4
14	Costa Rica	11		Oman	4
	Saudi Arabia	11		Senegal	4

Transport: *planes and trains*

Most air travel
Million passenger-km[a] per year

1	United States	984,697	16	Italy	37,623
2	Japan	154,402	17	Thailand	34,340
3	United Kingdom	152,126	18	Malaysia	29,372
4	Germany	90,424	19	Switzerland	28,847
5	France	89,306	20	Mexico	25,078
6	Chaina	75,279	21	India	24,723
7	Australia	73,661	22	New Zealand	19,014
8	Netherlands	69,133	23	Saudi Arabia	18,820
9	Canada	63,801	24	Indonesia	18,029
10	Singapore	58,083	25	South Africa	16,996
11	South Korea	47,711	26	Belgium	15,338
12	Brazil	46,162	27	Argentina	14,225
13	Russia	44,456	28	Turkey	13,033
14	Hong Kong	43,039	29	Philippines	12,909
15	Spain	40,042			

Busiest airports

	Total passengers, m			International passengers, m	
1	Atlanta, Hartsfield	77.9	1	London, Heathrow	53.1
2	Chicago, O'Hare	72.6	2	Paris, Charles de Gaulle	34.4
3	Los Angeles Intl.	63.9	3	Frankfurt/Main	34.3
4	London, Heathrow	62.3	4	Amsterdam, Schipol	33.8
5	Dallas/Ft. Worth	60.0	5	Hong Kong Intl.	27.2
6	Tokyo, Hanedo	54.3	6	London, Gatwick	26.3
7	Frankfurt/Main	45.9	7	Singapore, Changi	22.5
8	Paris, Charles de Gaulle	43.6	8	Tokyo, Narita	21.7
9	San Francisco Intl.	40.4	9	Brussels, Zaventem	18.4
10	Denver Intl.	38.0	10	New York, Kennedy	17.7
11	Amsterdam, Schipol	36.8		Zurich	17.7
12	Minneapolis, St Paul	34.2	12	Bangkok Intl.	17.0

Biggest airlines
No. of aeroplanes and average age of aeroplanes

		No.	Yrs.			No.	Yrs.
1	American	697	10.6	9	Lufthansa	298	7.5
2	United	594	9.9	10	Air France	223	9.3
3	Delta	584	12.0	11	Iberia	215	11.3
4	Northwest	409	19.9	12	KLM	202	8.3
5	US Airways	393	12.7	13	SAS	190	9.3
6	Continental	363	8.4	14	TWA	183	12.1
7	British Airways	357	8.0	15	Alitalia	155	9.1
8	Southwest	312	8.2		**Average age**[b]		**10.7**

a Air passenger–km data refer to the distance travelled by each aircraft of national origin.
b Weighted by number of aircraft.

Longest railway networks
'000 km, 1998

1	United States	232.2	21	Australia	9.5
2	Russia	86.2	22	Czech Republic	9.4
3	India	58.9	23	Turkey	8.6
4	China	57.6	24	Pakistan	8.2
5	Germany	38.1	25	Hungary	7.8
6	Argentina	34.2	26	Iran	6.3
7	France	31.7	27	Finland	5.9
8	Mexico	26.5	28	Austria	5.6
9	Poland	23.2	29	Belarus	5.5
10	South Africa	22.8	30	Egypt	5.0
11	Ukraine	22.5	31	Philippines	4.9
12	Brazil	22.1	32	Cuba	4.8
13	Japan	20.2	33	Sudan	4.6
14	United Kingdom	17.2	34	North Korea	4.5
15	Italy	16.1	35	Algeria	4.3
16	Canada	14.1		Serbia & Montenegro	4.3
17	Spain	13.7	37	Indonesia	4.2
18	Kazakhstan	13.6	38	Norway	4.0
19	Romania	11.4	39	New Zealand	3.9
20	Sweden	11.1	40	Slovakia	3.7

Most rail passengers
Km per year per person, 1998

1	Japan	1,921	11	Germany	722
2	Switzerland	1,817	12	Italy	721
3	Belarus	1,302	13	Luxembourg	714
4	France	1,091	14	Belgium	696
5	Egypt	1,046	15	Czech Republic	680
6	Denmark	1,013	16	Kazakhstan	677
7	Ukraine	989	17	Hungary	672
8	Austria	987	18	Russia	665
9	Netherlands	948	19	Finland	656
10	Sweden	792	20	United Kingdom	612

Most rail freight
Million tonnes-km per year, 1998

1	United States	2,010,027	11	Australia	30,449
2	China	1,226,152	12	Belarus	30,370
3	Russia	901,381	13	Japan	22,681
4	India	284,249	14	Italy	22,454
5	Ukraine	158,693	15	Czech Republic	18,286
6	South Africa	103,866	16	United Kingdom	18,175
7	Kazakhstan	99,877	17	Romania	17,854
8	Germany	73,613	18	Uzbekistan	15,672
9	Poland	60,937	19	Austria	14,487
10	France	53,959	20	Sweden	14,313

Transport: *sail away*

Largest merchant fleets

Number of vessels over 100 GRT [a] *Mid-1999*		*Gross tonnage[b]* *'000, mid-1999*	
1 Japan	8,462	1 Panama	105,248
2 Panama	6,143	2 Liberia	54,107
3 United States	5,642	3 Bahamas	29,483
4 Russia	4,694	4 Malta	28,205
5 China	3,285	5 Greece	24,833
6 South Korea	2,417	6 Cyprus	23,641
7 Indonesia	2,369	7 Norway	23,446
8 Norway	2,350	8 Singapore	21,780
9 Philippines	1,897	9 Japan	17,063
10 Singapore	1,736	10 China	16,315
11 Liberia	1,629	11 United States	12,026
12 Malta	1,574	12 Russia	10,649
13 Spain	1,562	13 Italy	8,048
14 Cyprus	1,556	14 Hong Kong	7,973
15 Honduras	1,551	15 Philippines	7,650
16 Greece	1,491	16 India	6,915
17 United Kingdom	1,391	17 Germany	6,514
18 Italy	1,389	18 Turkey	6,325
19 Bahamas	1,294	19 Denmark	5,913
20 Netherlands	1,276	20 South Korea	5,735
21 Turkey	1,152	21 Taiwan	5,371
22 Denmark	1,057	22 Malaysia	5,245
23 Germany	1,028	23 Netherlands	4,814
24 India	971	24 Bermuda	4,811
25 Ukraine	936	25 United Kingdom	4,331
26 Canada	857	26 Brazil	3,933
27 Malaysia	828	27 Iran	3,546
28 Peru	724	28 Indonesia	3,241
29 France	713	29 Sweden	2,947
30 Taiwan	684	30 Canada	2,496
31 Vietnam	640	31 Kuwait	2,456
32 Australia	621	32 Australia	2,084
Mexico	621	33 Thailand	1,956
34 Sweden	570	34 France	1,813
35 Thailand	551	35 Ukraine	1,775
36 Brazil	503	36 Finland	1,658
37 Morocco	496	37 Egypt	1,368
38 Argentina	493	38 Luxembourg	1,343
39 Hong Kong	479	39 Poland	1,319
40 Chile	472	40 Spain	1,269

a Gross Tonnage (GRT) = total volume within the hull and above deck. 1 GRT=100 cu ft.
b By country in which ships have registered.

Tourism

Most tourist arrivals
Number of arrivals, '000

1	France	70,000	21	Thailand	7,843
2	Spain	47,749	22	Ukraine	6,208
3	United States	46,395	23	Belgium	6,179
4	Italy	34,829	24	Ireland	6,064
5	United Kingdom	25,745	25	South Africa	5,898
6	China	25,073	26	Singapore	5,631
7	Mexico	19,810	27	Malaysia	5,551
8	Canada	18,837	28	Argentina	4,860
9	Poland	18,780	29	Brazil	4,818
10	Austria	17,352	30	Tunisia	4,718
11	Germany	16,511	31	Indonesia	4,606
12	Czech Republic	16,325	32	South Korea	4,250
13	Russia	15,805	33	Australia	4,167
14	Hungary	15,000	34	Croatia	4,112
15	Portugal	11,295	35	Japan	4,106
16	Greece	10,916	36	Macau	4,044
17	Switzerland	10,900	37	Morocco	3,243
18	Hong Kong	9,575	38	Egypt	3,213
19	Netherlands	9,320	39	India	2,359
20	Turkey	8,960	40	United Arab Emirates	2,184

Biggest tourist spenders
$m

1	United States	56,100	9	Austria	9,500
2	Germany	46,900	10	China	9,200
3	United Kingdom	32,300	11	Belgium	8,800
4	Japan	28,800	12	Russia	8,300
5	France	17,800	13	Sweden	7,700
6	Italy	17,600	14	Switzerland	7,100
7	Netherlands	11,200	15	Brazil	5,700
8	Canada	10,800			

Largest tourist receipts
$m

1	United States	71,250	16	Netherlands	6,803
2	France	29,931	17	Russia	6,508
3	Italy	29,809	18	Thailand	5,934
4	Spain	29,737	19	South Korea	5,890
5	United Kingdom	20,978	20	Belgium	5,437
6	Germany	16,429	21	Ukraine	5,407
7	China	12,602	22	Argentina	5,363
8	Austria	11,184	23	Greece	5,182
9	Canada	9,393	24	Singapore	5,162
10	Poland	7,946	25	Portugal	4,853
11	Mexico	7,897	26	Indonesia	4,045
12	Switzerland	7,815	27	Japan	3,742
13	Turkey	7,809	28	Czech Republic	3,719
14	Australia	7,335	29	Brazil	3,678
15	Hong Kong	7,083	30	Ireland	3,252

Education

Highest primary enrolment
Number enrolled as % of relevant age group, 1997

1	Gabon	162		Mexico	114
2	Malawi	134		Vietnam	114
3	South Africa	133	18	Cambodia	113
4	Namibia	131		Colombia	113
5	Portugal	128		Indonesia	113
6	Ecuador	127		Nepal	113
7	Brazil	125	22	Laos	112
8	China	123		Zimbabwe	112
	Peru	123	24	Argentina	111
10	Myanmar	121		Honduras	111
11	Togo	120		Lebanon	111
12	Tunisia	118		Libya	111
13	Philippines	117		Paraguay	111
14	United Kingdom	115	29	Sri Lanka	109
15	Congo-Brazzaville	114		Uruguay	109

Lowest primary enrolment
Number enrolled as % of relevant age group, 1997

1	Niger	29	15	Côte d'Ivoire	71
2	Burkina Faso	40		Jordan	71
3	Ethiopia	43		Senegal	71
4	Mali	49	18	Congo	72
5	Burundi	51	19	Pakistan	74
	Sudan	51		Uganda	74
7	Eritrea	53	21	Oman	76
8	Guinea	54		Saudi Arabia	76
9	Chad	58	23	Gambia, The	77
10	Mozambique	60		Kuwait	77
11	Guinea-Bissau	62	25	Benin	78
12	Tanzania	67		Uzbekistan	78
13	Serbia & Montenegro	69	27	Ghana	79
14	Yemen	70		Mauritania	79

Highest tertiary enrolment[a]
Number enrolled as % of relevant age group, 1997

1	Canada	90	12	Sweden	50
2	United States	81	13	Austria	48
3	Australia	80	14	Germany	47
4	Finland	74		Greece	47
5	South Korea	68		Italy	47
6	New Zealand	63		Netherlands	47
7	Norway	62	18	Denmark	45
8	Belgium	57		Estonia	45
9	United Kingdom	52	20	Belarus	44
10	France	51		Israel	44
	Spain	51	22	Japan	43

Notes: The gross enrolment ratios shown are the actual number enrolled as a percentage of the number of children in the official primary age group. They may exceed 100 when children outside the primary age group are receiving primary education either because they have not moved on to secondary education or because they have started primary education early.

Least literate
% adult literacy rate, 1997

1	Niger	14.3	16	Pakistan	40.9
2	Burkina Faso	20.7	17	Central African Rep	42.4
3	Gambia, The	33.1	18	Yemen	42.5
4	Afghanistan	33.4	19	Côte d'Ivoire	42.6
5	Guinea-Bissau	33.6	20	Bhutan	44.2
6	Benin	33.9	21	Burundi	44.6
7	Sierra Leone	34.3	22	Haiti	45.8
8	Senegal	34.6	23	Morocco	45.9
9	Ethiopia	35.4	24	Liberia	48.4
10	Mali	35.5	25	Chad	50.3
11	Guinea	37.9	26	Egypt	52.7
12	Nepal	38.1	27	Togo	53.2
13	Mauritania	38.4	28	Sudan	53.3
14	Bangladesh	38.9	29	India	53.5
15	Mozambique	40.5	30	Malawi	57.7

Highest education spending
% of GDP, 1997

1	Moldova	10.6		Saudi Arabia	7.5
2	Namibia	9.1	15	Jamaica	7.4
3	Zimbabwe	9.0		Norway	7.4
4	Botswana	8.6	17	New Zealand	7.3
5	Lesotho	8.4		Swaziland	7.3
6	Sweden	8.3		Ukraine	7.3
7	Denmark	8.1	20	Barbados	7.2
8	South Africa	7.9		Estonia	7.2
9	Tunisia	7.7	22	Yemen	7.0
	Uzbekistan	7.7	23	Canada	6.9
11	Israel	7.6	24	Jordan	6.8
12	Finland	7.5	25	Cuba	6.7
	Poland	7.5	26	Kenya	6.5

Lowest education spending
% of GDP, 1997

1	Nigeria	0.7	14	Bangladesh	2.2
2	Sudan	0.9		Mali	2.2
3	Myanmar	1.2		Tajikistan	2.2
4	Indonesia	1.4		Turkey	2.2
5	Burkina Faso	1.5		Zambia	2.2
6	Chad	1.7	19	China	2.3
	Guatemala	1.7		Dominican Republic	2.3
8	Eritrea	1.8		Niger	2.3
	United Arab Emirates	1.8	22	El Salvador	2.5
10	Guinea	1.9		Lebanon	2.5
	Madagascar	1.9	24	Uganda	2.6
12	Armenia	2.0	25	Pakistan	2.7
13	Laos	2.1			

a Tertiary education includes all levels of post-secondary education including courses
   leading to awards not equivalent to a university degree, courses leading to a first
   university degree and postgraduate courses.

Life: *the chances*

Highest life expectancy
Years

1	Japan	80		Singapore	77
2	Canada	79		United Kingdom	77
	Iceland	79		United States	77
	Martinique[a]	79	28	Barbados	76
	Sweden	79		Brunei	76
	Switzerland	79		Costa Rica	76
7	Australia	78		Cuba	76
	Cyprus	78		Denmark	76
	France	78		Ireland	76
	Greece	78		Kuwait	76
	Israel	78		Netherlands Antilles[a]	76
	Italy	78	36	Chile	75
	Macau[a]	78		Jamaica	75
	Netherlands	78		Portugal	75
	Norway	78		Réunion[a]	75
	Spain	78		United Arab Emirates	75
17	Austria	77	41	Bahamas	74
	Belgium	77		Czech Republic	74
	Finland	77		Panama	74
	Germany	77		Puerto Rico[a]	74
	Guadeloupe[a]	77		Slovenia	74
	Luxembourg	77		Trinidad & Tobago	74
	Malta	77		Uruguay	74
	New Zealand	77			

Highest male life expectancy
Years

1	Iceland	77		Italy	75
	Japan	77		Macau[a]	75
3	Canada	76		Malta	75
	Cyprus	76		Netherlands	75
	Greece	76		Norway	75
	Israel	76		Singapore	75
	Martinique[a]	76		Spain	75
	Sweden	76		Switzerland	75
9	Australia	75		United Kingdom	75

Highest female life expectancy
Years

1	Japan	83		Greece	81
2	Canada	82		Guadeloupe[a]	81
	France	82		Hong Kong[a]	81
	Martinique[a]	82		Iceland	81
	Spain	82		Italy	81
	Switzerland	82		Netherlands	81
7	Australia	81		Norway	81
	Belgium	81		Sweden	81
	Finland	81			

a 1995–2000

Lowest life expectancy
Years

1	Sierra Leone	38		26	Nigeria	50
2	Malawi	39		27	Congo	51
3	Uganda	40			Eritrea	51
	Zambia	40			Namibia	51
5	Rwanda	41		30	Gabon	52
6	Burundi	43			Kenya	52
	Ethiopia	43		32	Benin	53
8	Mozambique	44			Cambodia	53
	Zimbabwe	44			Laos	53
10	Burkina Faso	45			Senegal	53
	Central African Rep	45		36	Haiti	54
	Guinea-Bissau	45			Mali	54
13	Afghanistan	46			Mauritania	54
14	Angola	47			South Africa	54
	Botswana	47		40	Cameroon	55
	Chad	47			Sudan	55
	Côte d'Ivoire	47		42	Lesotho	56
	Gambia, The	47		43	Bangladesh	58
	Guinea	47			Madagascar	58
	Somalia	47			Nepal	58
21	Liberia	48			Papua New Guinea	58
	Tanzania	48			Yemen	58
23	Congo-Brazzaville	49		48	Ghana	60
	Niger	49			Myanmar	60
	Togo	49			Swaziland	60

Lowest male life expectancy
Years

1	Sierra Leone	36		Guinea-Bissau	43
2	Malawi	39	10	Burkina Faso	44
	Rwanda	39		Mozambique	44
	Uganda	39		Zimbabwe	44
5	Zambia	40	13	Afghanistan	45
6	Burundi	41		Angola	45
7	Ethiopia	42		Gambia, The	45
8	Central African Rep	43		Somalia	45

Lowest female life expectancy
Years

1	Sierra Leone	39	10	Afghanistan	46
2	Malawi	40		Guinea-Bissau	46
	Uganda	40	12	Central African Rep	47
4	Zambia	41		Côte d'Ivoire	47
5	Rwanda	42		Guinea	47
6	Burundi	44		Mozambique	47
	Ethiopia	44	16	Angola	48
8	Burkina Faso	45		Botswana	48
	Zimbabwe	45			

Death: *the chances*

Highest death rates
Number of deaths per 1,000 population

1	Sierra Leone	25		Denmark	12
2	Malawi	23		Haiti	12
3	Afghanistan	21		Kenya	12
	Uganda	21		Lesotho	12
5	Burundi	20		Lithuania	12
	Ethiopia	20		South Africa	12
	Guinea-Bissau	20	51	Croatia	11
	Zambia	20		Czech Republic	11
9	Angola	19		Germany	11
	Burkina Faso	19		Madagascar	11
	Central African Rep	19		Moldova	11
	Mozambique	19		Nepal	11
13	Chad	18		Portugal	11
	Somalia	18		Romania	11
	Zimbabwe	18		Sudan	11
16	Gambia, The	17		Sweden	11
	Guinea	17		United Kingdom	11
	Niger	17	62	Austria	10
	Rwanda	17		Bangladesh	10
20	Botswana	16		Belgium	10
	Congo-Brazzaville	16		Bhutan	10
	Côte d'Ivoire	16		Finland	10
	Gabon	16		Greece	10
	Mali	16		Italy	10
25	Congo	15		Norway	10
	Liberia	15		Papua New Guinea	10
	Nigeria	15		Poland	10
	Tanzania	15		Serbia & Montenegro	10
	Togo	15		Slovakia	10
30	Bulgaria	14		Slovenia	10
	Eritrea	14		Yemen	10
	Estonia	14	76	Bolivia	9
	Hungary	14		France	9
	Latvia	14		Georgia	9
	Namibia	14		Ghana	9
	Russia	14		India	9
	Ukraine	14		Kazakhstan	9
38	Belarus	13		Luxembourg	9
	Benin	13		Myanmar	9
	Cambodia	13		Netherlands	9
	Laos	13		Spain	9
	Mauritania	13		Swaziland	9
	Senegal	13		Switzerland	9
44	Cameroon	12		Uruguay	9

Note: Both death and, in particular, infant mortality rates can be underestimated in certain countries where not all deaths are officially recorded.

Highest infant mortality
Number of deaths per 1,000 live births

1	Sierra Leone	182	21	Mongolia	105
2	Angola	170		Rwanda	105
3	Niger	166	23	Cambodia	104
4	Afghanistan	165	24	Iraq	103
5	Liberia	157	25	Benin	101
6	Mali	144	26	Laos	96
7	Malawi	134	27	Madagascar	95
8	Guinea-Bissau	130		Pakistan	95
9	Mozambique	129	29	Cameroon	94
10	Congo	128		Lesotho	94
11	Somalia	125	31	Haiti	91
12	Guinea	124		Tanzania	91
13	Mauritania	120	33	Côte d'Ivoire	90
14	Chad	118	34	Yemen	87
15	Central African Rep	113	35	Gabon	85
16	Nigeria	112	36	Bhutan	84
	Zambia	112		Uganda	84
18	Ethiopia	110	38	Congo-Brazzaville	81
19	Burkina Faso	109		Togo	81
20	Burundi	106	40	Myanmar	80

Lowest death rates
No. deaths per 1,000 pop.

1	Kuwait	2
2	Brunei	3
	United Arab Emirates	3
4	Bahrain	4
	Costa Rica	4
	Fiji	4
	Oman	4
	Qatar	4
	Saudi Arabia	4
10	Bahamas	5
	Dominican Republic	5
	Honduras	5
	Iran	5
	Jordan	5
	Libya	5
	Macau	5
	Malaysia	5
	Mexico	5
	North Korea	5
	Panama	5
	Paraguay	5
	Singapore	5
	Syria	5
	Venezuela	5
	Réunion	5

Lowest infant mortality
No. deaths per 1,000 live births

1	Finland	4
	Japan	4
	Norway	4
	Singapore	4
	Sweden	4
6	Australia	5
	Austria	5
	Czech Republic	5
	Denmark	5
	France	5
	Germany	5
	Iceland	5
	Luxembourg	5
	Netherlands	5
	New Zealand	5
	Slovenia	5
	South Korea	5
	Switzerland	5
19	Belgium	6
	Canada	6
	Greece	6
	Ireland	6
	Israel	6
	Italy	6
	Malta	6
	Spain	6
	United Kingdom	6

Death and diseases

Cancer[a]

%

1	Netherlands	25.3
2	Belgium	24.6
	Canada	24.6
	France	24.6
5	Italy	24.0
6	Australia	23.9
7	United Kingdom	23.6
8	Ireland	22.9
9	Germany	22.7
10	Austria	22.5
	Norway	22.5
12	Singapore	22.3
13	United States	22.2
14	Spain	22.0
15	Israel	21.7
16	Slovenia	21.4
17	Hungary	21.2
18	Sweden	21.0
19	Costa Rica	20.7
20	Chile	19.9

Heart attack[a]

%

1	Azerbaijan	44.8
2	Lithuania	38.4
3	Macedonia	36.8
4	Austria	36.5
5	Estonia	34.6
6	Sweden	33.7
7	Israel	32.8
8	United States	32.7
9	Argentina	32.3
	Finland	32.3
11	Germany	32.1
12	Ireland	31.9
13	Australia	31.7
14	Kazakhstan	31.6
15	Moldova	31.4
16	Latvia	30.9
	Romania	30.9
18	Greece	30.6
19	Cuba	29.9
20	Mauritius	29.4
	Norway	29.4

Infectious disease[a]

%

1	Ecuador	6.7
2	Venezuela	4.8
3	Tajikistan	4.1
4	Argentina	3.4
5	Mexico	3.3
6	Kazakhstan	2.6
	Singapore	2.6
8	Chile	2.5
9	Azerbaijan	2.3
	Kirgizstan	2.3
11	Colombia	2.2
12	Costa Rica	2.0
13	Mauritius	1.8
14	Cuba	1.6
	Israel	1.6
16	France	1.4
	United States	1.4
18	Trinidad & Tobago	1.3
19	Latvia	1.2
	Russia	1.2

Motor accident[a]

%

1	Ecuador	2.1
2	Venezuela	2.0
3	Costa Rica	1.9
4	Colombia	1.7
	Greece	1.7
	Latvia	1.7
	Portugal	1.7
8	Estonia	1.5
	Mexico	1.5
	Slovenia	1.5
11	Cuba	1.4
	Mauritius	1.4
13	Lithuania	1.3
	Poland	1.3
	Russia	1.3
16	United States	1.2
17	Belgium	1.1
	Chile	1.1
	France	1.1
	Hungary	1.1
	Italy	1.1
	Moldova	1.1
	Spain	1.1

a Data refer to the chances a newborn baby has of eventually dying from one of the causes shown. Statistics are available for only a limited number of countries and many less developed countries are excluded. Latest available.

Tuberculosis
Cases per 100,000 pop.

1	Zambia[a]	481.8
2	Namibia	480.4
3	Swaziland[a]	433.3
4	Zimbabwe	415.5
5	South Africa	326.3
6	Botswana	303.4
7	Lesotho[b]	271.9
8	Papua New Guinea	245.5
9	Malawi	220.0
10	Philippines	219.2
11	Eritrea	217.7
12	Peru	176.3
13	Kenya	168.7
14	Tanzania	159.6
15	Cambodia	158.1
16	Guinea-Bissau[a]	155.6
17	Mauritania[b]	153.9
18	Uganda	142.2
19	Central African Rep	139.9
20	Iraq	139.1

Malaria
Cases per 100,000 pop., 1997

1	Malawi[c]	45,785.6
2	Zambia[a]	36,623.0
3	Gambia, The	26,489.4
4	Namibia	25,613.6
5	Rwanda	18,334.0
6	Kenya[d]	14,972.4
7	Burundi[d]	14,446.2
8	Guinea-Bissau[e]	13,673.4
9	Ghana	11,625.9
10	Benin	11,604.5
11	Guinea	10,933.8
12	Niger	9,712.8
13	Mauritania[d]	8,480.7
14	Yemen	8,257.8
15	Togo[c]	7,470.7
16	Senegal[d]	6,984.0
17	Côte d'Ivoire	6,878.6
18	Sudan	5,175.5
19	Chad	4,720.6
20	Cameroon	4,511.1

AIDS
Cases per 100,000 population[f]

1	Bahamas	1,046.6	21	Central African Rep	201.3
2	Zimbabwe	657.3	22	Eritrea	192.1
3	Botswana	646.0	23	Burundi	186.1
4	Bermuda	540.6	24	Guadeloupe	178.3
5	Zambia	511.8	25	Ghana	154.2
6	Malawi	492.7	26	Gabon	142.2
7	Namibia	408.7	27	Chad	139.2
8	Barbados	389.2	28	Spain	138.7
9	Swaziland	370.6	29	Honduras	133.7
10	Congo-Brazzaville	367.1	30	Cameroon	132.7
11	Lesotho	354.8	31	Netherlands Antilles	120.7
12	Tanzania	349.0	32	Burkina Faso	119.6
13	Côte d'Ivoire	346.6	33	Jamaica	117.2
14	Kenya	280.9	34	Martinique	112.1
15	Uganda	266.2	35	Haiti	111.9
16	United States	261.8	36	Congo	96.8
17	Togo	246.2	37	Switzerland	91.0
18	Rwanda	240.8	38	Brazil	87.6
19	Thailand	213.3	39	France	84.2
20	Trinidad & Tobago	203.7	40	Italy	77.6

a 1996 b 1997 c 1994 d 1995 e 1993
f AIDS data refer to the total number of cases reported to the World Health
  Organisation up to November 15 1999. The number of cases diagnosed and reported
  depends on the quality of medical practice and administration and is likely to be
  under-recorded in a number of countries.

Health

Highest health spending
As % of GDP[a]

1	United States	14.0
2	Uruguay	13.4
3	Germany	10.5
4	Croatia	10.1
5	Switzerland	9.8
6	Argentina	9.7
	France	9.7
8	Canada	9.2
9	Czech Republic	9.1
10	Australia	8.6
	Netherlands	8.6
	Nicaragua	8.6
13	Costa Rica	8.5
14	West Bank and Gaza	8.4
15	Macedonia	8.3
16	Portugal	8.2
17	Austria	8.0
	Iceland	8.0
19	Belgium	7.9
	Jordan	7.9
	Norway	7.9
	South Africa	7.9
23	Armenia	7.8
24	Spain	7.7
25	Italy	7.6
26	Finland	7.5
	Venezuela	7.5
28	Colombia	7.4
	Malta	7.4
30	Hungary	7.3
	Sweden	7.3

Lowest health spending
As % of GDP[a]

1	Sudan	0.3
2	Niger	1.0
3	Nigeria	1.3
4	Cameroon	1.4
5	Ghana	1.5
6	Indonesia	1.8
7	Sri Lanka	1.9
8	Eritrea	2.0
9	Bangladesh	2.4
	Philippines	2.4
11	Malaysia	2.5
	United Arab Emirates	2.5
	Yemen	2.5
14	Ethiopia	2.6
	Kenya	2.6
	Laos	2.6
17	Mali	2.7
18	Qatar	2.8
19	Botswana	2.9
20	Saudi Arabia	3.1
21	Guatemala	3.2
22	Kazakhstan	3.3
	Zambia	3.3
24	Fiji	3.4
	Morocco	3.4
	Togo	3.4
	Trinidad & Tobago	3.4
28	Bermuda	3.5
	Côte d'Ivoire	3.5
	Pakistan	3.5
	Singapore	3.5

Highest population per doctor
Latest available year

1	Chad	50,000		Central African Rep	16,667
	Eritrea	50,000	18	Cameroon	14,286
	Gambia, The	50,000		Senegal	14,286
	Malawi	50,000	20	Cambodia	10,000
5	Mozambique	33,333		Congo	10,000
	Niger	33,333		Côte d'Ivoire	10,000
7	Angola	25,000		Lesotho	10,000
	Ethiopia	25,000		Mali	10,000
	Ghana	25,000		Mauritania	10,000
	Rwanda	25,000		Papua New Guinea	10,000
	Somalia	25,000		Sudan	10,000
	Tanzania	25,000		Togo	10,000
	Uganda	25,000		Zambia	10,000
14	Nepal	20,000	30	Bahrain	9,091
15	Benin	16,667		Philippines	9,091
	Burundi	16,667			

Most hospital beds
Beds per 1,000 pop.

1	Switzerland	20.8	32	New Zealand	6.1
2	Japan	16.2	33	Israel	6.0
3	Norway	15.0	34	Croatia	5.9
4	Belarus	12.2	35	Slovenia	5.7
5	Moldova	12.1	36	Sweden	5.6
	Russia	12.1	37	Poland	5.4
7	Ukraine	11.8	38	Serbia & Montenegro	5.3
8	Mongolia	11.5	39	Macedonia	5.2
	Turkmenistan	11.5	40	Cuba	5.1
10	Netherlands	11.3		Trinidad & Tobago	5.1
11	Bulgaria	10.6	42	Greece	5.0
12	Latvia	10.3	43	Georgia	4.8
13	Azerbaijan	9.7	44	Denmark	4.7
14	Germany	9.6	45	South Korea	4.6
	Lithuania	9.6	46	United Kingdom	4.5
16	Kirgizstan	9.5	47	Uruguay	4.4
17	Austria	9.2	48	Libya	4.3
	Czech Republic	9.2	49	Canada	4.2
	Finland	9.2	50	Portugal	4.1
20	Hungary	9.1	51	Papua New Guinea	4.0
21	Tajikistan	8.8		United States	4.0
22	France	8.7	53	Spain	3.9
23	Australia	8.5	54	Vietnam	3.8
	Kazakhstan	8.5	55	Ireland	3.7
25	Uzbekistan	8.3	56	Singapore	3.6
26	Armenia	7.6	57	Congo-Brazzaville	3.4
	Romania	7.6	58	Argentina	3.3
28	Slovakia	7.5		Puerto Rico	3.3
29	Estonia	7.4	60	Albania	3.2
30	Belgium	7.2		Gabon	3.2
31	Italy	6.5			

Lowest population per doctor
Latest available year

1	Italy	182	16	Belgium	294
2	Cuba	189		Germany	294
3	Israel	217		Hungary	294
	Russia	217		Latvia	294
5	Ukraine	222	20	Uzbekistan	303
6	Belarus	233	21	Switzerland	313
7	Spain	238	22	Estonia	323
8	Greece	256		Kirgizstan	323
	Lithuania	256		Sweden	323
10	Azerbaijan	263	25	Armenia	333
11	Georgia	263		Portugal	333
12	Uruguay	270		Slovakia	333
13	Moldova	278	28	Czech Republic	345
14	Bulgaria	286		Denmark	345
	Kazakhstan	286		France	345

a Latest available year.

Till death us do part

Highest marriage rates[a]
Number of marriages per 1,000 population

1	Bermuda	15.7	32	Denmark	6.5
2	Barbados	13.5		Macedonia	6.5
3	United Kingdom	10.8		Russia	6.5
4	Egypt	10.2	35	Jordan	6.4
5	Fiji	9.9		Kazakhstan	6.4
6	Bangladesh	9.7		Romania	6.4
7	Mauritius	9.4	38	Japan	6.3
8	Bahamas	9.3	39	Azerbaijan	6.1
	Sri Lanka	9.3		Brunei	6.1
10	Puerto Rico	8.7		Israel	6.1
11	Syria	8.4		Ukraine	6.1
12	United States	8.1	43	Kirgizstan	6.0
13	Uzbekistan	7.9		Moldova	6.0
14	Cyprus	7.8		Mongolia	6.0
	Iran	7.8	46	Australia	5.9
	Taiwan	7.8	47	New Zealand	5.8
	Turkey	7.8	48	Bahrain	5.7
18	Belarus	7.5		Czech Republic	5.7
19	Jamaica	7.4		Ecuador	5.7
20	Mexico	7.1	51	Chile	5.6
21	South Korea	7.0		Trinidad & Tobago	5.6
	Thailand	7.0		Tunisia	5.6
23	China	6.9	54	Algeria	5.5
	Costa Rica	6.9		Netherlands	5.5
	Philippines	6.9		Suriname	5.5
26	Albania	6.8		Uruguay	5.5
	Tajikistan	6.8	58	Cuba	5.4
28	Malta	6.7		Greece	5.4
	Portugal	6.7		Iceland	5.4
	Singapore	6.7		Poland	5.4
31	Turkmenistan	6.6		Switzerland	5.4

Lowest marriage rates[a]
Number of marriages per 1,000 population

1	Dominican Republic	1.9	11	Argentina	3.9
2	Qatar	2.9		Latvia	3.9
3	Saudi Arabia	3.1		Luxembourg	3.9
4	Panama	3.4		South Africa	3.9
5	Georgia	3.6	15	Peru	4.0
	Sweden	3.6	16	Bulgaria	4.1
7	Estonia	3.7		Martinique	4.1
	Slovenia	3.7	18	Belgium	4.4
	Venezuela	3.7	19	Hungary	4.5
10	United Arab Emirates	3.8		Ireland	4.5

a Latest available year.

Note: Marriage rates refer to registered marriages only and, therefore, reflect the customs surrounding registry and efficiency of administration. The data are based on latest available figures and hence will be affected by the population age structure at the time.

Highest divorce rates[a]
Number of divorces per 1,000 population

1	Cuba	5.9	32	Iceland	1.9
2	Belarus	5.0		Israel	1.9
3	United States	4.5	34	Luxembourg	1.8
4	Russia	3.9		Taiwan	1.8
	Ukraine	3.9	36	Bahamas	1.7
6	Estonia	3.7		Japan	1.7
	Puerto Rico	3.7		Slovakia	1.7
8	Moldova	3.4	39	Hong Kong	1.6
9	United Kingdom	3.3		Kuwait	1.6
10	Lithuania	3.2		Singapore	1.6
	Uruguay	3.2	42	Egypt	1.5
12	Czech Republic	3.1		Portugal	1.5
13	New Zealand	3.0		Romania	1.5
14	Australia	2.8		Turkmenistan	1.5
15	Finland	2.7		Uzbekistan	1.5
	Norway	2.7	47	Barbados	1.4
17	Belgium	2.6		South Korea	1.4
	Latvia	2.6	49	Dominican Republic	1.3
	Netherlands Antilles	2.6		Réunion	1.3
20	Denmark	2.5	51	Bahrain	1.2
	Hungary	2.5		Jordan	1.2
	Suriname	2.5		Kirgizstan	1.2
	Switzerland	2.5		Poland	1.2
24	Germany	2.3	55	Brunei	1.1
	Kazakhstan	2.3		Costa Rica	1.1
	Sweden	2.3		Slovenia	1.1
27	Austria	2.1	58	Bulgaria	1.0
	Netherlands	2.1		Cyprus	1.0
29	Canada	2.0		Tunisia	1.0
	France	2.0		United Arab Emirates	1.0
	Guadeloupe	2.0			

Lowest divorce rates[a]
Number of divorces per 1,000 population

1	Colombia	0.1	17	Azerbaijan	0.8
2	Guatemala	0.2		China	0.8
3	Macedonia	0.3		South Africa	0.8
4	Chile	0.5		Syria	0.8
	El Salvador	0.5	21	Armenia	0.9
	Iran	0.5		Croatia	0.9
	Jamaica	0.5		Greece	0.9
	Libya	0.5		Martinique	0.9
	Mexico	0.5		Panama	0.9
	Turkey	0.5		Qatar	0.9
11	Bermuda	0.6		Spain	0.9
	Italy	0.6		Tajikistan	0.9
	Macau	0.6		Thailand	0.9
14	Brazil	0.7		Trinidad & Tobago	0.9
	Ecuador	0.7		Venezuela	0.9
	Mauritius	0.7			

Households and prices

Biggest households[a]
Population per dwelling

1	Bosnia	7.3		Ukraine	5.7
2	Jordan	7.2		Yemen	5.7
	United Arab Emirates	7.2	27	Afghanistan	5.6
4	Gabon	7.1		Laos	5.6
	Pakistan	7.1		Mozambique	5.6
6	Saudi Arabia	6.3		South Africa	5.6
7	Swaziland	6.2		Venezuela	5.6
8	North Korea	6.1	32	Bangladesh	5.5
	Togo	6.1		Sri Lanka	5.5
10	Congo-Brazzaville	6.0	34	Fiji	5.4
	Sudan	6.0		Liberia	5.4
12	Malawi	5.9		Madagascar	5.4
	Niger	5.9		Tanzania	5.4
	Papua New Guinea	5.9		Turkmenistan	5.4
	Uzbekistan	5.9		Uganda	5.4
16	Burundi	5.8	40	Central African Rep	5.3
	Croatia	5.8		Gambia, The	5.3
	Lesotho	5.8		Guinea-Bissau	5.3
	Réunion	5.8		Iraq	5.3
	Rwanda	5.8		Mali	5.3
	Senegal	5.8		Philippines	5.3
22	Ghana	5.7		Somalia	5.3
	Guinea	5.7	47	Haiti	5.2
	Sierra Leone	5.7		Kirgizstan	5.2

Highest cost of living[b]
December 1999, USA=100

1	Japan	164	17	Argentina	92
2	Hong Kong	120		Côte d'Ivoire	92
3	Gabon	114		Finland	92
4	Norway	112		South Korea	92
	Switzerland	112	21	Germany	90
6	United Kingdom	109	22	Netherlands	89
7	France	108	23	Belgium	87
8	Austria	101		Russia	87
	Denmark	101	25	Australia	84
10	Taiwan	100		Egypt	84
	United States	100		Jordan	84
12	Libya	99	28	Bahrain	83
	Sweden	99		Ireland	83
14	China	98	30	Luxembourg	81
15	Singapore	96		Nigeria	81
16	Israel	93			

a Latest available year.
b The cost of living index shown is compiled by The Economist Intelligence Unit for
  use by companies in determining expatriate compensation: it is a comparison of the
  cost of maintaining a typical international lifestyle in the country rather than a
  comparison of the purchasing power of a citizen of the country. The index is based
  on typical urban prices an international executive and family will face abroad. The

Smallest households[a]
Population per dwelling

1	Sweden	2.2	26	Cyprus	3.0
2	Denmark	2.3		Czech Republic	3.0
	Finland	2.3		Japan	3.0
	Germany	2.3		New Zealand	3.0
	Iceland	2.3		Romania	3.0
	Netherlands	2.3	31	Malta	3.1
	Norway	2.3	32	Hong Kong	3.2
8	Austria	2.4		Macau	3.2
	Belgium	2.4		Myanmar	3.2
10	France	2.5	35	Belarus	3.3
	Italy	2.5		South Korea	3.3
	Switzerland	2.5	37	Albania	3.4
13	Australia	2.6		Serbia & Montenegro	3.4
	Canada	2.6	39	Taiwan	3.5
	Hungary	2.6	40	Estonia	3.6
	Uruguay	2.6		Nicaragua	3.6
17	Argentina	2.7	42	Cameroon	3.7
	Portugal	2.7		China	3.7
	Spain	2.7		Lithuania	3.7
	United Kingdom	2.7	45	Botswana	3.8
	United States	2.7		Congo	3.8
22	Russia	2.8		Oman	3.8
23	Bulgaria	2.9		Slovenia	3.8
	Greece	2.9		Zimbabwe	3.8
	Luxembourg	2.9			

Lowest cost of living[b]
December 1999, USA=100

1	India	41	18	Brazil	60
2	Zimbabwe	42		Indonesia	60
3	Ecuador	46		Zambia	60
4	Pakistan	48	21	Bangladesh	61
5	Philippines	49	22	Tunisia	63
	Romania	49	23	Brazil	64
7	Iran	51	24	Peru	65
8	Hungary	52	25	Chile	66
9	Paraguay	54		Croatia	66
	South Africa	54	27	Turkey	67
11	Kenya	55	28	Kuwait	68
12	Sri Lanka	57	29	Panama	69
	Thailand	57	30	Guatemala	70
14	Colombia	58		Serbia & Montenegro	70
15	Czech Republic	59		Uraguay	70
	Malaysia	59		Vietnam	70
	Poland	59			

prices are for products of international comparable quality found in a supermarket or department store. Prices found in local markets and bazaars are not used unless the available merchandise is of the specified quality and the shopping area itself is safe for executive and family members. New York City prices are used as the base, so United States = 100.

Consumer goods: *ownership*

TV

Colour TVs per 100 households

1	Japan	99.6		26	United Arab Emirates	95.4
2	Taiwan	99.5		27	Italy	94.2
3	Canada	99.4		28	Austria	92.5
4	Hong Kong	99.3		29	Slovakia	92.0
5	South Africa	99.1		30	Slovenia	91.0
6	Ireland	99.0		31	Jordan	90.7
7	United Kingdom	98.3		32	Estonia	90.0
8	New Zealand	98.2			Hungary	90.0
	South Korea	98.2		34	Mexico	89.8
10	Netherlands	98.1		35	Argentina	89.6
	United States	98.1		36	Greece	89.4
12	Czech Republic	98.0		37	Malaysia	89.2
	Norway	98.0		38	Azerbaijan	89.0
14	Belgium	97.8		39	Israel	87.5
15	Australia	97.5			Venezuela	87.5
16	Denmark	97.0		41	Brazil	87.2
	Germany	97.0		42	Spain	87.0
	Poland	97.0		43	Kuwait	86.0
	Saudi Arabia	97.0		44	Croatia	84.0
	Sweden	97.0		45	Chile	83.3
21	Switzerland	96.7		46	Colombia	83.0
22	Portugal	96.4		47	Lithuania	82.0
23	Finland	96.0		48	Latvia	79.0
24	France	95.8		49	Russia	79.0
25	China	95.6		50	Thailand	78.2

Telephone

Telephone lines per 100 people

1	Bermuda	84.0		23	Malta	49.9
2	Luxembourg	69.2		24	Austria	49.1
3	Sweden	67.4			New Zealand	49.1
	Switzerland	67.4		26	Israel	47.1
5	United States	66.1		27	Italy	45.3
6	Denmark	66.0		28	Guadeloupe	44.5
	Norway	66.0		29	Martinique	44.3
8	Iceland	64.7		30	Ireland	43.5
9	Canada	63.5		31	South Korea	43.3
10	Netherlands	59.3		32	Barbados	42.2
11	France	57.0		33	Portugal	41.4
12	Germany	56.8			Spain	41.4
13	Singapore	56.2		35	Macau	40.4
14	Hong Kong	55.8		36	United Arab Emirates	38.9
15	United Kingdom	55.7		37	Slovenia	38.0
16	Finland	55.3		38	Netherlands Antilles	36.6
17	Cyprus	54.5		39	Czech Republic	36.4
18	Taiwan	52.4		40	Bahamas	35.8
19	Greece	52.2		41	Réunion	35.6
20	Australia	50.9		42	Croatia	34.8
21	Japan	50.3		43	Puerto Rico	34.6
22	Belgium	50.0		44	Estonia	34.4

Video cassette recorder
Per 100 households

#	Country		#	Country	
1	Australia	91	12	Japan	77
2	South Korea	89		Netherlands	77
3	Canada	88	14	Hong Kong	76
4	Singapore	86	15	Sweden	75
	South Africa	86	16	Norway	73
6	Denmark	83	17	Switzerland	71
	New Zealand	83	18	Venezuela	67
8	United Kingdom	82	19	Finland	66
	United States	82	20	Belgium	64
10	Germany	81	21	Brazil	61
11	Ireland	78		Mexico	61

Computer
Computers per 100 people

#	Country		#	Country	
1	Luxembourg	73.2	18	Hong Kong	25.4
2	Singapore	45.8	19	Slovenia	25.1
3	United States	45.5	20	Japan	23.7
4	Switzerland	42.1	21	Austria	23.3
5	Australia	41.1	22	Israel	21.7
6	Denmark	37.7	23	Guadeloupe	18.1
7	Norway	37.3	24	Italy	17.4
8	Sweden	36.1	25	Taiwan	15.9
9	Finland	34.9	26	South Korea	15.7
10	Canada	33.1	27	Spain	14.5
11	Iceland	32.6	28	Qatar	12.1
12	Netherlands	31.8	29	Croatia	11.2
13	New Zealand	28.8	30	United Arab Emirates	10.6
14	Belgium	28.6	31	Kuwait	10.5
15	Ireland	27.2	32	Martinique	10.3
16	United Kingdom	26.3	33	Czech Republic	9.7
17	Malta	26.0	34	Uruguay	9.1

Mobile telephone
Subscribers per 100 people

#	Country		#	Country	
1	Finland	57.1	16	Ireland	25.7
2	Hong Kong	47.5	17	United Kingdom	25.2
3	Norway	47.4	18	Austria	24.9
4	Sweden	46.4	19	Switzerland	23.5
5	Japan	37.4	20	Taiwan	21.6
6	Denmark	36.4	21	Netherlands	21.3
7	Israel	35.9	22	United Arab Emirates	21.0
8	Italy	35.7	23	New Zealand	20.7
9	Singapore	34.6	24	Bermuda	19.6
10	Iceland	33.1	25	Greece	19.4
11	United States	31.3	26	France	18.8
12	Portugal	30.9	27	Spain	17.9
13	Luxembourg	30.8	28	Canada	17.6
14	South Korea	30.2	29	Macau	17.5
15	Australia	28.5	30	Belgium	17.3

Books and newspapers

Book sales

$m, 1998			Per head, $		
1	United States	26,025	1	Norway	130
2	Germany	8,928	2	Germany	109
3	Japan	8,708	3	Finland	98
4	United Kingdom	4,636	4	Belgium	97
5	Brazil	3,150	5	United States	95
6	France	2,903	6	Switzerland	93
7	Italy	2,648	7	United Kingdom	78
8	Spain	2,617	8	Denmark	71
9	China	2,246		Singapore	71
10	South Korea	1,429		Sweden	71
11	Canada	1,426	11	Japan	69
12	Australia	1,061	12	Spain	66
13	Netherlands	1,014	13	Netherlands	65
14	Belgium	983	14	New Zealand	62
15	Argentina	695	15	Australia	57
16	Switzerland	682		Ireland	57
17	Sweden	633	17	Austria	54
18	Taiwan	628	18	France	49
19	Mexico	574	19	Canada	47
20	Norway	573	20	Italy	46
21	Poland	517	21	Portugal	36
22	Finland	505	22	South Korea	31
23	Austria	436	23	Taiwan	29
24	South Africa	380	24	Israel	27
25	Denmark	373	25	Greece	21
26	Vietnam	360	26	Argentina	19
27	Portugal	352		Brazil	19

Daily newspapers

Copies per '000 population, latest year

1	Hong Kong	800	21	United States	212
2	Norway	593	22	Slovenia	206
3	Japan	580		Venezuela	206
4	Iceland	535	24	Hungary	189
5	Finland	455	25	Malaysia	163
6	Sweden	446	26	Belgium	160
7	South Korea	394	27	Canada	159
8	United Kingdom	332	28	Greece	153
9	Switzerland	330		Ireland	153
10	Luxembourg	327	30	Argentina	123
11	Singapore	324	31	Poland	113
12	Denmark	311	32	Russia	105
	Germany	311	33	Italy	104
14	Netherlands	305	34	Chile	99
15	Australia	297		Spain	99
16	Austria	294	36	Mexico	97
17	Israel	291	37	Turkey	92
18	Czech Republic	256	38	Philippines	82
19	New Zealand	223	39	Portugal	75
20	France	216	40	Thailand	65

Music and the Internet

Music sales[a]

$m, 1999			*$ per head*	
1	United States	15,104	1 Iceland	64
2	Japan	6,437	2 Norway	59
3	United Kingdom	2,909	3 United States	55
4	Gabon	2,833	4 Japan	51
5	France	1,983	5 Denmark	50
6	Canada	884	United Kingdom	50
7	Brazil	668	7 Sweden	40
8	Australia	656	Austria	40
9	Spain	640	9 Switzerland	38
10	Mexico	626	10 Australia	35
11	Italy	607	11 Belgium	34
12	Netherlands	522	France	34
13	Sweden	357	Germany	34
14	Belgium	342	14 Netherlands	33
15	Austria	323	15 Ireland	31
16	Taiwan	307	16 Canada	29
17	Switzerland	277	17 New Zealand	26
18	Argentina	270	18 Finland	25
19	Denmark	264	19 Cyprus	23
20	Norway	261	20 Portugal	18
21	South Korea	236	21 United Arab Emirates	17
22	South Africa	181	22 Spain	16

Internet hosts

By country, January 1999			*Per 1,000 pop., January 1999*	
1	United States[b]	46,304,342	1 United States[b]	168.98
2	Japan	2,636,541	2 Finland	122.48
3	United Kingdom	1,901,812	3 Iceland	108.54
4	Germany	1,702,486	4 Norway	90.95
5	Canada	1,669,664	5 New Zealand	71.39
6	Australia	1,090,468	6 Sweden	67.00
7	Netherlands	820,944	7 Denmark	63.93
8	France	779,879	8 Australia	58.88
9	Italy	658,307	9 Canada	54.63
10	Finland	631,248	10 Netherlands	52.36
11	Taiwan	597,036	11 Singapore	42.65
12	Sweden	594,627	12 Switzerland	41.93
13	Brazil	446,444	13 Austria	33.68
14	Spain	415,641	14 United Kingdom	32.43
15	Mexico	404,873	15 Belgium	31.64
16	Norway	401,889	16 Taiwan	27.30
17	Denmark	336,928	17 Israel	23.39
18	Belgium	320,840	18 Japan	20.88
19	Switzerland	306,073	19 Estonia	20.77
20	South Korea	283,459	20 Germany	20.73
21	Austria	274,173	21 Hong Kong	17.25
22	New Zealand	271,003	22 Ireland	16.21
23	Russia	214,704	23 France	13.29

a Includes vinyl, tape and compact disc sales.
b Includes all hosts ending ".com", ".net" and ".org", which exaggerates the numbers.

Nobel prize winners: *1901–99*

Peace

1	United States	16
2	United Kingdom	11
3	France	9
4	Sweden	5
5	Germany	4
	Belgium	4
7	Norway	3
	South Africa	3
9	Argentina	2
	Austria	2
	Israel	2
	Russia	2
	Switzerland	2

Economics[a]

1	United States	23
2	United Kingdom	8
3	Norway	2
	Sweden	2
5	France	1
	Germany	1
	Netherlands	1
	Russia	1

Literature

1	France	13
2	United States	12
3	United Kingdom	8
4	Germany	7
5	Spain	6
	Sweden	6
7	Italy	5
8	Norway	3
	Poland	3
	Russia	3

Physiology or medicine

1	United States	44
2	United Kingdom	18
3	Germany	14
4	France	6
	Sweden	6
	Switzerland	6
7	Austria	5
	Denmark	5
9	Belgium	3
	Italy	3

Physics

1	United States	41
2	United Kingdom	19
3	Germany	17
4	France	8
5	Netherlands	6
6	Russia	4
	Sweden	4
	Switzerland	4
9	Austria	3
	Italy	3
	Japan	3

Chemistry

1	United States	36
2	United Kingdom	22
3	Germany	14
4	France	6
5	Sweden	5
	Switzerland	5
7	Canada	4
8	Argentina	1
	Austria	1
	Belgium	1
	Czech Republic	1
	Denmark	1
	Finland	1
	Italy	1
	Japan	1
	Netherlands	1
	Norway	1
	Russia	1

a 1969–99
Prizes by country of residence at time awarded. When prizes have been shared in the same field, one credit given to each country. Only top rankings in each field are included.

Olympic medal winners

Summer games, 1896–1996

		Gold	Silver	Bronze
1	United States	833	634	548
2	Soviet Union[a]	485	395	354
3	Germany	360	375	391
4	United Kingdom	177	233	225
5	France	176	181	205
6	Italy	166	136	142
7	Hungary	142	128	155
8	Sweden	134	152	173
9	Finland	99	80	113
10	Japan	93	89	98
11	Australia	87	85	122
12	Romania	63	77	99
13	China	52	63	49
14	Poland	50	67	110
15	Canada	49	77	91
16	Netherlands	49	57	81
17	Switzerland	46	68	60
18	Bulgaria	43	76	63
19	Denmark	39	60	57
20	Belgium	37	50	49

Winter games, 1924–1998

		Gold	Silver	Bronze
1	Germany	96	89	80
2	Soviet Union[a]	87	63	67
3	Norway	83	87	69
4	United States	59	59	41
5	Austria	39	53	53
6	Sweden	39	28	25
7	Finland	38	49	48
8	Switzerland	29	31	32
9	Italy	27	27	23
10	Canada	25	25	29
11	Russia	21	14	7
12	Netherlands	19	23	19
13	France	18	17	26
14	South Korea	9	3	4
15	Japan	8	9	12
16	United Kingdom	7	4	13
17	Poland	1	1	2
18	Czech Republic	1	1	1
19	Bulgaria	1	0	0
20	China	0	10	4

a Includes unified team in 1992.

Drinking and smoking

Beer drinkers
Litres consumed per head

1	Czech Republic	161.8
2	Ireland	150.5
3	Germany	127.4
4	Luxembourg	110.9
5	Austria	108.6
6	Denmark	105.0
7	United Kingdom	99.4
8	Belgium	98.0
9	Australia	94.5
10	Slovakia	91.8
11	New Zealand	84.7
12	Netherlands	84.2
13	United States	82.0
14	Finland	80.1
15	Venezuela	78.8
16	Canada	67.9
17	Spain	66.4
18	Portugal	64.6
19	Switzerland	59.7
20	Hungary	59.3
21	South Africa	58.1
22	Sweden	57.3

Wine drinkers
Litres consumed per head

1	Luxembourg	70.0
2	France	58.1
3	Portugal	53.2
4	Italy	52.0
5	Switzerland	43.2
6	Argentina	38.8
7	Greece	35.9
8	Spain	35.6
9	Austria	30.1
10	Denmark	29.1
11	Hungary	29.0
12	Ireland	25.6
13	Romania	25.2
14	Belgium	25.0
15	Germany	22.8
16	Bulgaria	22.1
17	Uruguay	20.9
18	Australia	19.7
19	Netherlands	18.1
20	Chile	18.1
21	Czech Republic	16.9
22	New Zealand	16.1

Pure alcohol
Litres consumed per head

1	Luxembourg	13.3
2	Portugal	11.2
3	France	10.8
	Ireland	10.8
5	Germany	10.6
6	Czech Republic	10.2
7	Spain	10.1
8	Denmark	9.5
	Romania	9.5
10	Hungary	9.4
11	Austria	9.2
	Switzerland	9.2
13	Greece	9.1
14	Belgium	8.9
15	Slovakia	8.3
16	Netherlands	8.1
17	Russia	7.9
18	Italy	7.7
19	Australia	7.6
	New Zealand	7.6
21	United Kingdom	7.5
22	Finland	7.1
	Latvia	7.1

Smokers
Av. ann. consumption of cigarettes per head per day

1	Greece	7.8
2	Japan	7.1
3	Bulgaria	6.6
	Poland	6.6
5	South Korea	6.3
6	Hungary	6.1
	Estonia	6.1
8	Spain	6.0
9	Switzerland	5.9
10	Czech Republic	5.3
	Taiwan	5.3
12	Russia	5.2
13	Austria	5.1
14	Ireland	4.8
15	United States	4.7
16	Germany	4.6
	Turkey	4.6
18	Belgium[a]	4.5
	Portugal	4.5
20	Slovakia	4.4

a Including Luxembourg.

Crime and punishment

Serious assault[a]
No. per 100,000 pop., 1996

1	Australia	713.68
2	Belgium	535.75
3	Jamaica	511.36
4	Swaziland	474.23
5	Namibia	466.80
6	Israel	463.04
7	Fiji	418.83
8	Ghana	408.57
9	United Kingdom	379.18
10	Brazil	255.67
11	Luxembourg	251.83
12	Netherlands	242.77
13	Slovakia	204.64
14	Zimbabwe	179.85
15	Tunisia	169.13
16	Barbados	168.23
17	Lebanon	152.83
18	France	148.38
19	Canada	142.25
20	Germany	134.39

Theft[a]
No. per 100,000 pop., 1996

1	Denmark	7,797
2	Australia	6,206
3	United Kingdom	6,062
4	Netherlands	5,303
5	Norway[c]	4,740
6	Switzerland	4,260
7	Canada	4,229
8	Germany	4,129
9	Israel	3,994
10	France	3,917
11	Belgium	3,839
12	Hungary	2,975
13	Finland	2,919
14	Luxembourg	2,750
15	Iceland	2,732
16	Austria	2,617
17	Italy	2,568
18	Estonia	2,534
19	Bahamas	2,494
20	Uruguay	2,088

Prisoners[b]
Total prison pop., 1997

1	United States	1,802,496
2	Russia	1,009,172
3	South Africa	122,006
4	Germany	79,251
5	United Kingdom	73,304
6	Poland	59,180
7	France	53,607
8	Japan	52,711
9	Italy	49,864
10	Spain	44,370
11	Canada	34,166
12	Czech Republic	22,067
13	Australia	18,334
14	Portugal	14,330
15	Hungary	14,181
16	Netherlands	11,699
17	Belgium	7,860
18	Greece	7,129
19	Austria	6,891
20	Switzerland	5,980

Per 100,000 pop., 1997

1	Russia	690
2	United States	668
3	South Africa	310
4	Czech Republic	215
5	Poland	153
6	Portugal	144
7	Hungary	140
8	United Kingdom	124
9	Canada	113
10	Spain	111
11	Luxembourg[c]	105
12	Australia	98
13	Germany	97
14	France	89
15	Italy	87
16	Austria	85
17	Switzerland	84
18	Belgium	77
19	Netherlands	75
20	Ireland	71

a Crime statistics are based on offences recorded by the police. The number will therefore depend partly on the efficiency of police administration systems, the definition of offences, and the proportion of crimes reported, and therefore may not be strictly comparable.
b Only developed countries and other countries in Europe considered.
c 1997

Stars...

Space missions
Firsts and selected events

1957	Man-made satellite
	Dog in space, Laika
1961	Human in space, Yuri Garagin
	Entire day in space, Gherman Titov
1963	Woman in space, Valentina Tereshkova
1964	Space crew, one pilot and two passengers
1965	Space walk, Alexei Leonov
	Computer guidance system
	Eight days in space achieved (needed to travel to moon and back)
1966	Docking between space craft and target vehicle
	Autopilot re-entry and landing
1968	Live television broadcast from space
	Moon orbit
1969	Astronaut transfer from one craft to another in space
	Moon landing
1971	Space station, Salyut
	Drive on the moon
1973	Space laboratory, Skylab
1978	Non-Amercian, non-Soviet, Vladimir Remek (Czechoslovakia)
1982	Space shuttle, Columbia (first craft to carry four crew members)
1983	Five crew mission
1984	Space walk, untethered
	Capture, repair and redeployment of satellite in space
	Seven crew mission
1985	Classified US Defence Department mission
1986	Space shuttle explosion, Challenger
	Mir space station activated
1990	Hubble telescope deployed

Astronauts
Longest time in space, hours

United States			
John Blaha	3,864	Yuri Ramanenko	10,344
Andrew Thomas	3,268	Alexandr Volkov	9,384
David Wolf	3,216	Leonid Kizin	9,024
Edward Gibson	2,017		
William Pogue	2,017	**Other nations**	
		Jean-Loup Chrétien	784
Russia		Ulf Merbold	441
Musa Manarov	12,984	Pedro Duque	381
Sergi Krikalev	11,064	Jean-François Clervoy	262

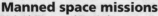

Manned space missions
United States and Russia[ab]

1961 63 65 67 69 71 73 75 77 79 81 83 85 87 89 91 93 95 97 99

...and Wars

Defence spending
As % of GDP, 1998

#	Country	Value	#	Country	Value
1	Eritrea	35.61	21	Bahrain	6.70
2	Saudi Arabia	15.71	22	Albania	6.67
3	Afghanistan	14.71	23	Congo-Brazzaville	6.62
4	North Korea	14.29	24	Yemen	6.60
5	Oman	12.68	25	Pakistan	6.56
6	Kuwait	12.59	26	Iran	6.52
7	Angola	11.79		United Arab Emirates	6.52
8	Israel	11.65	28	Botswana	6.40
9	Qatar	11.61	29	Sri Lanka	6.13
10	Croatia	8.33	30	Ethiopia	5.92
	Tajikistan	8.33	31	Libya	5.77
12	Armenia	8.28	32	Chad	5.73
13	Bosnia	8.10	33	Cyprus	5.48
14	Jordan	7.72	34	Guinea-Bissau	5.40
15	Syria	7.30	35	Uzbekistan	5.39
16	Burundi	7.27	36	Cuba	5.36
17	Rwanda	7.05	37	China	5.33
18	Brunei	6.87	38	Russia	5.00
19	Iraq	6.84		Singapore	5.00
20	Myanmar	6.77	40	Zimbabwe	4.95

Armed forces

#	Country	'000	% conscripts	#	Country	'000	% conscripts
1	China	2,480.0	51	20	Indonesia	298.0	
2	United States	1,371.5		21	Brazil	291.0	17
3	India	1,173.0		22	Italy	265.5	47
4	Russia	1,004.1	33	23	Poland	240.7	59
5	South Korea	672.0	24	24	Japan	236.3	
6	Turkey	639.0	83	25	United Kingdom	212.4	
7	Pakistan	587.0		26	Romania	207.0	52
8	Iran	545.6	46	27	Eritrea	200.0	75
9	Vietnam	484.0		28	Morocco	196.3	51
10	Egypt	450.0	71	29	Spain	186.5	55
11	Myanmar	429.0		30	Mexico	178.8	34
12	Taiwan	376.0		31	Israel	173.5	62
13	Iraq	375.0		32	Greece	165.7	64
14	Germany	332.8	43	33	Cambodia	149.0	
15	Ethiopia	325.5		34	Colombia	144.0	52
16	France	317.3	33	35	Bangladesh	137.0	
17	Syria	316.0		36	Algeria	122.0	61
18	Ukraine	311.4		37	Peru	115.0	56
19	Thailand	306.0					

a Previously Soviet Union.   b United States only from 1994.

Environment: *trees and disasters*

Top deforesters
Average annual rate, km² 1990–95

1	Brazil	25,544	21	Papua New Guinea	1,332
2	Indonesia	10,844	22	Madagascar	1,300
3	Bolivia	5,814	23	Cameroon	1,292
4	Mexico	5,080	24	Central African Rep	1,282
5	Venezuela	5,034	25	Nigeria	1,214
6	Malaysia	4,002	26	Ghana	1,172
7	Myanmar	3,874	27	Mozambique	1,162
8	Sudan	3,526	28	Mali	1,138
9	Thailand	3,294	29	Honduras	1,022
10	Paraguay	3,266	30	Chad	942
11	Tanzania	3,226	31	Gabon	910
12	Zambia	2,644	32	Argentina	894
13	Philippines	2,624	33	China	866
14	Colombia	2,622	34	Guatemala	824
15	Angola	2,370	35	Guinea	748
16	Peru	2,168	36	Botswana	708
17	Ecuador	1,890	37	Panama	636
18	Cambodia	1,638	38	Ethiopia	624
19	Nicaragua	1,508	39	Benin	596
20	Vietnam	1,352	40	Uganda	592

Top reafforesters
Average annual rate, km² 1990–95

1	United States	5,886	6	Greece	1,408
2	Uzbekistan	2,260	7	Belarus	688
3	Kazakhstan	1,928	8	New Zealand	434
4	Canada	1,764	9	Latvia	250
5	France	1,608	10	Portugal	240

Fastest forest depletion
% average annual decrease in forested area, 1990–95

1	Lebanon	7.8		Panama	2.1
2	Jamaica	7.2	18	Iran	1.7
3	Philippines	3.5	19	Cambodia	1.6
4	Haiti	3.4		Dominican Republic	1.6
5	El Salvador	3.3		Ecuador	1.6
6	Costa Rica	3.0		Malawi	1.6
	Sierra Leone	3.0	23	Trinidad & Tobago	1.5
8	Pakistan	2.9	24	Myanmar	1.4
9	Paraguay	2.6		Togo	1.4
	Thailand	2.6		Vietnam	1.4
11	Jordan	2.5	27	Ghana	1.3
	Nicaragua	2.5	28	Algeria	1.2
13	Malaysia	2.4		Benin	1.2
14	Honduras	2.3		Bolivia	1.2
15	Syria	2.2		Cuba	1.2
16	Guatemala	2.1			

Most forested countries
% of total area covered with forest, 1995

1	Suriname[a]	90.5	13	Slovenia	55.0
2	Guinea-Bissau	82.1	14	Bosnia	52.9
3	Papua New Guinea	81.5	15	Peru	52.8
4	South Korea	76.8	16	North Korea	51.7
5	Gabon	69.4	17	Colombia	51.0
6	Japan	66.6	18	Greece	50.4
7	Finland	65.6	19	Venezuela	49.9
8	Brazil	65.2	20	Central African Rep	48.0
9	Indonesia	60.6	21	Estonia	47.6
10	Sweden	59.2	22	Malaysia	47.1
11	Congo-Brazzaville	57.0	23	Austria	47.0
12	Cambodia	55.4	24	Latvia	46.8

Oil tanker spills

	Country affected	Oil spilled '000 tonnes	Name	Flag	Year
1	Trinidad & Tobago	276	Atlantic Express	Greece	1979
2	Italy	260	ABT Summer	Cyprus	1991
3	South Africa	256	Castello de Belvar	Spain	1983
4	France	228	Amoco Cadiz	Liberia	1978
5	Canada	140	Odyssey	Liberia	1988
6	United Kingdom	121	Torrey Canyon	Liberia	1967
7	Oman	120	Sea Star	South Korea	1972
8	Greece	102	Irenes Serenade	Greece	1980
9	Spain	101	Urquiola	Spain	1976
10	United States	99	Hawaiian Patriot	Liberia	1977
11	Turkey	95	Independenta	Romania	1979
12	United Kingdom	84	Braer	Liberia	1993

Industrial disasters, 1990–99[b]

	Location	Origin of accident	Deaths
1990	Bangkok, Thailand	explosion (lorry)	54
	Patna, India	explosion (train)	100
1991	Thailand	explosives	171
	Livorno, Italy	oil explosion	140
1992	Kozlu, Turkey	gas explosion	270
1993	Shenzhen, China	fire (toy factory)	84
	Thailand	fire (toy factory)	189
1996	Dusseldorf, Germany	fire	16
	Lima, Peru	explosives	12
1997	Sichuan, China	explosives	21
	Columbus, USA	chemical fire	25
1998	Jilin, China	hotel fire	22
	Yaounde, Cameroon	train collision	200
	Mombasa, Kenya	school fire	24
	Rawalpindi, Pakistan	explosion	14
1999	Tambelan, Indonesia	ship sinking	313
	West Bongal, India	explosion (train)	286
	Nantucket Island, USA	air crash	217

a 1992 b Not ranked due to difficulties in comparing the effects of each.

Environment: *pollution and waste*

Carbon dioxide emissions
Tonnes per head, 1996

#	Country		#	Country	
1	United Arab Emirates	33.3	22	Japan	9.3
2	Kuwait[a]	31.5	23	Israel	9.2
3	Singapore	21.6		Poland	9.2
4	United States	20.0	25	South Korea	9.0
5	Trinidad & Tobago	17.5	26	Libya	8.0
6	Australia	16.7		New Zealand	8.0
7	Norway	15.3	28	Ukraine	7.8
8	Canada	13.8	29	Greece	7.7
	Saudi Arabia	13.8	30	Austria	7.4
10	Czech Republic	12.3		Slovakia	7.4
11	Finland	11.5		Turkmenistan	7.4
12	North Korea	11.3	33	South Africa	7.3
13	Estonia	11.2	34	Italy	7.0
14	Kazakhstan	10.9		Oman	7.0
15	Denmark	10.7	36	Bulgaria	6.6
	Russia	10.7	37	Slovenia	6.5
17	Germany	10.5		Venezuela	6.5
18	Belgium	10.4	39	Macedonia	6.4
19	Netherlands	10.0	40	Switzerland	6.3
20	Ireland	9.6	41	France	6.2
21	United Kingdom	9.5	42	Sweden	6.1

Nitrogen oxide emissions in cities
Micrograms per cubic metre

#	City		#	City	
1	Milan, Italy	248	11	Cape Town, South Africa	72
2	Mexico City, Mexico	130	12	Bucharest, Romania	71
3	Sofia, Bulgaria	122	13	Tokyo, Japan	68
	Beijing, China	122	14	Athens, Greece	64
5	Cordoba, Argentina	97	15	Seoul, South Korea	60
6	Sao Paulo, Brazil	83	16	Amsterdam, Netherlands	58
7	Santiago, Chile	81	17	Paris, France	57
8	Katowice, Poland	79		Caracas, Venezuela	57
	New York, USA	79	19	Copenhagen, Denmark	54
10	London, UK	77	20	Munich, Germany	53

Sulphur dioxide emissions in cities
Micrograms per cubic metre

#	City		#	City	
1	Tehran, Iran	209	11	Sao Paulo, Brazil	43
2	Rio de Janeiro, Brazil	129	12	Sofia, Bulgaria	39
3	Istanbul, Turkey	120		Budapest, Hungary	39
4	Moscow, Russia	109	14	Athens, Greece	34
5	Beijing, China	90	15	Bombay, India	33
6	Katowice, Poland	83		Caracas, Venezuela	33
7	Tianjin, China	82	17	Prague, Czech Republic	32
8	Mexico City, Mexico	74	18	Zagreb, Croatia	31
9	Cairo, Egypt	69		Quito, Ecuador	31
10	Seoul, South Korea	44		Milan, Italy	31

a 1995

Water pollution

Emissions of organic pollutants[a], '000kg per day, latest available

1	China	7,396.0	21	Bangladesh	186.9
2	United States	2,584.8	22	Argentina	186.8
3	India	1,664.2	23	Philippines	178.2
4	Russia	1,615.3	24	Turkey	177.2
5	Japan	1,468.5	25	Australia	173.3
6	Germany	811.3	26	Cuba	173.0
7	Indonesia	727.5	27	Malaysia	167.0
8	Brazil	690.9	28	Czech Republic	162.6
9	United Kingdom	642.4	29	Mexico	142.9
10	France	585.4	30	Hungary	139.5
11	Ukraine	539.5	31	Portugal	137.4
12	Poland	385.3	32	Netherlands	126.9
13	Italy	359.6	33	Switzerland	123.8
14	Thailand	355.8	34	Serbia & Montenegro	123.2
15	South Korea	340.0	35	Pakistan	114.7
16	Spain	335.2	36	Belgium	113.5
17	Romania	333.2	37	Colombia	111.1
18	Canada	295.5	38	Algeria	103.0
19	South Africa	241.8	39	Iran	101.9
20	Egypt	216.1			

Municipal waste generated

	'000 tonnes, latest available			*Kg per head, latest available*	
1	United States	190,204	1	United States	720
2	Japan	50,536	2	Norway	630
3	Russia	50,000	3	Switzerland	600
4	Germany	36,976	4	Denmark	560
5	Mexico	29,272		Iceland	560
6	France	28,800		Ireland	560
7	United Kingdom	28,000		Netherlands	560
8	Italy	26,605	8	Austria	510
9	Turkey	20,253	9	Hungary	500
10	South Korea	18,223	10	Canada	490
11	Spain	15,307	11	Belgium	480
12	Canada	14,740		France	480
13	Poland	12,183		United Kingdom	480
14	Netherlands	8,716	14	Germany	460
15	Hungary	5,000		Italy	460
16	Belgium	4,852		Luxembourg	460
17	Switzerland	4,277	17	Finland	410
18	Austria	4,110	18	Japan	400
19	Greece	3,900		South Korea	400
20	Portugal	3,800	20	Spain	390
21	Czech Republic	3,200	21	Portugal	380
	Sweden	3,200	22	Greece	370
23	Denmark	2,951	23	Sweden	360
24	Norway	2,721	24	Russia	340
25	Finland	2,100		Slovakia	340

a Industrial emissions.

Environment: *recycling and water*

Glass recycling
Recovery rates, %, 1997

1	Switzerland	91	11	Finland	62
2	Austria	88	12	Japan[a]	56
3	Netherlands	82	13	France	52
4	Germany	79	14	Portugal	44
5	Norway	76	15	Australia[b]	42
	Sweden	76	16	Slovakia	40
7	Belgium	75	17	Ireland	38
	Iceland[a]	75	18	Spain	37
9	Denmark	70	19	New Zealand[c]	36
10	South Korea	68	20	Italy	34

Paper recycling
Recovery rates, %, 1997

1	Germany	70		Denmark	50
2	Austria	69	12	Hungary[f]	49
3	New Zealand[d]	66	13	Norway	44
4	Switzerland	63	14	Spain	42
5	Netherlands	62	15	France	41
	Sweden	62		United States[f]	41
7	Finland[b]	57	17	Portugal	40
	South Korea	57		United Kingdom	40
9	Japan	54	19	Turkey	36
10	Australia[e]	50	20	Slovakia	34

Freshwater resources
Cubic metres per head

1	Congo-Brazzaville	298,963	11	Cambodia	41,407
2	Papua New Guinea	177,940	12	Central African Rep	41,250
3	Gabon	138,942	13	Bolivia	38,625
4	Canada	92,142	14	Uruguay	37,971
5	Norway	88,673	15	Nicaragua	37,467
6	Paraguay	61,750	16	Sierra Leone	32,957
7	Venezuela	57,821	17	Chile	32,007
8	Laos	56,638	18	Guinea	31,910
9	Panama	52,961	19	Russia	30,619
10	Brazil	42,459	20	Argentina	27,865

Least access to safe water
% of population, latest available

1	Eritrea	7		Mozambique	32
2	Cambodia	13	12	Sierra Leone	34
3	Central African Rep	19		Uganda	34
4	Chad	24	14	Vietnam	36
5	Congo	27	15	Mali	37
	Ethiopia	27	16	Myanmar	38
7	Haiti	28	17	Laos	39
	Papua New Guinea	28		Nigeria	39
9	Madagascar	29		Paraguay	39
10	Angola	32		Yemen	39

a 1992   b 1995   c 1994   d 1993   e 1991   f 1996

Part II
COUNTRY PROFILES

ALGERIA

Area	2,381,741 sq km	Capital	Algiers
Arable as % of total land	3	Currency	Algerian dinar (AD)

People

Population	30.1m	Life expectancy: men	68 yrs
Pop. per sq km	13	women	70 yrs
Av. ann. growth		Adult literacy	61.6%
in pop. 1990–2000	2.33%	Fertility rate (per woman)	3.8
Pop. under 15	36.7%	Urban population	60.3%
Pop. over 65	3.8%		*per 1,000 pop.*
No. of men per 100 women	102.5	Crude birth rate	29.2
Human Development Index	66.5	Crude death rate	6

The economy

GDP[a]	AD2,982bn	GDP per head	$1,550
GDP	$46bn	GDP per head in purchasing	
Av. ann. growth in real		power parity (USA=100)	15.7
GDP 1990–98	1.2%	Economic freedom index	3.45

Origins of GDP

	% of total
Agriculture	11.2
Industry, of which:	43.1
manufacturing	9.4
Services	45.7

Components of GDP

	% of total
Private consumption	41.4
Public consumption	15.0
Investment	41.4
Exports	30.2
Imports	-28.0

Structure of employment[b]

	% of total		% of labour force
Agriculture	25	Unemployed 1997	28.0
Industry	26	Av. ann. rate 1990–97	24.5
Services	49		

Energy

	m TCE		
Total output	179.209	% output exported	70.3
Total consumption	47.461	% consumption imported	2.6
Consumption per head,			
kg coal equivalent	1,649		

Inflation and finance

Consumer price		*av. ann. increase 1993–98*	
inflation 1997	3.7%	Narrow money (M1)	12.7%
Av. ann. inflation 1990–97	23.2%	Broad money	14.7%
Money market rate, 1999	10.40%		

Exchange rates

	end 1999		December 1999
AD per $	69.31	Effective rates	1995 = 100
AD per SDR	69.65	– nominal	86.63
AD per euro	69.66	– real	109.11

Principal exports

	$bn fob
Energy & products	8.2
Total including others	**10.1**

Principal imports[c]

	$bn cif
Food	2.5
Machinery	2.1
Total incl. others	**8.7**

Main export destinations

	% of total
Italy	22.9
United States	16.1
France	13.9
Spain	12.6
Netherlands	6.5
Brazil	6.4

Main origins of imports

	% of total
France	32.5
Italy	10.8
United States	8.0
Spain	7.6
Germany	6.9
Turkey	5.9

Balance of payments[c], reserves and debt, $bn

Visible exports fob	13.8	Overall balance	1.2
Visible imports fob	-8.1	Change in reserves	-1.2
Trade balance	5.7	Level of reserves	
Invisibles inflows	1.4	end Dec.	8.5
Invisibles outflows	-4.7	No. months of import cover	7.7
Net transfers	1.1	Foreign debt	30.7
Current account balance	3.5	– as % of GDP	68
– as % of GDP	7.5	Debt service paid	4.6
Capital balance	-2.3	Debt service ratio	46

Health and education

Health spending, % of GDP	4.6	Education spending, % of GDP	5.2
Doctors per 1,000 pop.	0.8	Enrolment, %: primary	108
Hospital beds per 1,000 pop.	3.2	secondary	63
Safe water access, % of pop.	90	tertiary	13

Society

No. of households	6.5m	Colour TVs per 100 households	65.0
Av. no. per household	5.6	Telephone lines per 100 pop.	4.9
Marriages per 1,000 pop.	5.5	Mobile telephone subscribers	
Divorces per 1,000 pop.	...	per 100 pop.	0.1
Cost of living, Dec. 1999		Computers per 100 pop.	0.4
New York = 100	...	Internet hosts per 100 pop.	...

a Estimate.
b 1996
c 1997

ARGENTINA

Area	2,766,889 sq km	Capital	Buenos Aires
Arable as % of total land	10	Currency	Peso (P)

People

Population	36.1m	Life expectancy: men	70 yrs
Pop. per sq km	13	women	77 yrs
Av. ann. growth		Adult literacy	96.5%
in pop. 1990–2000	1.3%	Fertility rate (per woman)	2.6
Pop. under 15	27.7%	Urban population	89.9%
Pop. over 65	9.7%		per 1,000 pop.
No. of men per 100 women	96.3	Crude birth rate	19.9
Human Development Index	82.7	Crude death rate	8

The economy

GDP	P298bn	GDP per head	$8,030
GDP	$290bn	GDP per head in purchasing	
Av. ann. growth in real		power parity (USA=100)	40.1
GDP 1990–98	5.6%	Economic freedom index	2.10

Origins of GDP[a]		Components of GDP	
	% of total		% of total
Agriculture	7.3	Private consumption[b]	83.0
Industry, of which:	36.4	Public consumption	...
manufacturing	24.8	Investment	24.1
Services	56.3	Exports	14.5
		Imports	-21.7

Structure of employment

	% of total		% of labour force
Agricultural	8	Unemployed 1997	14.9
Industry	20	Av. ann. rate 1990–97	11.3
Services	72		

Energy

	m TCE		
Total output	101.409	% output exported	27.4
Total consumption	73.837	% consumption imported	9.5
Consumption per head			
kg coal equivalent	2,097		

Inflation and finance

Consumer price		av. ann. increase 1993–98	
inflation 1999	-1.2%	Narrow money (M1)	7.3%
Av. ann. inflation 1990–99	16.8%	Broad money	13.5%
Money market rate, 1999	6.99%		

Exchange rates

	end 1999		December 1999
		Effective rates	1995 = 100
P per $	1.00		
P per SDR	1.37	– nominal	...
P per euro	1.01	– real	...

Principal exports

	$bn fob
Agricultural products	14.8
Manufactures	8.3
Fuels	3.3
Total incl. others	**26.4**

Principal imports

	$bn cif
Intermediate goods	10.3
Capital goods	5.4
Consumer goods	4.1
Fuels	2.0
Total incl. others	**31.4**

Main export destinations

	% of total
Brazil	30.3
United States	8.1
Chile	6.7
Netherlands	4.2
Uruguay	3.2

Main origins of imports

	% of total
Brazil	22.6
United States	19.4
Germany	6.0
France	5.1
Italy	5.1

Balance of payments, reserves and debt, $bn

Visible exports fob	26.4	Overall balance	4.1
Visible imports fob	-29.6	Change in reserves	2.4
Trade balance	-3.1	Level of reserves	
Invisibles inflows	10.6	end Dec.	24.9
Invisibles outflows	-22.4	No. months of import cover	5.7
Net transfers	0.4	Foreign debt	144.1
Current account balance	-14.5	– as % of GDP	49
– as % of GDP	-5.0	Debt service paid	19.1
Capital balance	19.2	Debt service ratio	58

Health and education

Health spending, % of GDP	9.6	Education spending, % of GDP	3.5
Doctors per 1,000 pop.	2.7	Enrolment, %: primary	111
Hospital beds per 1,000 pop.	3.3	secondary	73
Safe water access, % of pop.	71	tertiary	42

Society

No. of households	13.2m	Colour TVs per 100 households	89.6
Av. no. per household	2.7	Telephone lines per 100 pop.	19.7
Marriages per 1,000 pop.	3.9	Mobile telephone subscribers	
Divorces per 1,000 pop.	...	per 100 pop.	7.0
Cost of living, Dec. 1999		Computers per 100 pop.	4.4
New York = 100	92	Internet hosts per 100 pop.	4.5

a 1997
b Including public consumption.

AUSTRALIA

Area	7,682,300 sq km	Capital	Canberra
Arable as % of total land	6	Currency	Australian dollar (A$)

People

Population	18.5m	Life expectancy: men	75 yrs
Pop. per sq km	2	women	81 yrs
Av. ann. growth		Adult literacy	99.0%
in pop. 1990–2000	1.1%	Fertility rate (per woman)	1.8
Pop. under 15	20.6%	Urban population	84.7%
Pop. over 65	12.1%		per 1,000 pop.
No. of men per 100 women	98.7	Crude birth rate	13.5
Human Development Index	92.2	Crude death rate	8

The economy

GDP	A$579bn	GDP per head	$20,640
GDP	$387bn	GDP per head in purchasing	
Av. ann. growth in real		power parity (USA=100)	74.5
GDP 1990–98	3.8%	Economic freedom index	1.90

Origins of GDP

Components of GDP

	% of total		% of total
Agriculture & mining	5.6	Private consumption	59.2
Industry, of which:	21.4	Public consumption	18.2
manufacturing	15.5	Investment	24.3
Services	73.0	Exports	19.9
		Imports	-21.6

Structure of employment

	% of total		% of labour force
Agriculture	5	Unemployed 1998	8.0
Industry	21	Av. ann. rate 1990–98	8.9
Services	74		

Energy

	m TCE		
Total output	267.597	% output exported	58.4
Total consumption	151.156	% consumption imported	21.2
Consumption per head,			
kg coal equivalent	8,371		

Inflation and finance

Consumer price		av. ann. increase 1993–98	
inflation 1999	1.5%	Narrow money (M1)	10.1%
Av. ann. inflation 1990–99	2.0%	Broad money	9.0%
Treasury bill rate, 1999	4.76%		

Exchange rates

	end 1999		December 1999
A$ per $	1.53	Effective rates	1995 = 100
A$ per SDR	2.10	– nominal	98.8
A$ per euro	1.54	– real	

Principal exports

	$bn fob
Ores & minerals	11.8
Coal & oil	9.2
Machinery	6.5
Gold	5.0
Total incl. others	**56.0**

Principal imports

	$bn cif
Machinery	17.5
Consumer goods	13.7
Transport equipment	11.2
Energy & products	2.8
Chemicals	2.1
Total incl. others	**60.7**

Main export destinations

	% of total
Japan	19.6
EU15	13.8
Asean[a]	11.3
United States	9.6

Main origins of imports

	% of total
EU15	23.9
United States	22.3
Japan	13.8
Asean[a]	12.1

Balance of payments, reserves and aid, $bn

Visible exports fob	55.8	Capital balance	16.3
Visible imports fob	-61.2	Overall balance	-1.9
Trade balance	-5.4	Change in reserves	-1.4
Invisibles inflows	22.6	Level of reserves	
Invisibles outflows	-35.2	end Dec.	16.1
Net transfers	-0.1	No. months of import cover	2.0
Current account balance	-18.0	Aid given	0.96
– as % of GDP	-4.7	– as % of GDP	0.27

Health and education

Health spending, % of GDP	8.4	Education spending, % of GDP	5.4
Doctors per 1,000 pop.	2.5	Enrolment, %: primary	101
Hospital beds per 1,000 pop.	8.5	secondary[b]	153
Safe water access, % of pop.	…	tertiary	80

Society

No. of households	7.1m	Colour TVs per 100 households	97.5
Av. no. per household	2.6	Telephone lines per 100 pop.	50.9
Marriages per 1,000 pop.	5.9	Mobile telephone subscribers	
Divorces per 1,000 pop.	2.8	per 100 pop.	28.5
Cost of living, Dec. 1999		Computers per 100 pop.	41.2
New York = 100	84	Internet hosts per 100 pop.	58.9

a Brunei, Indonesia, Laos, Malaysia, Myanmar, Philippines, Singapore, Thailand,
  Vietnam.
b Includes training for unemployed.

AUSTRIA

Area	83,855 sq km	Capital	Vienna
Arable as % of total land	18	Currency	Schilling (ASch)

People

Population	8.1m	Life expectancy: men	74 yrs
Pop. per sq km	98	women	80 yrs
Av. ann. growth		Adult literacy	99.0%
in pop. 1990–2000	0.64%	Fertility rate (per woman)	1.4
Pop. under 15	17.0%	Urban population	64.7%
Pop. over 65	14.7%		per 1,000 pop.
No. of men per 100 women	97.5	Crude birth rate	10.3
Human Development Index	90.4	Crude death rate	10

The economy

GDP	ASch2,623bn	GDP per head	$26,830
GDP	$217bn	GDP per head in purchasing	
Av. ann. growth in real		power parity (USA=100)	79.2
GDP 1990–98	1.9%	Economic freedom index	2.05

Origins of GDP

	% of total
Agriculture	1.3
Industry, of which:	32.4
manufacturing	…
Services	66.3

Components of GDP

	% of total
Private consumption	55.3
Public consumption	18.8
Investment	25.7
Exports	43.7
Imports	-43.5

Structure of employment[a]

	% of total		% of labour force
Agriculture	7	Unemployed 1998	4.2
Industry	30	Av. ann. rate 1990–98	4.0
Services	63		

Energy

	m TCE		
Total output	8.157	% output exported	29.7
Total consumption	35.344	% consumption imported	86.5
Consumption per head,			
kg coal equivalent	4,360		

Inflation and finance

			av. ann. increase 1993–98
Consumer price			
inflation 1999	0.6%	Euro area:	
Av. ann. inflation 1990–99	2.3%	Narrow money (M1)	6.4%
Deposit rate, 1999	2.21%	Broad money	4.0%

Exchange rates

	end 1999		December 1999
ASch per $	13.59	Effective rates	1995 = 100
ASch per SDR	18.62	– nominal	94.6
ASch per euro	13.66	– real	84.9

Principal exports

	$bn fob
Machinery & transport equipment	26.0
Manufactured goods	16.5
Consumer goods	8.5
Chemicals	5.8
Food, drink & tobacco	2.8
Raw materials	2.1
Total incl. others	**62.5**

Principal imports

	$bn cif
Machinery & transport equipment	27.0
Manufactured products	12.3
Consumer goods	11.3
Chemicals	7.3
Food, drink & tobacco	4.1
Fuel & energy	2.8
Total incl. others	**66.5**

Main export destinations

	% of total
Germany	36.0
Italy	8.6
Switzerland	5.0
Hungary	4.9
EU15	63.9

Main origins of imports

	% of total
Germany	41.8
Italy	8.0
France	4.9
United States	4.8
EU15	69.6

Balance of payments, reserves and aid, $bn

Visible exports fob	62.8	Capital balance	8.4
Visible imports fob	-66.5	Overall balance	3.5
Trade balance	-3.7	Change in reserves	3.2
Invisibles inflows	43.1	Level of reserves	
Invisibles outflows	-42.2	end Dec.	25.2
Net transfers	-1.9	No. months of import cover	2.8
Current account balance	-4.6	Aid given	0.46
– as % of GDP	-2.1	– as % of GDP	0.22

Health and education

Health spending, % of GDP	8.3	Education spending, % of GDP	5.4
Doctors per 1,000 pop.	2.8	Enrolment, %: primary	100
Hospital beds per 1,000 pop.	9.2	secondary	103
Safe water access, % of pop.	…	tertiary	48

Society

No. of households	3.4m	Colour TVs per 100 households	92.5
Av. no. per household	2.4	Telephone lines per 100 pop.	49.1
Marriages per 1,000 pop.	4.8	Mobile telephone subscribers	
Divorces per 1,000 pop.	2.1	per 100 pop.	24.9
Cost of living, Dec. 1999		Computers per 100 pop.	23.3
New York = 100	101	Internet hosts per 100 pop.	33.7

a 1997

BANGLADESH

Area	143,998 sq km	Capital	Dhaka
Arable as % of total land	75	Currency	Taka (Tk)

People

Population	124.8m	Life expectancy: men	58 yrs
Pop. per sq km	897	women	58 yrs
Av. ann. growth		Adult literacy	38.9%
in pop. 1990–2000	1.66%	Fertility rate (per woman)	3.1
Pop. under 15	35.1%	Urban population	24.5%
Pop. over 65	3.2%		*per 1,000 pop.*
No. of men per 100 women	104.9	Crude birth rate	27.6
Human Development Index	44.0	Crude death rate	10

The economy

GDP[a]	Tk1,749bn	GDP per head	$350
GDP	$44bn	GDP per head in purchasing	
Av. ann. growth in real		power parity (USA=100)	4.8
GDP 1990–98	4.7%	Economic freedom index	3.75

Origins of GDP[a]		**Components of GDP**[a]	
	% of total		*% of total*
Agriculture	30.0	Private consumption	76.4
Industry, of which:	14.9	Public consumption	14.0
manufacturing	8.9	Investment	14.0
Services	55.1	Exports	18.5
		Imports	-22.9

Structure of employment[b]

	% of total		*% of labour force*
Agriculture	63	Unemployed 1996[b]	2.5
Industry	10	Av. ann. rate 1990–96	...
Services	27		

Energy

	m TCE		
Total output	10.051	% output exported	0.0
Total consumption	12.991	% consumption imported	28.0
Consumption per head,			
kg coal equivalent	108		

Inflation and finance

Consumer price		*av. ann. increase 1993–98*	
inflation 1997	8.3%	Narrow money (M1)	11.9%
Av. ann. inflation 1990–97	4.8%	Broad money	12.6%
Deposit rate, 1999	8.74%		

Exchange rates

	end 1999		*December 1999*
Tk per $	51.00	Effective rates	*1995 = 100*
Tk per SDR	70.00	– nominal	...
Tk per euro	51.26	– real	...

Principal exports[a]

	$bn fob
Clothing	2.7
Fish & fish products	0.3
Jute goods	0.2
Leather	0.2
Total incl. others	**3.7**

Principal imports[a]

	$bn cif
Textiles	1.7
Machinery & transport equipment	0.9
Cereal & dairy products	0.9
Iron & steel	0.3
Fuels	0.3
Total incl. others	**7.6**

Main export destinations

	% of total
United States	35.7
Germany	10.5
United Kingdom	9.0
France	6.6
Italy	6.1
Netherlands	4.9

Main origins of imports

	% of total
India	16.7
China	7.8
Japan	6.5
Hong Kong	6.4
Singapore	6.1
South Korea	4.7

Balance of payments, reserves and debt, $bn

Visible exports fob	5.1	Overall balance	0.2
Visible imports fob	-6.9	Change in reserves	0.3
Trade balance	-1.7	Level of reserves	
Invisibles inflows	0.8	end Dec.	1.9
Invisibles outflows	-1.5	No. months of import cover	2.8
Net transfers	2.2	Foreign debt	16.4
Current account balance	-0.2	– as % of GDP	37
– as % of GDP	-0.4	Debt service paid	0.6
Capital balance	0.3	Debt service ratio	8

Health and education

Health spending, % of GDP	3.5	Education spending, % of GDP	2.2
Doctors per 1,000 pop.	0.2	Enrolment, %: primary	…
Hospital beds per 1,000 pop.	0.3	secondary	…
Safe water access, % of pop.	95	tertiary	6

Society

No. of households	22.9m	Colour TVs per 100 households	0.6
Av. no. per household	5.5	Telephone lines per 100 pop.	0.3
Marriages per 1,000 pop.[c]	9.7	Mobile telephone subscribers	
Divorces per 1,000 pop.	…	per 100 pop.	0.1
Cost of living, Dec. 1999		Computers per 100 pop.	…
New York = 100	61	Internet hosts per 100 pop.	…

a Fiscal year ending June 30 1999.
b Fiscal year ending June 30 1996.
c 1997

BELGIUM

Area	30,520 sq km	Capital	Brussels
Arable as % of total land	25	Currency	Belgian franc (BFr)

People

Population	10.1m	Life expectancy: men	74 yrs
Pop. per sq km	333	women	81 yrs
Av. ann. growth		Adult literacy	99.0%
in pop. 1990–2000	0.2%	Fertility rate (per woman)	1.6
Pop. under 15	17.1%	Urban population	97.3%
Pop. over 65	16.7%		*per 1,000 pop.*
No. of men per 100 women	96.0	Crude birth rate	10.7
Human Development Index	92.3	Crude death rate	10

The economy

GDP	BFr9,089bn	GDP per head	$25,380
GDP	$259bn	GDP per head in purchasing	
Av. ann. growth in real		power parity (USA=100)	80.8
GDP 1990–98	1.6%	Economic freedom index	2.10

Origins of GDP

	% of total	### Components of GDP	*% of total*
Agriculture	1.4	Private consumption	54.0
Industry, of which:	26.1	Public consumption	21.1
manufacturing	21.4	Investment	21.1
Services	72.5	Exports	75.4
		Imports	-71.5

Structure of employment

	% of total		*% of labour force*
Agriculture	3	Unemployed 1998	9.1
Industry	28	Av. ann. rate 1990–98	8.4
Services	69		

Energy

	m TCE		
Total output	16.488	% output exported[a]	178.3
Total consumption	73.299	% consumption imported[a]	134.6
Consumption per head,			
kg coal equivalent	7,215		

Inflation and finance

Consumer price		*av. ann. increase 1993–98*	
inflation 1999	1.1%	Euro area:	
Av. ann. inflation 1990–99	2.0%	Narrow money (M1)	6.4%
Treasury bill rate, 1999	2.72%	Broad money	4.0%

Exchange rates

	end 1999		*December 1999*
BFr per $	39.86	Effective rates	*1995 = 100*
BFr per SDR	54.61	– nominal	91.8
BFr per euro	40.06	– real	90.8

Principal exports

	$bn fob
Vehicles	26.9
Machinery & electrical goods	26.3
Chemicals	26.0
Metals & products	16.1
Rubber & plastic goods	14.5
Total incl. others	**176.2**

Principal imports

	$bn cif
Machinery & electrical products	27.5
Vehicles	19.6
Chemicals	18.6
Mineral products	12.2
Precious stones & jewellery	11.8
Total incl. others	**155.9**

Main export destinations

	% of total
Germany	19.0
France	17.7
Netherlands	12.5
United Kingdom	9.8
EU15	76.2

Main origins of imports

	% of total
Germany	17.9
Netherlands	16.7
France	13.5
United Kingdom	8.6
EU15	71.0

Balance of payments[b], reserves and aid, $bn

Visible exports fob	153.8	Capital balance	-15.7
Visible imports fob	-146.3	Overall balance	1.6
Trade balance	7.5	Change in reserves	0.4
Invisibles inflows	102.9	Level of reserves	
Invisibles outflows	-93.9	end Dec.	21.0
Net transfers	-4.4	No. months of import cover	1.1
Current account balance	12.1	Aid given	0.88
– as % of GDP	4.3	– as % of GDP	0.35

Health and education

Health spending, % of GDP	7.6	Education spending, % of GDP	3.1
Doctors per 1,000 pop.	3.4	Enrolment, %: primary	103
Hospital beds per 1,000 pop.	7.2	secondary[c]	146
Safe water access, % of pop.	…	tertiary	57

Society

No. of households	4.2m	Colour TVs per 100 households	97.8
Av. no. per household	2.4	Telephone lines per 100 pop.	50.0
Marriages per 1,000 pop.	4.4	Mobile telephone subscribers	
Divorces per 1,000 pop.	2.6	per 100 pop.	17.3
Cost of living, Dec. 1999		Computers per 100 pop.	28.6
New York = 100	87	Internet hosts per 100 pop.	31.6

a Energy trade data are distorted by transitory and oil refining activities.
b Including Luxembourg.
c Includes training for unemployed.

BRAZIL

Area	8,511,965 sq km	Capital	Brasilia
Arable as % of total land	6	Currency	Real (R)

People

Population	165.9m	Life expectancy: men	63 yrs
Pop. per sq km	20	women	71 yrs
Av. ann. growth		Adult literacy	84.0%
in pop. 1990–2000	1.4%	Fertility rate (per woman)	2.3
Pop. under 15	28.8%	Urban population	81.3%
Pop. over 65	5.1%		*per 1,000 pop.*
No. of men per 100 women	97.6	Crude birth rate	20.3
Human Development Index	73.9	Crude death rate	7

The economy

GDP	R900bn	GDP per head	$4,630
GDP	$768bn	GDP per head in purchasing	
Av. ann. growth in real		power parity (USA=100)	22.1
GDP 1990–98	3.2%	Economic freedom index	3.50

Origins of GDP[a]		Components of GDP	
	% of total		*% of total*
Agriculture	8.9	Private consumption	63.6
Industry, of which:	37.5	Public consumption	17.8
manufacturing	23.5	Investment	21.3
Services	53.6	Exports	7.4
		Imports	-10.1

Structure of employment

	% of total		*% of labour force*
Agriculture	26	Unemployed 1998	7.6
Industry	23	Av. ann. rate 1994–98	5.7
Services	51		

Energy

	m TCE		
Total output	102.014	% output exported	2.4
Total consumption	154.330	% consumption imported	46.9
Consumption per head,			
kg coal equivalent	958		

Inflation and finance

Consumer price		*av. ann. increase 1993–98*	
inflation 1999	4.9%	Narrow money (M1)	127%
Av. ann. inflation 1990–98	236%	Broad money	105%
Money market rate, 1999	26.26%		

Exchange rates

	end 1999		*December 1999*
R per $	1.79	Effective rates	*1995 = 100*
R per SDR	2.46	– Nominal	...
R per euro	1.80	– Real	...

Principal exports

	$bn fob
Transport equipment	7.6
Metal goods	5.4
Soyabeans etc.	4.8
Chemical products	3.7
Iron ore	3.5
Total incl. others	**51.1**

Principal imports

	$bn fob
Machines & electrical equipment	18.5
Chemical products	9.3
Transport equipment & parts	6.8
Fuels & lubricants	4.3
Total incl. others	**57.7**

Main export destinations

	% of total
United States	19.3
Argentina	13.2
Germany	5.9
Netherlands	5.4
Japan	4.3

Main origins of imports

	% of total
United States	23.7
Argentina	13.9
Germany	9.1
Japan	5.7
Italy	5.6

Balance of payments, reserves and debt, $bn

Visible exports fob	51.1	Overall balance	-16.3
Visible imports fob	-57.7	Change in reserves	-7.8
Trade balance	-6.6	Level of reserves	
Invisibles inflows	12.5	end Dec.	43.9
Invisibles outflows	-41.2	No. months of import cover	5.3
Net transfers	1.4	Foreign debt	232.0
Current account balance	-33.8	– as % of GDP	31
– as % of GDP	-4.4	Debt service paid	46.4
Capital balance	19.7	Debt service ratio	73

Health and education

Health spending, % of GDP	7.3	Education spending, % of GDP	5.1
Doctors per 1,000 pop.	1.3	Enrolment, %: primary	125
Hospital beds per 1,000 pop.	3.1	secondary	62
Safe water access, % of pop.	76	tertiary	15

Society

No. of households	40.2m	Colour TVs per 100 households	87.2
Av. no. per household	4.1	Telephone lines per 100 pop.	12.1
Marriages per 1,000 pop.	4.6	Mobile telephone subscribers	
Divorces per 1,000 pop.	0.7	per 100 pop.	4.7
Cost of living, Dec. 1999		Computers per 100 pop.	2.5
New York = 100	60	Internet hosts per 100 pop.	2.8

a 1997

BULGARIA

Area	110,994 sq km	Capital	Sofia
Arable as % of total land	39	Currency	Lev (BGL)

People

Population	8.3m	Life expectancy: men	68 yrs
Pop. per sq km	74	women	75 yrs
Av. ann. growth		Adult literacy	98.2%
in pop. 1990–2000	-0.59%	Fertility rate (per woman)	1.2
Pop. under 15	16.3%	Urban population	69.6%
Pop. over 65	15.9%		*per 1,000 pop.*
No. of men per 100 women	94.6	Crude birth rate	8.8
Human Development Index	75.8	Crude death rate	14

The economy

GDP	BGL22bn	GDP per head	$1,220
GDP	$10bn	GDP per head in purchasing	
Av. ann. growth in real		power parity (USA=100)	16.0
GDP 1990–98	-3.1%	Economic freedom index	3.40

Origins of GDP		**Components of GDP**	
	% of total		*% of total*
Agriculture	21.1	Private consumption	79.8
Industry, of which:	28.7	Public consumption	8.2
manufacturing	19.1	Investment	14.8
Services	50.2	Exports	45.2
		Imports	-46.3

Structure of employment[a]

	% of total		*% of labour force*
Agriculture	14	Unemployed 1998	14.4
Industry	50	Av. ann. rate 1990–98	14.3
Services	36		

Energy

	m TCE		
Total output	14.796	% output exported	17.3
Total consumption	31.215	% consumption imported	69.0
Consumption per head,			
kg coal equivalent	3,686		

Inflation and finance

Consumer price		*av. ann change 1993–98*	
inflation 1999	-5.5%	Narrow money (M1)	123%
Av. ann. inflation 1990–98	124%	Broad money	93%
Money market rate 1998	2.93%		

Exchange rates

	end 1999		*December 1999*
BGL per $	1.95	Effective rates	*1995 = 100*
BGL per SDR	2.67	– Nominal	5.91
BGL per euro	1.96	– Real	123.96

Principal exports

	$bn fob
Base metals	0.8
Textiles	0.7
Chemicals	0.5
Machinery & transport equipment	0.5
Total incl. others	**4.3**

Principal imports

	$bn fob
Mineral products & fuels	1.3
Machinery & transport equip.	1.0
Textiles	0.6
Chemicals	0.5
Total incl. others	**4.3**

Main export destinations

	% of total
Italy	12.8
Germany	10.5
Greece	8.8
Turkey	7.9
Russia	5.5
EU15	49.7

Main origins of imports

	% of total
Russia	20.1
Germany	14.0
Italy	7.7
Greece	5.8
United States	4.0
EU15	45.1

Balance of payments, reserves and debt, $bn

Visible exports fob	4.2	Overall balance	-0.1
Visible imports fob	-4.6	Change in reserves	0.6
Trade balance	-0.4	Level of reserves	
Invisibles inflows	2.1	end Dec.	3.1
Invisibles outflows	-2.0	No. months of import cover	5.7
Net transfers	0.2	Foreign debt	9.9
Current account balance	-0.1	– as % of GDP	83
– as % of GDP	-0.6	Debt service paid	1.0
Capital balance	0.3	Debt service ratio	22

Health and education

Health spending, % of GDP	4.0	Education spending, % of GDP	3.2
Doctors per 1,000 pop.	3.5	Enrolment, %: primary	99
Hospital beds per 1,000 pop.	10.6	secondary	77
Safe water access, % of pop.	...	tertiary	41

Society

No. of households	3.0m	Colour TVs per 100 households	72.0
Av. no. per household	2.9	Telephone lines per 100 pop.	32.9
Marriages per 1,000 pop.	4.1	Mobile telephone subscribers	
Divorces per 1,000 pop.	1.0	per 100 pop.	1.5
Cost of living, Dec. 1999		Computers per 100 pop.	...
New York = 100	...	Internet hosts per 100 pop.	...

a 1990

CAMEROON

Area	475,442 sq km	Capital	Yaoundé
Arable as % of total land	15	Currency	CFA franc (CFAfr)

People

Population	14.3m	Life expectancy: men	53 yrs
Pop. per sq km	32	women	56 yrs
Av. ann. growth		Adult literacy	71.4%
in pop. 1990–2000	2.74%	Fertility rate (per woman)	5.3
Pop. under 15	43.5%	Urban population	48.9%
Pop. over 65	3.6%		per 1,000 pop.
No. of men per 100 women	98.9	Crude birth rate	39.4
Human Development Index	53.6	Crude death rate	12

The economy

GDP[a]	CFAfr5,604bn	GDP per head	$610
GDP	$8.7bn	GDP per head in purchasing	
Av. ann. growth in real		power parity (USA=100)	4.8
GDP 1990–98	0.6%	Economic freedom index	3.40

Origins of GDP[b]

	% of total
Agriculture	42.1
Industry, of which:	22.1
manufacturing	6.6
Services	35.8

Components of GDP[b]

	% of total
Private consumption	70.4
Public consumption	6.6
Investment	17.0
Exports	26.6
Imports	-20.8

Structure of employment[c]

	% of total		% of labour force
Agriculture	70	Unemployed 1998	...
Industry	9	Av. ann. rate 1990–98	...
Services	21		

Energy

	m TCE		
Total output	8.667	% output exported	82.3
Total consumption	1.955	% consumption imported	7.2
Consumption per head,			
kg coal equivalent	144		

Inflation and finance

Consumer price			av. ann. change 1993–98
inflation 1998	0.1%	Narrow money (M1)	12.7%
Av. ann. inflation 1990–98	5.9%	Broad money	6.4%
Deposit rate, 1999	5.00%		

Exchange rates

	end 1999		December 1999
			1995 = 100
CFAfr per $	652.95	Effective rates	
CFAfr per SDR	896.19	– nominal	99.5
CFAfr per euro	656.21	– real	108.1

Principal exports[b]

	$m fob
Crude oil	850
Timber	291
Cocoa	148
Cotton	132
Total incl. others	**2,005**

Principal imports[b]

	$m fob
Capital goods	315
Food	119
Fuel	26
Total incl. others	**1,297**

Main export destinations[d]

	% of total
Italy	25.4
Spain	20.4
France	16.1
Netherlands	7.1

Main origins of imports[d]

	% of total
France	25.0
Nigeria	8.5
United States	8.5
Germany	6.4

Balance of payments[e], reserves and debt, $bn

Visible exports fob	1.7	Overall balance	0.0
Visible imports fob	-1.1	Change in reserves	0.00
Trade balance	0.6	Level of reserves	
Invisibles inflows	0.3	end Dec.	0.01
Invisibles outflows	-0.9	No. months of import cover	0.1
Net transfers	0.1	Foreign debt	9.8
Current account balance	0.1	– as % of GDP	119
– as % of GDP	1.0	Debt service paid	0.5
Capital balance	0.1	Debt service ratio	22

Health and education

Health spending, % of GDP	5.0	Education spending, % of GDP	2.9
Doctors per 1,000 pop.	0.1	Enrolment, %: primary	85
Hospital beds per 1,000 pop.	2.6	secondary	27
Safe water access, % of pop.	54	tertiary	4

Society

No. of households	3.9m	Colour TVs per 100 households	3.2
Av. no. per household	3.7	Telephone lines per 100 pop.[d]	0.5
Marriages per 1,000 pop.	...	Mobile telephone subscribers	
Divorces per 1,000 pop.	...	per 100 pop.	...
Cost of living, Dec. 1999		Computers per 100 pop.	...
New York = 100	72	Internet hosts per 100 pop.	...

a Fiscal year ending June 30 1998.
b Fiscal year ending June 30 1997.
c 1990
d 1997
e 1995

CANADA

Area[a]	9,970,610 sq km	Capital	Ottawa
Arable as % of total land	5	Currency	Canadian dollar (C$)

People

Population	30.6m	Life expectancy: men	76 yrs
Pop. per sq km	3	women	82 yrs
Av. ann. growth		Adult literacy	99.0%
in pop. 1990–2000	1.14%	Fertility rate (per woman)	1.6
Pop. under 15	18.9%	Urban population	77.1%
Pop. over 65	12.8%		per 1,000 pop.
No. of men per 100 women	98.0	Crude birth rate	11.5
Human Development Index	93.2	Crude death rate	7

The economy

GDP	C$896bn	GDP per head	$19,170
GDP	$581bn	GDP per head in purchasing	
Av. ann. growth in real		power parity (USA=100)	78.0
GDP 1990–98	2.2%	Economic freedom index	2.00

Origins of GDP		**Components of GDP**	
	% of total		% of total
Agriculture	2.4	Private consumption	59.6
Industry, of which:	30.5	Public consumption	19.3
manufacturing & mining	21.7	Investment	19.6
Services	67.1	Exports	41.5
		Imports	-40.2

Structure of employment

	% of total		% of labour force
Agriculture	4	Unemployed 1998	8.3
Industry	22	Av. ann. rate 1990–98	9.8
Services	74		

Energy

	m TCE		
Total output	489.507	% output exported	49.1
Total consumption	326.505	% consumption imported	20.7
Consumption per head,			
kg coal equivalent	11,001		

Inflation and finance

Consumer price		av. ann. increase 1993–98	
inflation 1999	1.7%	Narrow money (M1)	8.8%
Av. ann. inflation 1990–99	1.9%	Broad money	6.0%
Money market rate, 1999	4.76%		

Exchange rates

	end 1999		December 1999
C$ per $	1.44	Effective rates	1995 = 100
C$ per SDR	1.99	– nominal	95.8
C$ per euro	1.45	– real	92.3

Principal exports

	$bn fob
Motor vehicles & parts	53.5
Machinery & industrial equipment	53.2
Industrial supplies	38.8
Forest products	24.0
Agric. products & foodstuffs	17.0
Energy products	15.6
Total incl. others	**218.5**

Principal imports

	$bn fob
Machinery & industrial equipment	68.6
Motor vehicles & parts	45.1
Industrial supplies	40.7
Consumer goods	23.4
Agric. products	11.7
Energy products	5.9
Total incl. others	**205.4**

Main export destinations

	% of total
United States	83.7
Japan	3.0
United Kingdom	1.5
EU15	5.5

Main origins of imports

	% of total
United States	77.0
Japan	3.2
United Kingdom	2.0
EU15	8.4

Balance of payments, reserves and aid, $bn

Visible exports fob	217.2	Capital balance	14.9
Visible imports fob	-204.6	Overall balance	5.0
Trade balance	12.6	Change in reserves	5.3
Invisibles inflows	51.5	Level of reserves	
Invisibles outflows	-75.9	end Dec.	24.0
Net transfers	0.5	No. months of import cover	1.0
Current account balance	-11.2	Aid given	1.69
– as % of GDP	-1.9	– as % of GDP	0.29

Health and education

Health spending, % of GDP	9.2	Education spending, % of GDP	6.9
Doctors per 1,000 pop.	2.1	Enrolment, %: primary	102
Hospital beds per 1,000 pop.	4.2	secondary	105
Safe water access, % of pop.	…	tertiary	90

Society

No. of households	11.7m	Colour TVs per 100 households	99.4
Av. no. per household	2.6	Telephone lines per 100 pop.	63.5
Marriages per 1,000 pop.	5.0	Mobile telephone subscribers	
Divorces per 1,000 pop.	2.0	per 100 pop.	17.6
Cost of living, Dec. 1999		Computers per 100 pop.	33.0
New York = 100	76	Internet hosts per 100 pop.	54.6

a Including freshwater.

CHILE

Area	756,945 sq km	Capital	Santiago
Arable as % of total land	5	Currency	Chilean peso (Ps)

People

Population	14.8m	Life expectancy: men	72 yrs
Pop. per sq km	20	women	78 yrs
Av. ann. growth		Adult literacy	95.2%
in pop. 1990–2000	1.5%	Fertility rate (per woman)	2.4
Pop. under 15	28.5%	Urban population	85.7%
Pop. over 65	7.2%		per 1,000 pop.
No. of men per 100 women	98.1	Crude birth rate	19.9
Human Development Index	84.4	Crude death rate	6

The economy

GDP	33,513bn pesos	GDP per head	$4,990
GDP	$74bn	GDP per head in purchasing	
Av. ann. growth in real		power parity (USA=100)	29.1
GDP 1990–98	7.9%	Economic freedom index	2.00

Origins of GDP

	% of total
Agriculture	8.8
Industry, of which:	37.1
manufacturing	17.7
Services	54.1

Components of GDP

	% of total
Private consumption	69.0
Public consumption	7.7
Investment	35.1
Exports	39.4
Imports	-51.2

Structure of employment

	% of total		% of labour force
Agriculture	15	Unemployed 1998	7.2
Industry	25	Av. ann. rate 1990–98	5.4
Services	60		

Energy

	m TCE		
Total output	7.581	% output exported	2.2
Total consumption	24.181	% consumption imported	69.6
Consumption per head,			
kg coal equivalent	1,677		

Inflation and finance

Consumer price			av. ann. increase 1993–98
inflation 1999	3.3%	Narrow money (M1)	11.4%
Av. ann. inflation 1990–99	10.0%	Broad money	16.4%
Deposit rate, 1999	8.55%		

Exchange rates

	end 1999		December 1999
Ps per $	530.1	Effective rates	1995 = 100
Ps per SDR	727.5	– nominal	88.4
Ps per Ecu	532.8	– real	99.2

Principal exports

	$bn fob
Industrial goods	6.7
Copper	5.5
Agricultural goods	1.5
Total incl. others	**14.9**

Principal imports

	$bn fob
Intermediate goods	10.2
Capital goods	5.0
Consumer goods	3.6
Total incl. others	**18.8**

Main export destinations

	% of total
United States	17.7
Japan	13.3
United Kingdom	7.9
Brazil	5.3
Argentina	5.0
Italy	4.5
Taiwan	3.6

Main origins of imports

	% of total
United States	23.3
Argentina	11.0
Brazil	6.3
Japan	5.8
Mexico	4.9
Germany	4.7
China	4.4

Balance of payments, reserves and debt, $bn

Visible exports fob	14.8	Overall balance	-2.1
Visible imports fob	-17.3	Change in reserves	-1.8
Trade balance	-2.5	Level of reserves	
Invisibles inflows	5.3	end Dec.	16.0
Invisibles outflows	-7.3	No. months of import cover	7.8
Net transfers	0.5	Foreign debt	36.3
Current account balance	-4.1	– as % of GDP	48
– as % of GDP	-5.6	Debt service paid	4.0
Capital balance	3.2	Debt service ratio	22

Health and education

Health spending, % of GDP	3.9	Education spending, % of GDP	3.6
Doctors per 1,000 pop.	1.1	Enrolment, %: primary	101
Hospital beds per 1,000 pop.	2.7	secondary	75
Safe water access, % of pop.	91	tertiary	31

Society

No. of households	3.4m	Colour TVs per 100 households	83.3
Av. no. per household	4.4	Telephone lines per 100 pop.	18.6
Marriages per 1,000 pop.	5.6	Mobile telephone subscribers	
Divorces per 1,000 pop.	0.5	per 100 pop.	6.5
Cost of living, Dec. 1999		Computers per 100 pop.	4.8
New York = 100	66	Internet hosts per 100 pop.	2.8

CHINA

Area	9,560,900 sq km	Capital	Beijing
Arable as % of total land	10	Currency	Yuan

People

Population	1,255.7m	Life expectancy: men	68 yrs
Pop. per sq km	133	women	72 yrs
Av. ann. growth		Adult literacy	82.9%
in pop. 1990–2000	1.01%	Fertility rate (per woman)	1.8
Pop. under 15	24.9%	Urban population	32.1%
Pop. over 65	6.8%		*per 1,000 pop.*
No. of men per 100 women	105.9	Crude birth rate	16.2
Human Development Index	70.1	Crude death rate	7

The economy

GDP	Yuan7,985bn	GDP per head	$750
GDP	$924bn	GDP per head in purchasing	
Av. ann. growth in real		power parity (USA=100)	10.4
GDP 1990–98	11.2%	Economic freedom index	3.40

Origins of GDP		**Components of GDP**	
	% of total		*% of total*
Agriculture	18.4	Private consumption	44.1
Industry, of which:	48.7	Public consumption	11.2
manufacturing	…	Investment	37.1
Services	32.9	Exports	22.0
		Imports	-18.2

Structure of employment

	% of total		*% of labour force*
Agriculture	50	Unemployed 1998	3.1
Industry	23	Av. ann. rate 1990–98	2.7
Services	27		

Energy

	m TCE		
Total output	1,276.595	% output exported	5.1
Total consumption	1,225.474	% consumption imported	4.9
Consumption per head,			
kg coal equivalent	1,012		

Inflation and finance

Consumer price		*av. ann. increase 1993–98*	
inflation 1999	-1.4%	Narrow money (M1)	20.9%
Av. ann. inflation 1991–99	8.0%	Broad money	24.9%
Deposit rate, 1999	2.25%		

Exchange rates

	end 1999		*December 1999*
Yuan per $	8.28	Effective rates	*1995 = 100*
Yuan per SDR	11.36	– nominal	112.5
Yuan per euro	8.32	– real	114.5

Principal exports

	$bn fob
Machinery & transport equipment	50.2
Textiles & clothing	40.5
Chemicals	9.6
Food & tobacco	4.3
Total incl. others	**183.6**

Principal imports

	$bn cif
Machinery & transport equipment	56.8
Textiles	11.1
Chemicals	20.2
Fuels	6.8
Iron & steel	6.5
Total incl. others	**140.3**

Main export destinations

	% of total
Hong Kong	21.1
United States	20.7
Japan	14.5
Germany	4.0
South Korea	3.4
Netherlands	2.8
United Kingdom	2.5
Singapore	2.1

Main origins of imports

	% of total
Japan	20.1
United States	12.1
Taiwan	11.9
South Korea	10.7
Germany	5.0
Hong Kong	4.8
Singapore	3.0
Russia	2.6

Balance of payments, reserves and debt, $bn

Visible exports fob	183.5	Overall balance	6.2
Visible imports fob	-136.9	Change in reserves	6.4
Trade balance	46.6	Level of reserves	
Invisibles inflows	29.6	end Dec.	152.8
Invisibles outflows	-51.2	No. months of import cover	9.8
Net transfers	4.3	Foreign debt	154.6
Current account balance	29.3	– as % of GDP	16
– as % of GDP	3.2	Debt service paid	16.8
Capital balance	-6.3	Debt service ratio	9

Health and education

Health spending, % of GDP	4.5	Education spending, % of GDP	2.3
Doctors per 1,000 pop.	2.0	Enrolment, %: primary	123
Hospital beds per 1,000 pop.	2.9	secondary	70
Safe water access, % of pop.	67	tertiary	6

Society

No. of households	340.3m	Colour TVs per 100 households	95.6
Av. no. per household	3.7	Telephone lines per 100 pop.	7.0
Marriages per 1,000 pop.	6.9	Mobile telephone subscribers	
Divorces per 1,000 pop.	0.8	per 100 pop.	1.9
Cost of living, Dec. 1999		Computers per 100 pop.	0.9
New York = 100	98	Internet hosts per 100 pop.	0.1

COLOMBIA

Area	1,141,748 sq km	Capital	Bogota
Arable as % of total land	5	Currency	Colombian peso (peso)

People

Population	40.8m	Life expectancy: men	67 yrs
Pop. per sq km	37	women	74 yrs
Av. ann. growth		Adult literacy	90.9%
in pop. 1990–2000	1.91%	Fertility rate (per woman)	2.8
Pop. under 15	32.7%	Urban population	73.9%
Pop. over 65	4.7%		*per 1,000 pop.*
No. of men per 100 women	97.7	Crude birth rate	24.5
Human Development Index	76.8	Crude death rate	6

The economy

GDP[a]	121,708bn pesos	GDP per head	$2,470
GDP	$101bn	GDP per head in purchasing	
Av. ann. growth in real		power parity (USA=100)	20.0
GDP 1990–98	3.9%	Economic freedom index	2.90

Origins of GDP		**Components of GDP**	
	% of total		*% of total*
Agriculture	12.5	Private consumption	64.9
Industry, of which:	19.0	Public consumption	19.9
manufacturing	16.0	Investment	21.0
Services	68.5	Exports	14.8
		Imports	-20.8

Structure of employment[b]

	% of total		*% of labour force*
Agriculture	19	Unemployed 1998	15
Industry	25	Av. ann. rate 1990–98	10.3
Services	56		

Energy

	m TCE		
Total output	85.456	% output exported	60.5
Total consumption	31.554	% consumption imported	5.1
Consumption per head,			
kg coal equivalent	866		

Inflation and finance

Consumer price		*av. ann. increase 1993–98*	
inflation 1999	11.2%	Narrow money (M1)	15.5%
Av. ann. inflation 1990–99	21.6%	Broad money	23.1%
Money market rate, 1999	18.8%		

Exchange rates

	end 1999		*December 1999*
Peso per $	1,874	Effective rates	*1995 = 100*
Peso per SDR	2,572	– nominal	56.7
Peso per euro	1,883	– real	94.7

Principal exports

	$bn fob
Petroleum & products	2.3
Coffee	1.9
Coal	0.9
Gold	0.1
Total incl. others	**11.0**

Principal imports

	$bn fob
Industrial supplies	6.2
Capital goods	5.6
Consumer goods	2.8
Total	**14.6**

Main export destinations

	% of total
United States	38.3
Venezuela	10.6
Germany	6.3
Ecuador	5.3

Main origins of imports

	% of total
United States	35.0
Venezuela	9.6
Japan	5.8
Germany	5.1

Balance of payments, reserves and debt, $bn

Visible exports fob	11.5	Overall balance	-1.4
Visible imports fob	-14.0	Change in reserves	-1.2
Trade balance	-2.6	Level of reserves	
Invisibles inflows	3.0	end Dec.	8.4
Invisibles outflows	-6.2	No. months of import cover	5.0
Net transfers	0.4	Foreign debt	33.3
Current account balance	-5.3	– as % of GDP	33
– as % of GDP	-5.3	Debt service paid	4.2
Capital balance	5.1	Debt service ratio	30

Health and education

Health spending, % of GDP	9.4	Education spending, % of GDP	4.1
Doctors per 1,000 pop.	1.1	Enrolment, %: primary	113
Hospital beds per 1,000 pop.	1.5	secondary	67
Safe water access, % of pop.	85	tertiary	17

Society

No. of households	8.7m	Colour TVs per 100 households	83.0
Av. no. per household	4.7	Telephone lines per 100 pop.	16.1
Marriages per 1,000 pop.	...	Mobile telephone subscribers	
Divorces per 1,000 pop.	0.1	per 100 pop.	4.7
Cost of living, Dec. 1999		Computers per 100 pop.	2.8
New York = 100	58	Internet hosts per 100 pop.	1.0

a 1997
b Main cities.

CÔTE D'IVOIRE

Area	322,463 sq km	Capital	Abidjan/Yamoussoukro
Arable as % of total land	12	Currency	CFA franc (CFAfr)

People

Population	14.3m	Life expectancy: men		46 yrs
Pop. per sq km	46	women		47 yrs
Av. ann. growth		Adult literacy		42.6%
in pop. 1990–2000	2.4%	Fertility rate (per woman)		5.1
Pop. under 15	43.4%	Urban population		46.4%
Pop. over 65	2.9%			*per 1,000 pop.*
No. of men per 100 women	103.5	Crude birth rate		37.3
Human Development Index	42.2	Crude death rate		16

The economy

GDP	CFAfr6,893bn	GDP per head	$700
GDP	$10.2bn	GDP per head in purchasing	
Av. ann. growth in real		power parity (USA=100)	5.1
GDP 1990–98	3.5%	Economic freedom index	3.45

Origins of GDP		**Components of GDP**	
	% of total		*% of total*
Agriculture	32.1	Private consumption	64.8
Industry, of which:	17.9	Public consumption	10.6
manufacturing	...	Investment	18.2
Services	50.0	Exports	44.2
		Imports	-37.8

Structure of employment[a]

	% of total		*% of labour force*
Agriculture	60	Unemployed 1998	...
Industry	10	Av. ann. rate 1990–98	...
Services	30		

Energy

	m TCE		
Total output	1.941	% output exported	20.7
Total consumption	3.296	% consumption imported	146.6
Consumption per head,			
kg coal equivalent	235		

Inflation and finance

Consumer price		*av. ann. change 1993–98*	
inflation 1999	0.8%	Narrow money (M1)	19.8%
Av. ann. inflation 1990–99	6.6%	Broad money	15.6%
Money market rate, 1999	4.95%		

Exchange rates

	end 1999		*December 1999*
CFAfr per $	653.0	Effective rates	*1995 = 100*
CFAfr per SDR	896.2	– nominal	98.6
CFAfr per euro	656.3	– real	102.1

Principal exports

	$bn fob
Cocoa beans & products	1.6
Coffee & products	0.4
Petroleum products	0.4
Fish	0.3
Total incl. others	**4.4**

Principal imports

	$bn cif
Raw materials & semi-processed goods	0.9
Capital goods	0.8
Consumer goods	0.6
Fuel	0.6
Total incl. others	**3.0**

Main export destinations

	% of total
France	17.1
Netherlands	12.2
United States	9.0
Italy	5.9
Ghana	5.7

Main origins of imports

	% of total
France	28.6
Italy	5.2
United States	5.0
Germany	4.6
Netherlands	3.7

Balance of payments, reserves and debt, $bn

Visible exports fob	4.5	Overall balance	-0.6
Visible imports fob	-2.7	Change in reserves	0.2
Trade balance	1.8	Level of reserves	
Invisibles inflows	0.7	end Dec.	0.9
Invisibles outflows	-2.3	No. months of import cover	2.1
Net transfers	-0.5	Foreign debt	14.9
Current account balance	-0.3	– as % of GDP	145
– as % of GDP	-3.0	Debt service paid	1.3
Capital balance	-0.5	Debt service ratio	26

Health and education

Health spending, % of GDP	3.7	Education spending, % of GDP	5.0
Doctors per 1,000 pop.	0.1	Enrolment, %: primary	71
Hospital beds per 1,000 pop.	0.8	secondary	25
Safe water access, % of pop.	42	tertiary	5

Society

No. of households	3.1m	Colour TVs per 100 households	38.7
Av. no. per household	4.6	Telephone lines per 100 pop.	1.2
Marriages per 1,000 pop.	...	Mobile telephone subscribers	
Divorces per 1,000 pop.	...	per 100 pop.	0.6
Cost of living, Dec. 1999		Computers per 100 pop.	3.9
New York = 100	92	Internet hosts per 100 pop.	...

a 1990

CZECH REPUBLIC

Area	78,864 sq km	Capital	Prague
Arable as % of total land	43	Currency	Koruna (Kc)

People

Population	10.3m	Life expectancy: men	70 yrs
Pop. per sq km	130	women	77 yrs
Av. ann. growth		Adult literacy	99.0%
in pop. 1990–2000	-0.06	Fertility rate (per woman)	1.2
Pop. under 15	16.5%	Urban population	74.7%
Pop. over 65	13.6%		per 1,000 pop.
No. of men per 100 women	94.9	Crude birth rate	8.9
Human Development Index	83.3	Crude death rate	11

The economy

GDP	Kcs1,798bn	GDP per head	$5,150
GDP	$53bn	GDP per head in purchasing	
Av. ann. growth in real		power parity (USA=100)	41.7
GDP 1990–98	0.9%	Economic freedom index	2.20

Origins of GDP

Components of GDP

	% of total		% of total
Agriculture	4.5	Private consumption	52.2
Industry, of which:	41.8	Public consumption	19.3
manufacturing	...	Investment	29.9
Services	53.7	Exports	60.0
		Imports	-61.4

Structure of employment

	% of total		% of labour force
Agriculture	5	Unemployed 1998	6.5
Industry	40	Av. ann. rate 1993–98	5.4
Services	55		

Energy

	m TCE		
Total output	45.077	% output exported	27.1
Total consumption	58.376	% consumption imported	50.2
Consumption per head,			
kg coal equivalent	5,695		

Inflation and finance

Consumer price		av. ann. increase 1993–98	
inflation 1999	2.1%	Narrow money (M1)	8.5%
Av. ann. inflation 1990–99	14.4%	Broad money	11.7%
Refinancing rate, 1999	7.50%		

Exchange rates

	end 1999		December 1999
Kc per $	35.98	Effective rates	1995 = 100
Kc per SDR	49.38	– nominal	99.8
Kc per euro	36.16	– real	114.5

Principal exports

	$bn fob
Machinery & transport equipment	10.9
Semi-manufactures	7.0
Chemicals	2.0
Raw materials & fuels	1.8
Total incl. others	**26.4**

Principal imports

	$bn fob
Machinery & transport equipment	11.4
Semi-manufactures	6.0
Chemicals	3.4
Raw materials & fuels	3.0
Total incl. others	**28.8**

Main export destinations

	% of total
Germany	38.5
Slovakia	10.6
Austria	6.3
Poland	5.7
Italy	3.8

Main origins of imports

	% of total
Germany	34.4
Slovakia	7.2
Austria	5.9
Russia	5.5
Italy	5.2

Balance of payments, reserves and debt, $bn

Visible exports fob	26.4	Overall balance	1.9
Visible imports fob	-29.0	Change in reserves	2.6
Trade balance	-2.6	Level of reserves	
Invisibles inflows	8.9	end Dec.	12.6
Invisibles outflows	-8.1	No. months of import cover	4.1
Net transfers	0.4	Foreign debt	25.3
Current account balance	-1.4	– as % of GDP	45
– as % of GDP	-2.6	Debt service paid	5.0
Capital balance	2.9	Debt service ratio	15

Health and education

Health spending, % of GDP	7.0	Education spending, % of GDP	5.1
Doctors per 1,000 pop.	2.9	Enrolment, %: primary	104
Hospital beds per 1,000 pop.	9.2	secondary	99
Safe water access, % of pop.	…	tertiary	24

Society

No. of households	3.5m	Colour TVs per 100 households	98.0
Av. no. per household	3.0	Telephone lines per 100 pop.	36.4
Marriages per 1,000 pop.	5.7	Mobile telephone subscribers	
Divorces per 1,000 pop.	3.1	per 100 pop.	9.4
Cost of living, Dec. 1999		Computers per 100 pop.	9.7
New York = 100	59	Internet hosts per 100 pop.	11.7

DENMARK

Area	43,075 sq km	Capital	Copenhagen
Arable as % of total land	60	Currency	Danish krone (DKr)

People

Population	5.3m	Life expectancy: men	73 yrs
Pop. per sq km	123	women	78 yrs
Av. ann. growth		Adult literacy	99.0%
in pop. 1990–2000	0.3	Fertility rate (per woman)	1.7
Pop. under 15	17.9%	Urban population	85.3%
Pop. over 65	15.2%		per 1,000 pop.
No. of men per 100 women	97.8	Crude birth rate	12.2
Human Development Index	90.5	Crude death rate	12

The economy

GDP	DKr1,167bn	GDP per head	$33,040
GDP	$175bn	GDP per head in purchasing	
Av. ann. growth in real		power parity (USA=100)	81.6
GDP 1990–98	2.9%	Economic freedom index	2.25

Origins of GDP[a]		Components of GDP	
	% of total		% of total
Agriculture	3.5	Private consumption	51.2
Industry, of which:	26.8	Public consumption	25.5
manufacturing	17.7	Investment	21.4
Services	69.7	Exports	34.9
		Imports	-33.1

Structure of employment

	% of total		% of labour force
Agriculture	5	Unemployed 1998	5.5
Industry	26	Av. ann. rate 1990–98	7.8
Services	69		

Energy

	m TCE		
Total output	23.350	% output exported	81.4
Total consumption	23.999	% consumption imported	105.2
Consumption per head,			
kg coal equivalent	4,583		

Inflation and finance

Consumer price		av. ann. increase 1993–98	
inflation 1999	2.5%	Narrow money (M1)	5.0%
Av. ann. inflation 1990–99	2.1%	Broad money	2.7%
Money market rate, 1999	3.37%		

Exchange rates

	end 1999		December 1999
			1995 = 100
DKr per $	7.40	Effective rates	
DKr per SDR	10.16	– nominal	94.1
DKr per euro	7.44	– real	98.1

Principal exports

	$bn fob
Manufactured goods	36.8
Agric. products	6.3
Energy & products	1.6
Ships	0.8
Total incl. others	**48.2**

Principal imports

	$bn cif
Intermediate goods	21.2
Consumer goods	12.8
Capital goods	5.7
Transport equipment	3.2
Total incl. others	**46.1**

Main export destinations

	% of total
Germany	21.4
Sweden	11.2
United Kingdom	9.2
Norway	6.0
France	5.2
United States	4.7
EU15	66.6

Main origins of imports

	% of total
Germany	22.5
Sweden	12.9
United Kingdom	7.9
Netherlands	7.4
France	5.9
Norway	4.6
EU15	72.5

Balance of payments, reserves and aid, $bn

Visible exports fob	48.0	Capital balance	-1.5
Visible imports fob	-44.2	Overall balance	-4.2
Trade balance	3.7	Change in reserves	-3.9
Invisibles inflows	24.7	Level of reserves	
Invisibles outflows	-29.0	end Dec.	15.8
Net transfers	-1.5	No. months of import cover	2.6
Current account balance	-2.1	Aid given	1.70
– as % of GDP	-1.2	– as % of GDP	0.99

Health and education

Health spending, % of GDP	8.0	Education spending, % of GDP	8.1
Doctors per 1,000 pop.	2.9	Enrolment, %: primary	102
Hospital beds per 1,000 pop.	4.7	secondary	121
Safe water access, % of pop.	...	tertiary	45

Society

No. of households	2.3m	Colour TVs per 100 households	97.0
Av. no. per household	2.3	Telephone lines per 100 pop.	66.0
Marriages per 1,000 pop.	6.5	Mobile telephone subscribers	
Divorces per 1,000 pop.	2.5	per 100 pop.	36.4
Cost of living, Dec. 1999		Computers per 100 pop.	37.7
New York = 100	101	Internet hosts per 100 pop.	63.9

a 1997

EGYPT

Area	1,000,250 sq km	Capital	Cairo
Arable as % of total land	2	Currency	Egyptian pound (£E)

People

Population	66.0m	Life expectancy: men	65 yrs
Pop. per sq km	68	women	68 yrs
Av. ann. growth		Adult literacy	52.7%
in pop. 1990–2000	1.95%	Fertility rate (per woman)	3.4
Pop. under 15	35.4%	Urban population	45.2%
Pop. over 65	4.1%		*per 1,000 pop.*
No. of men per 100 women	102.9	Crude birth rate	26.3
Human Development Index	61.6	Crude death rate	7

The economy

GDP[a]	£E280bn	GDP per head	$1,290
GDP	$79.2bn	GDP per head in purchasing	
Av. ann. growth in real		power parity (USA=100)	10.8
GDP 1990–98	4.2%	Economic freedom index	3.50

Origins of GDP[a]

	% of total
Agriculture	17.5
Industry, of which:	32.3
manufacturing	...
Services	50.2

Components of GDP[a]

	% of total
Private consumption	70.0
Public consumption	11.2
Investment	22.9
Exports	28.5
Imports	-32.6

Structure of employment[b]

	% of total		% of labour force
Agriculture	34	Unemployed 1995	11.3
Industry	22	Av. ann. rate 1990–95	10.1
Services	44		

Energy

	m TCE		
Total output	84.662	% output exported	38.1
Total consumption	50.602	% consumption imported	3.3
Consumption per head,			
kg coal equivalent	800		

Inflation and finance

Consumer price			*av. ann. increase 1993–98*
inflation 1999	3.1%	Narrow money (M1)	11.1%
Av. ann. inflation 1990–99	9.7%	Broad money	10.7%
Treasury bill rate, 1999	9.0%		

Exchange rates

	end 1999		December 1999
£E per $	3.41	Effective rates	1995 = 100
£E per SDR	4.67	– nominal	...
£E per euro	3.43	– real	...

Principal exports[a]

	$m fob
Petroleum & products	1,728
Cotton yarn & textiles	759
Industrial goods	445
Other agric. products	140
Raw cotton	103
Total incl. others	**4,930**

Principal imports[a]

	$m fob
Machinery & transport equipment	4,530
Agric. products & foodstuffs	2,506
Chemicals & rubber	1,840
Wood, paper & textiles	1,566
Base metals & manufactures	1,414
Total incl. others	**16,899**

Main export destinations

	% of total
United States	38.3
EU15	29.3

Main origins of imports

	% of total
EU15	43.1
United States	18.2

Balance of payments, reserves and debt, $bn

Visible exports fob	4.4	Overall balance	-1.4
Visible imports fob	-14.6	Change in reserves	-0.5
Trade balance	-10.2	Level of reserves	
Invisibles inflows	10.2	end Dec.	18.8
Invisibles outflows	-7.6	No. months of import cover	10.2
Net transfers	5.0	Foreign debt	32.0
Current account balance	-2.6	– as % of GDP	37
– as % of GDP	-3.2	Debt service paid	1.6
Capital balance	1.9	Debt service ratio	8

Health and education

Health spending, % of GDP	3.8	Education spending, % of GDP	4.8
Doctors per 1,000 pop.	2.1	Enrolment, %: primary	101
Hospital beds per 1,000 pop.	2.0	secondary	78
Safe water access, % of pop.	87	tertiary	23

Society

No. of households	15.0m	Colour TVs per 100 households	16.0
Av. no. per household	4.4	Telephone lines per 100 pop.	6.0
Marriages per 1,000 pop.	10.2	Mobile telephone subscribers	
Divorces per 1,000 pop.	1.5	per 100 pop.	0.1
Cost of living, Dec. 1999		Computers per 100 pop.	0.9
New York = 100	84	Internet hosts per 100 pop.	0.4

a Year ending June 30, 1998.
b 1995
c Year ending June 30, 1999.

FINLAND

Area	338,145 sq km	Capital	Helsinki
Arable as % of total land	8	Currency	Markka (Fmk)

People

Population	5.2m	Life expectancy: men	73 yrs
Pop. per sq km	15	women	81 yrs
Av. ann. growth		Adult literacy	99.0%
in pop. 1990–2000	0.37%	Fertility rate (per woman)	1.7
Pop. under 15	18.0%	Urban population	67.3%
Pop. over 65	14.9%		*per 1,000 pop.*
No. of men per 100 women	95.2	Crude birth rate	11.4
Human Development Index	91.3	Crude death rate	10

The economy

GDP	Fmk687bn	GDP per head	$24,280
GDP	$125bn	GDP per head in purchasing	
Av. ann. growth in real		power parity (USA=100)	70.6
GDP 1990–98	2.0%	Economic freedom index	2.20

Origins of GDP

	% of total
Agriculture	3.8
Industry, of which:	33.7
manufacturing & mining	25.6
Services	62.5

Components of GDP

	% of total
Private consumption	50.2
Public consumption	21.0
Investment	19.1
Exports	42.6
Imports	-32.9

Structure of employment

	% of total		% of labour force
Agriculture	6	Unemployed 1998	11.3
Industry	28	Av. ann. rate 1990–98	13.2
Services	65		

Energy

	m TCE		
Total output	11.871	% output exported[a]	58.3
Total consumption	39.506	% consumption imported[a]	78.1
Consumption per head,			
kg coal equivalent	7,707		

Inflation and finance

Consumer price		*av. ann. increase 1993–98*	
inflation 1999	1.2%	Euro area:	
Av. ann. inflation 1990–99	1.7%	Narrow money (M1)	6.4%
Money market rate, 1999	2.97%	Broad money	4.0%

Exchange rates

	end 1999		December 1999
Fmk per $	5.88	Effective rates	1995 = 100
Fmk per SDR	8.06	– nominal	90.3
Fmk per euro	5.91	– real	86.3

Principal exports

	$bn fob
Metals, machinery & transport equipment	11.7
Electrical equipment	11.2
Paper & products	10.2
Wood & products	2.7
Total incl. others	**43.2**

Principal imports

	$bn cif
Intermediate goods	13.5
Capital goods	8.9
Consumer goods	7.6
Energy & products	2.5
Total incl. others	**32.4**

Main export destinations

	% of total
Germany	11.8
Sweden	9.4
United Kingdom	9.2
United States	7.3
Russia	6.0
France	5.1
EU15	56.1

Main origins of imports

	% of total
Germany	15.2
Sweden	11.7
United States	8.2
United Kingdom	7.3
Russia	6.2
Japan	5.7
EU15	59.7

Balance of payments, reserves and aid, $bn

Visible exports fob	43.4	Capital balance	-2.0
Visible imports fob	-30.9	Overall balance	0.3
Trade balance	12.5	Change in reserves	1.4
Invisibles inflows	10.9	Level of reserves	
Invisibles outflows	-14.9	end Dec.	10.3
Net transfers	-1.1	No. months of import cover	2.7
Current account balance	7.4	Aid given	0.40
– as % of GDP	5.9	– as % of GDP	0.32

Health and education

Health spending, % of GDP	7.4	Education spending, % of GDP	7.5
Doctors per 1,000 pop.	2.8	Enrolment, %: primary	99
Hospital beds per 1,000 pop.	9.2	secondary	118
Safe water access, % of pop.	…	tertiary	74

Society

No. of households	2.2m	Colour TVs per 100 households	96.0
Av. no. per household	2.3	Telephone lines per 100 pop.	55.3
Marriages per 1,000 pop.	4.7	Mobile telephone subscribers	
Divorces per 1,000 pop.	2.7	per 100 pop.	57.1
Cost of living, Dec. 1999		Computers per 100 pop.	34.9
New York = 100	92	Internet hosts per 100 pop.	122.5

a Energy trade data are distorted by transitory and oil refinery activities.

FRANCE

Area	543,965 sq km	Capital	Paris
Arable as % of total land	35	Currency	Franc (FFr)

People

Population	58.7m	Life expectancy: men	74 yrs
Pop. per sq km	107	women	82 yrs
Av. ann. growth		Adult literacy	99.0%
in pop. 1990–2000	0.41%	Fertility rate (per woman)	1.7
Pop. under 15	18.7%	Urban population	75.6%
Pop. over 65	15.9%		per 1,000 pop.
No. of men per 100 women	95.1	Crude birth rate	12.2
Human Development Index	91.8	Crude death rate	9

The economy

GDP	FFr8,565bn	GDP per head	$24,210
GDP	$1,465bn	GDP per head in purchasing	
Av. ann. growth in real		power parity (USA=100)	72.6
GDP 1990–98	1.5%	Economic freedom index	2.50

Origins of GDP		**Components of GDP**	
	% of total		% of total
Agriculture	3.3	Private consumption	55.0
Industry, of which:	26.1	Public consumption	23.6
manufacturing	…	Investment	18.8
Services	70.6	Exports	26.0
		Imports	-23.3

Structure of employment

	% of total		% of labour force
Agriculture	4	Unemployed 1998	11.8
Industry	25	Av. ann. rate 1990–98	11.1
Services	71		

Energy

	m TCE		
Total output	171.168	% output exported	18.9
Total consumption	326.649	% consumption imported	64.1
Consumption per head,			
kg coal equivalent	5,597		

Inflation and finance

Consumer price		av. ann. increase 1993–98	
inflation 1999	0.5%	Euro area:	
Av. ann. inflation 1990–99	1.7%	Narrow money (M1)	6.4%
Treasury bill rate, 1999	2.72%	Broad money	4.0%

Exchange rates

	end 1999		December 1999
FFr per $	6.48	Effective rates	1995 = 100
FFr per SDR	8.88	– nominal	94.7
FFr per euro	6.51	– real	86.6

Principal exports

	$bn fob
Capital equipment	91.2
Non-durable consumer goods	46.3
Chemicals	43.2
Motor vehicles & other transport equipment	43.0
Agric. products & foodstuffs	40.1
Total incl. others	**304.8**

Principal imports

	$bn cif
Capital equipment	80.9
Non-durable consumer goods	47.7
Chemicals	44.4
Motor vehicles & other transport equipment	32.9
Agric. products & foodstuffs	30.2
Total incl. others	**286.3**

Main export destinations

	% of total
Germany	15.9
United Kingdom	10.0
Italy	9.1
Spain	8.7
Belgium & Luxembourg	7.7
United States	7.4
EU15	62.9

Main origins of imports

	% of total
Germany	17.2
Italy	9.9
United States	8.8
United Kingdom	8.4
Belgium & Luxembourg	7.7
Spain	7.1
EU15	62.4

Balance of payments, reserves and aid, $bn

Visible exports fob	301.7	Capital balance	-29.1
Visible imports fob	-275.5	Overall balance	19.8
Trade balance	26.2	Change in reserves	19.1
Invisibles inflows	147.8	Level of reserves	
Invisibles outflows	-124.7	end Dec.	73.8
Net transfers	-9.1	No. months of import cover	2.2
Current account balance	40.2	Aid given[a]	5.74
– as % of GDP	2.7	– as % of GDP	0.40

Health and education

Health spending, % of GDP	9.6	Education spending, % of GDP	6.0
Doctors per 1,000 pop.	2.9	Enrolment, %: primary	105
Hospital beds per 1,000 pop.	8.7	secondary	111
Safe water access, % of pop.	…	tertiary	51

Society

No. of households	24.0m	Colour TVs per 100 households	95.8
Av. no. per household	2.5	Telephone lines per 100 pop.	57.0
Marriages per 1,000 pop.	4.8	Mobile telephone subscribers	
Divorces per 1,000 pop.	2.0	per 100 pop.	18.8
Cost of living, Dec. 1999		Computers per 100 pop.	20.8
New York = 100	108	Internet hosts per 100 pop.	13.3

a Including aid to French overseas territories.

GERMANY

Area	357,868 sq km	Capital	Berlin
Arable as % of total land	34	Currency	Deutschemark (DM)

People

Population	82.1m	Life expectancy: men	74 yrs
Pop. per sq km	230	women	80 yrs
Av. ann. growth		Adult literacy	99.0%
in pop. 1990–2000	0.41%	Fertility rate (per woman)	1.3
Pop. under 15	15.5%	Urban population	87.5%
Pop. over 65	16.4%		*per 1,000 pop.*
No. of men per 100 women	96.0	Crude birth rate	9.2
Human Development Index	90.6	Crude death rate	11

The economy

GDP	DM3,784bn	GDP per head	$26,570
GDP	$2,180bn	GDP per head in purchasing	
Av. ann. growth in real		power parity (USA=100)	75.3
GDP 1990–98	1.5%	Economic freedom index	2.20

Origins of GDP

	% of total
Agriculture	1.1
Industry, of which:	31.9
manufacturing	...
Services	67.0

Components of GDP

	% of total
Private consumption	57.2
Public consumption	18.9
Investment	21.8
Exports	27.5
Imports	-25.3

Structure of employment

	% of total		% of labour force
Agriculture	3	Unemployed 1998	9.7
Industry	35	Av. ann. rate 1991–98	8.1
Services	62		

Energy

	m TCE		
Total output	197.884	% output exported	15.5
Total consumption	478.089	% consumption imported	68.5
Consumption per head,			
kg coal equivalent	5,836		

Inflation and finance

Consumer price		*av. ann. increase 1993–98*	
inflation 1999	0.6%	Euro area:	
Av. ann. inflation 1990–99	2.5%	Narrow money (M1)	6.4%
Money market rate, 1999	2.73%	Broad money	4.0%

Exchange rates

	end 1999		December 1999
			1995 = 100
DM per $	1.93	Effective rates	
DM per SDR	2.64	– nominal	89.9
DM per euro	1.94	– real	83.8

Principal exports

	$bn fob
Road vehicles	95.6
Non-electrical machinery	84.1
Electrical machinery	69.0
Chemicals	68.7
Metals & manufactures	44.2
Textiles & clothing	20.3
Total incl. others	**537.8**

Principal imports

	$bn cif
Electrical machinery	54.9
Road vehicles	45.9
Food, drink & tobacco	42.3
Chemicals	41.7
Non-electrical machinery	32.7
Total incl. others	**462.0**

Main export destinations

	% of total
France	11.1
United States	9.4
United Kingdom	8.6
Italy	7.4
Netherlands	6.8
Belgium & Luxembourg	5.7
EU15	56.4

Main origins of imports

	% of total
France	11.1
United States	8.3
Netherlands	8.0
Italy	7.8
United Kingdom	6.9
Belgium & Luxembourg	5.6
EU15	53.6

Balance of payments, reserves and aid, $bn

Visible exports fob	540.0	Capital balance	12.6
Visible imports fob	-461.0	Overall balance	4.0
Trade balance	79.0	Change in reserves	3.1
Invisibles inflows	162.6	Level of reserves	
Invisibles outflows	-214.8	end Dec.	108.3
Net transfers	-30.3	No. months of import cover	1.9
Current account balance	-3.4	Aid given	5.58
– as % of GDP	-0.2	– as % of GDP	0.26

Health and education

Health spending, % of GDP	10.7	Education spending, % of GDP	4.8
Doctors per 1,000 pop.	3.4	Enrolment, %: primary	104
Hospital beds per 1,000 pop.	9.6	secondary	104
Safe water access, % of pop.	...	tertiary	47

Society

No. of households	36.0m	Colour TVs per 100 households	97.0
Av. no. per household	2.3	Telephone lines per 100 pop.	56.7
Marriages per 1,000 pop.	5.1	Mobile telephone subscribers	
Divorces per 1,000 pop.	2.3	per 100 pop.	17.0
Cost of living, Dec. 1999		Computers per 100 pop.	30.5
New York = 100	90	Internet hosts per 100 pop.	20.7

GREECE

Area	131,957 sq km	Capital	Athens
Arable as % of total land	27	Currency	Drachma (Dr)

People

Population	10.6m	Life expectancy: men	76 yrs
Pop. per sq km	81	women	81 yrs
Av. ann. growth		Adult literacy	96.6%
in pop. 1990–2000	0.41%	Fertility rate (per woman)	1.3
Pop. under 15	14.9%	Urban population	60.1%
Pop. over 65	17.9%		*per 1,000 pop.*
No. of men per 100 women	96.9	Crude birth rate	9.3
Human Development Index	86.7	Crude death rate	10

The economy

GDP	Dr35,911bn	GDP per head	$11,740
GDP	$123.4bn	GDP per head in purchasing	
Av. ann. growth in real		power parity (USA=100)	47.9
GDP 1990–98	1.7%	Economic freedom index	2.75

Origins of GDP

Components of GDP

	% of total		*% of total*
Agriculture	8.3	Private consumption	71.8
Industry, of which:	29.4	Public consumption	14.6
manufacturing	...	Investment	21.8
Services	62.3	Exports	16.4
		Imports	-24.6

Structure of employment

	% of total		*% of labour force*
Agriculture	21	Unemployed 1998	11.2
Industry	24	Av. ann. rate 1990–98	9.4
Services	55		

Energy

	m TCE		
Total output	12.421	% output exported[a]	43.3
Total consumption	35.683	% consumption imported[a]	93.3
Consumption per head,			
kg coal equivalent	3,402		

Inflation and finance

Consumer price		*av. ann. increase 1993–98*	
inflation 1999	2.6%	Narrow money (M1)	16.0%
Av. ann. inflation 1990–99	10.0%	Broad money	13.4%
Treasury bill rate, 1999	9.50%		

Exchange rates

	end 1999		*December 1999*
Dr per $	328.4	Effective rates	*1995 = 100*
Dr per SDR	450.8	– nominal	88.2
Dr per euro	330.0	– real	103.8

Principal exports[b]

	$bn fob
Manufactured products	2.9
Food & beverages	1.0
Petroleum products	0.6
Raw materials & industrial supplies	0.3
Minerals	0.2
Total incl. others	**10.8**

Principal imports[b]

	$bn cif
Manufactured consumer goods	9.4
Capital goods	5.6
Foodstuffs	3.1
Petroleum	2.1
Chemicals & products	1.0
Iron & steel	0.7
Total incl. others	**25.2**

Main export destinations[b]

	% of total
Germany	25.2
United States	15.8
Italy	10.8
United Kingdom	7.7
France	6.0
EU15	56.5

Main origins of imports[b]

	% of total
Italy	15.6
Germany	15.5
United States	11.1
France	8.3
United Kingdom	6.6
EU15	60.9

Balance of payments[b], reserves and debt, $bn

Visible exports fob	5.6	Overall balance	-4.5
Visible imports fob	-21.0	Change in reserves	5.8
Trade balance	-15.4	Level of reserves	
Invisibles inflows	10.5	end Dec.	19.5
Invisibles outflows	-7.5	No. months of import cover	8.2
Net transfers	7.5	Aid given	0.18
Current account balance	-4.9	– as % of GDP	0.15
– as % of GDP	-4.0		
Capital balance	0.1		

Health and education

Health spending, % of GDP	8.9	Education spending, % of GDP	3.1
Doctors per 1,000 pop.	3.9	Enrolment, %: primary	93
Hospital beds per 1,000 pop.	5.0	secondary	95
Safe water access, % of pop.	…	tertiary	47

Society

No. of households	3.6m	Colour TVs per 100 households	89.4
Av. no. per household	2.9	Telephone lines per 100 pop.	52.2
Marriages per 1,000 pop.	5.4	Mobile telephone subscribers	
Divorces per 1,000 pop.	0.9	per 100 pop.	19.4
Cost of living, Dec. 1999		Computers per 100 pop.	5.2
New York = 100	…	Internet hosts per 100 pop.	7.6

a Energy trade figures are distorted by transitory and oil refining activities.
b 1997

HONG KONG

Area	1,075 sq km	Capital	Victoria
Arable as % of total land	7	Currency	Hong Kong dollar (HK$)

People

Population	6.7m	Life expectancy[a]: men	76 yrs
Pop. per sq km	6,628	women	81 yrs
Av. ann. growth		Adult literacy	92.4%
in pop. 1990–2000	1.94%	Fertility rate (per woman)	1.3
Pop. under 15	17.2%	Urban population	100.0%
Pop. over 65	10.5%		per 1,000 pop.
No. of men per 100 women	112.4	Crude birth rate	10.4
Human Development Index	88.0	Crude death rate[a]	6

The economy

GDP	HK$1,267bn	GDP per head	$23,660
GDP	$158.2bn	GDP per head in purchasing	
Av. ann. growth in real		power parity (USA=100)	71.0
GDP 1990–98	4.4%	Economic freedom index	1.30

Origins of GDP

Components of GDP

	% of total		% of total
Agriculture	0.1	Private consumption	60.5
Industry, of which:	14.7	Public consumption	9.3
manufacturing	6.5	Investment	29.7
Services	85.2	Exports	127.4
		Imports	-126.9

Structure of employment

	% of total		% of labour force
Agriculture	0	Unemployed 1998	4.7
Industry	13	Av. ann. rate 1990–98	2.4
Services	87		

Energy

	m TCE		
Total output	nil	% output exported	nil
Total consumption	10.035	% consumption imported	285.9
Consumption per head,			
kg coal equivalent	1,621		

Inflation and finance

Consumer price		av. ann. increase 1993–98	
inflation 1999	-4.0%	Narrow money (M1)	1.2%
Av. ann. inflation 1990–99	6.3%	Broad money	10.9%
Money market rate, 1999	5.75%		

Exchange rates

	end 1999		December 1999
HK$ per $	7.77	Effective rates	1995 = 100
HK$ per SDR	10.64	– nominal	...
HK$ per euro	7.81	– real	...

Principal exports[b]

	$bn fob
Clothing	9.7
Electrical machinery & apparatus	3.4
Watches, clocks & photographic equipment	1.6
Textiles	1.4
Total incl. others	**24.3**

Principal imports

	$bn cif
Consumer goods	66.0
Raw materials & semi-manufactured products	62.4
Capital goods	44.7
Agric. products & foodstuffs	8.3
Fuels	3.0
Total incl. others	**184.4**

Main export destinations[c]

	% of total
China	34.4
United States	23.4
Japan	5.2
Germany	3.9
United Kingdom	3.9

Main origins of imports

	% of total
China	40.6
Japan	12.6
United States	7.5
Taiwan	7.3
Singapore	4.8

Balance of payments, reserves and debt[d], $bn

Visible exports fob	174.0	Overall balance	...
Visible imports cif	-184.9	Change in reserves	-3.2
Trade balance	-10.9	Level of reserves end Dec.	89.7
Services inflows	34.5	No. months of import cover	5.2
Services outflows	-22.5	Foreign debt	40.3
Net transfers	...	– as % of GDP	24
Current account balance[e]	0.8	Debt service paid	3.4
– as % of GDP	0.5	Debt service ratio	2
Capital balance	...		

Health and education

Health spending, % of GDP	5.0	Education spending, % of GDP	2.9
Doctors per 1,000 pop.	1.3	Enrolment, %: primary	94
Hospital beds per 1,000 pop.	...	secondary	73
Safe water access, % of pop.	...	tertiary	23

Society

No. of households	2.1m	Colour TVs per 100 households	99.3
Av. no. per household	3.2	Telephone lines per 100 pop.	55.8
Marriages per 1,000 pop.	4.7	Mobile telephone subscribers per 100 pop.	47.5
Divorces per 1,000 pop.	1.6	Computers per 100 pop.	25.4
Cost of living, Dec. 1999 New York = 100	120	Internet hosts per 100 pop.	17.3

a 1995–2000.
b Domestic.
c Including re-exports.
d 1997
e Goods and services.
Note: Hong Kong became a Special Administrative Region of China from July 1 1997.

HUNGARY

Area	93,030 sq km	Capital	Budapest
Arable as % of total land	53	Currency	Forint (Ft)

People

Population	10.1m	Life expectancy: men	67 yrs
Pop. per sq km	108	women	75 yrs
Av. ann. growth		Adult literacy	99.0%
in pop. 1990–2000	-0.33%	Fertility rate (per woman)	1.4
Pop. under 15	17.0%	Urban population	64.0%
Pop. over 65	14.7%		per 1,000 pop.
No. of men per 100 women	91.5	Crude birth rate	9.9
Human Development Index	79.5	Crude death rate	14

The economy

GDP	Ft10,163bn	GDP per head	$4,510
GDP	$45.7bn	GDP per head in purchasing	
Av. ann. growth in real		power parity (USA=100)	33.6
GDP 1990–98	0.5%	Economic freedom index	2.55

Origins of GDPª		Components of GDP	
	% of total		% of total
Agriculture	5.2	Private consumption	62.2
Industry, of which:	29.1	Public consumption	10.1
manufacturing	…	Investment	30.9
Services	65.7	Exports	49.3
		Imports	-52.5

Structure of employment

	% of total		% of labour force
Agriculture	8	Unemployed 1998	7.8
Industry	35	Av. ann. rate 1992–98	8.8
Services	57		

Energy

	m TCE		
Total output	19.111	% output exported	11.9
Total consumption	36.786	% consumption imported	62.6
Consumption per head,			
kg coal equivalent	3,661		

Inflation and finance

Consumer price		*av. ann. increase 1993–98*	
inflation 1999	10.3%	Narrow money (M1)	14.7%
Av. ann. inflation 1990–99	21.3%	Broad money	21.2%
Treasury bill rate, 1999	14.7%		

Exchange rates

	end 1999		December 1999
Ft per $	252.5	Effective rates	1995 = 100
Ft per SDR	346.6	– nominal	65.5
Ft per euro	253.8	– real	111.5

Principal exports

	$bn fob
Machinery & transport equipment	11.9
Other manufactures	7.5
Food & beverages	2.4
Raw materials	0.7
Total incl. others	**23.0**

Principal imports

	$bn cif
Machinery & transport equipment	12.0
Other manufactures	10.3
Fuels	1.7
Food & food products	1.0
Total incl. others	**25.7**

Main export destinations

	% of total
Germany	36.6
Austria	10.6
Italy	5.8
Netherlands	4.7

Main origins of imports

	% of total
Germany	28.2
Austria	9.6
Italy	7.6
Russia	6.5

Balance of payments, reserves and debt, $bn

Visible exports fob	20.7	Overall balance	1.0
Visible imports fob	-23.1	Change in reserves	0.9
Trade balance	-2.4	Level of reserves	
Invisibles inflows	6.0	end Dec.	9.3
Invisibles outflows	-7.0	No. months of import cover	3.7
Net transfers	1.0	Foreign debt	28.6
Current account balance	-2.3	– as % of GDP	62
– as % of GDP	-5.0	Debt service paid	6.9
Capital balance	3.0	Debt service ratio	27

Health and education

Health spending, % of GDP	6.4	Education spending, % of GDP	4.6
Doctors per 1,000 pop.	3.4	Enrolment, %: primary	103
Hospital beds per 1,000 pop.	9.1	secondary	98
Safe water access, % of pop.	…	tertiary	25

Society

No. of households	3.9m	Colour TVs per 100 households	90.0
Av. no. per household	2.6	Telephone lines per 100 pop.	33.6
Marriages per 1,000 pop.	4.5	Mobile telephone subscribers	
Divorces per 1,000 pop.	2.5	per 100 pop.	10.5
Cost of living, Dec. 1999		Computers per 100 pop.	5.9
New York = 100	52	Internet hosts per 100 pop.	11.2

a 1997

INDIA

Area	3,287,263 sq km	Capital	New Delhi
Arable as % of total land	57	Currency	Indian rupee (Rs)

People

Population	982.2m	Life expectancy: men	62 yrs
Pop. per sq km	308	women	63 yrs
Av. ann. growth		Adult literacy	53.5%
in pop. 1990–2000	1.75%	Fertility rate (per woman)	3.1
Pop. under 15	33.3%	Urban population	28.4%
Pop. over 65	5.0%		per 1,000 pop.
No. of men per 100 women	106.7	Crude birth rate	25.5
Human Development Index	54.5	Crude death rate	9

The economy

GDP[a]	Rs17,626bn	GDP per head	$440
GDP	$427.4bn	GDP per head in purchasing	
Av. ann. growth in real		power parity (USA=100)	7.0
GDP 1990–98	6.1%	Economic freedom index	3.80

Origins of GDP[a]

	% of total
Agriculture	26.8
Industry, of which:	26.5
manufacturing	17.5
Services	46.6

Components of GDP[a]

	% of total
Private consumption	64.0
Public consumption	11.9
Investment	24.2
Exports	12.3
Imports	-13.4

Structure of employment[b]

	% of total		% of labour force
Agriculture	60	Unemployed 1998	...
Industry	18	Av. ann. rate 1990–98	...
Services	22		

Energy

	m TCE		
Total output	340.393	% output exported	0.2
Total consumption	400.122	% consumption imported	21.8
Consumption per head,			
kg coal equivalent	424		

Inflation and finance

Consumer price			av. ann. increase 1993–98
inflation 1999	4.7%	Narrow money (M1)	15.2%
Av. ann. inflation 1990–99	9.6%	Broad money	17.1%
Bank rate, 1999	8.00%		

Exchange rates

	end 1999		December 1999
Rs per $	43.49	Effective rates	1995 = 100
Rs per SDR	59.69	– nominal	...
Rs per euro	43.71	– real	...

Principal exports[c]

	$bn fob
Textiles	8.1
Gems & jewellery	5.1
Engineering goods	5.0
Chemicals	3.6
Total incl. others	**34.0**

Principal imports[c]

	$bn cif
Crude oil & products	8.2
Capital goods	7.1
Gems	3.1
Iron & steel	1.5
Total incl. others	**41.0**

Main export destinations

	% of total
United States	20.6
Germany	5.7
United Kingdom	5.6
Japan	5.2
Hong Kong	4.6
United Arab Emirates	4.4

Main origins of imports

	% of total
United States	9.6
Belgium & Luxembourg	6.7
Japan	6.4
Saudi Arabia	6.2
Germany	5.8
United Kingdom	5.8

Balance of payments, reserves and debt, $bn

Visible exports fob	34.1	Overall balance	3.1
Visible imports fob	-44.8	Change in reserves	2.3
Trade balance	-10.8	Level of reserves	
Invisibles inflows	13.5	end Dec.	30.6
Invisibles outflows	-20.0	No. months of import cover	5.7
Net transfers	10.3	Foreign debt	98.2
Current account balance	-6.9	– as % of GDP	23
– as % of GDP	-1.6	Debt service paid	11.3
Capital balance	8.6	Debt service ratio	18

Health and education

Health spending, % of GDP	5.2	Education spending, % of GDP	3.2
Doctors per 1,000 pop.	0.4	Enrolment, %: primary	100
Hospital beds per 1,000 pop.	0.8	secondary	49
Safe water access, % of pop.	81	tertiary	7

Society

No. of households	194.6m	Colour TVs per 100 households	26.0
Av. no. per household	5.1	Telephone lines per 100 pop.	2.2
Marriages per 1,000 pop.	...	Mobile telephone subscribers	
Divorces per 1,000 pop.	...	per 100 pop.	0.1
Cost of living, Dec. 1999		Computers per 100 pop.	0.3
New York = 100	41	Internet hosts per 100 pop.	...

a Year ending March 31, 1999.
b 1998
c Year ending March 31, 1998.

INDONESIA

Area[a]	1,904,443 sq km	Capital	Jakarta
Arable as % of total land	17	Currency	Rupiah (Rp)

People

Population	206.3m	Life expectancy: men	63 yrs
Pop. per sq km	111	women	67 yrs
Av. ann. growth		Adult literacy	85.0%
in pop. 1990–2000	1.49%	Fertility rate (per woman)	2.6
Pop. under 15	30.7%	Urban population	40.9%
Pop. over 65	4.7%		*per 1,000 pop.*
No. of men per 100 women	99.6	Crude birth rate	22.7
Human Development Index	68.1	Crude death rate	7

The economy

GDP	Rp1,107trn	GDP per head	$640
GDP	$130.6bn	GDP per head in purchasing	
Av. ann. growth in real		power parity (USA=100)	8.2
GDP 1990–98	5.8%	Economic freedom index	3.50

Origins of GDP

	% of total		*% of total*
Agriculture	19.5	Private consumption	71.2
Industry, of which:	44.1	Public consumption	7.1
manufacturing	24.9	Investment	21.1
Services	36.4	Exports	35.8
		Imports	-35.2

Components of GDP

Structure of employment

	% of total		*% of total*
Agriculture	43	Unemployed 1998	5.5
Industry	17	Av. ann. rate 1990–98	...
Services	40		

Energy

	m TCE		
Total output	299.913	% output exported	48.5
Total consumption	131.790	% consumption imported	20.6
Consumption per head,			
kg coal equivalent	657		

Inflation and finance

Consumer price		*av. ann. increase 1993–98*	
inflation 1999	20.5%	Narrow money (M1)	20.9%
Av. ann. inflation 1990–99	14.6%	Broad money	31.8%
Money market rate, 1999	23.58%		

Exchange rates

	end 1999		*December 1999*
Rp per $	7,085	Effective rates	*1995 = 100*
Rp per SDR	9,724	– nominal	...
Rp per euro	7,120	– real	...

Principal exports

	$bn fob
Petroleum & products	4.1
Natural gas	3.8
Electrical appliances	3.3
Garments	2.6
Total incl. others	**48.8**

Principal imports

	$bn cif
Raw materials	11.2
Machinery & transport equipment	10.8
Fuels	2.7
Food, drink & tobacco	2.5
Total incl. others	**27.3**

Main export destinations

	% of total
Japan	18.0
United States	15.6
Singapore	10.6
South Korea	6.2
China	4.5
Germany	3.4

Main origins of imports

	% of total
Japan	15.7
Singapore	11.6
South Korea	8.3
United States	7.8
Germany	6.5
Australia	5.3

Balance of payments, reserves and debt, $bn

Visible exports fob	50.4	Overall balance	-3.7
Visible imports fob	-31.9	Change in reserves	6.1
Trade balance	18.4	Level of reserves	
Invisibles inflows	6.4	end Dec.	23.6
Invisibles outflows	-22.1	No. months of import cover	6.2
Net transfers	1.3	Foreign debt	147.5
Current account balance	4.1	– as % of GDP	173
– as % of GDP	3.1	Debt service paid	17.5
Capital balance	-9.6	Debt service ratio	33

Health and education

Health spending, % of GDP	1.3	Education spending, % of GDP	1.4
Doctors per 1,000 pop.	0.2	Enrolment, %: primary	113
Hospital beds per 1,000 pop.	0.7	secondary	56
Safe water access, % of pop.	74	tertiary	11

Society

No. of households	48.2m	Colour TVs per 100 households	36.1
Av. no. per household	4.3	Telephone lines per 100 pop.	2.7
Marriages per 1,000 pop.	...	Mobile telephone subscribers	
Divorces per 1,000 pop.	...	per 100 pop.	0.5
Cost of living, Dec. 1999		Computers per 100 pop.	0.8
New York = 100	60	Internet hosts per 100 pop.	0.1

a Excludes East Timor, 14,874 sq km.

IRAN

Area	1,648,000 sq km	Capital	Tehran
Arable as % of total land	11	Currency	Rial (IR)

People

Population	65.8m	Life expectancy: men	69 yrs
Pop. per sq km	41	women	70 yrs
Av. ann. growth		Adult literacy	73.3%
in pop. 1990–2000	1.85%	Fertility rate (per woman)	2.8
Pop. under 15	36.2%	Urban population	61.6%
Pop. over 65	4.4%		per 1,000 pop.
No. of men per 100 women	103.0	Crude birth rate	22.0
Human Development Index	71.5	Crude death rate	5

The economy

GDPa	IR328,338bn	GDP per head	$1,650
GDP	$102.2bn	GDP per head in purchasing	
Av. ann. growth in real		power parity (USA=100)	17.5
GDP 1990–98	3.6%	Economic freedom index	4.55

Origins of GDPb

	% of total
Agriculture	23.6
Industry, of which:	37.3
manufacturing	...
Services	39.1

Components of GDPb

	% of total
Private consumption	66.3
Public consumption	14.2
Investment	5.1
Net exports	14.4

Structure of employmentc

	% of total		% of labour force
Agriculture	39	Unemployed 1998	...
Industry	23	Av. ann. rate 1990–98	...
Services	38		

Energy

	m TCE		
Total output	321.416	% output exported	60.0
Total consumption	127.269	% consumption imported	5.7
Consumption per head,			
kg coal equivalent	1,819		

Inflation and finance

Consumer price		av. ann. increase 1993–98	
inflation 1999	21.0%	Narrow money (M1)	29.8%
Av. ann. inflation 1990–99	25.4%	Broad money	27.9%

Exchange rates

	end 1999		December 1999
IR per $	1,752	Effective rates	1995 = 100
IR per SDR	2,405	– nominal	140.90
IR per euro	1,761	– real	264.68

Principal exports[d]

	$bn fob
Oil & gas	15.1
Carpets	0.9
Fruit	0.5
Total incl. others	**18.4**

Principal imports[e]

	$bn cif
Raw materials & intermediate goods	12.6
Capital goods	5.1
Consumer goods	2.2
Total incl. others	**20.0**

Main export destinations

	% of total
Japan	16.6
Italy	8.6
Greece	7.5
United Arab Emirates	5.6
France	4.9
China	3.7
Germany	3.3

Main origins of imports

	% of total
Germany	11.8
Italy	7.8
Japan	7.5
China	5.6
France	5.4
United Kingdom	4.8
United Arab Emirates	4.3

Balance of payments[a], reserves and debt, $bn

Visible exports fob	13.0	Overall balance	-1.6
Visible imports fob	-13.6	Change in reserves	...
Trade balance	-0.6	Level of reserves	
Invisibles inflows	1.5	end Dec.	...
Invisibles outflows	-3.3	No. months of import cover	...
Net transfers	0.5	Foreign debt	14.4
Current account balance	-1.9	– as % of GDP	13
– as % of GDP	-1.9	Debt service paid	2.7
Capital balance	3.1	Debt service ratio	20

Health and education

Health spending, % of GDP	4.3	Education spending, % of GDP	4.0
Doctors per 1,000 pop.	0.9	Enrolment, %: primary	98
Hospital beds per 1,000 pop.	1.6	secondary	77
Safe water access, % of pop.	95	tertiary	18

Society

No. of households	12.8m	Colour TVs per 100 households	15.7
Av. no. per household	5.1	Telephone lines per 100 pop.	11.2
Marriages per 1,000 pop.[f]	7.8	Mobile telephone subscribers	
Divorces per 1,000 pop.	0.5	per 100 pop.	0.6
Cost of living, Dec. 1999		Computers per 100 pop.	3.2
New York = 100	51	Internet hosts per 100 pop.	...

a Iranian year ending March 20, 1999, estimated.
b Iranian year ending March 20, 1997, estimated.
c 1990
d Iranian year ending March 20, 1996, estimated.
e Iranian year ending March 20, 1994, estimated.
f 1996

IRAQ

Area	438,317 sq km	Capital	Baghdad
Arable as % of total land	12	Currency	Iraqi dinar (ID)

People

Population	21.8m	Life expectancy: men	61 yrs
Pop. per sq km	53	women	64 yrs
Av. ann. growth		Adult literacy	58.0%
in pop. 1990–2000	2.46%	Fertility rate (per woman)	5.3
Pop. under 15	41.3%	Urban population	76.8%
Pop. over 65	3.1%		*per 1,000 pop.*
No. of men per 100 women	103.5	Crude birth rate	36.4
Human Development Index	58.6	Crude death rate	8

The economy

GDP	ID3.6bn	GDP per head	...
GDP	$12bn	GDP per head in purchasing	
Av. ann. growth in real		power parity (USA=100)	...
GDP 1985–95	-9.3%	Economic freedom index	4.90

Origins of GDP[a]		**Components of GDP**[a]	
	% of total		*% of total*
Agriculture	6.1	Private consumption	72.3
Industry, of which:	13.1	Public consumption	13.9
manufacturing	...	Investment	15.5
Services	80.8	Exports	1.3
		Imports	-3.0

Structure of employment[b]

	% of total		*% of labour force*
Agriculture	16	Unemployed 1998	...
Industry	18	Av. ann. rate 1990–98	...
Services	66		

Energy

	m TCE		
Total output	58.653	% output exported	13.1
Total consumption	36.873	% consumption imported	nil
Consumption per head,			
kg coal equivalent	1,789		

Inflation and finance

Consumer price		*av. ann. increase 1993–98*	
inflation 1999	...	Narrow money (M1)	...
Av. ann. inflation 1990–99	...	Broad money	...

Exchange rates

	end 1999		*December 1999*
ID per $	0.31	Effective rates	*1995 = 100*
ID per SDR	0.43	– nominal	...
ID per euro	0.31	– real	...

Principal exports[c]

	$bn fob
Crude oil	5.9
Total incl. others	**5.9**

Principal imports[d]

	$bn cif
Civilian goods	3.7
Military goods	0.9
Total incl. others	**4.6**

Main export destinations[d]

	% of total
Spain	16.8
United States	15.6
France	12.5
Italy	8.0

Main origins of imports[d]

	% of total
Australia	31.6
United States	11.7
Thailand	8.6
China	8.5

Balance of payments[ce], reserves and debt, $bn

Visible exports fob	1.5	Overall balance	...
Visible imports fob	-1.8	Change in reserves	...
Trade balance	-0.3	Level of reserves	
Invisibles inflows	...	end Dec.	...
Invisibles outflows	...	No. months of import cover	...
Net transfers	...	Foreign debt	...
Current account balance	-0.3	– as % of GDP	...
– as % of GDP	-4.3	Debt service	...
Capital balance	...	Debt service ratio	...

Health and education

Health spending, % of GDP	...	Education spending, % of GDP	...
Doctors per 1,000 pop.	0.6	Enrolment, %: primary	85
Hospital beds per 1,000 pop.	1.5	secondary	42
Safe water access, % of pop.	81	tertiary	11

Society

No. of households	4.1m	Colour TVs per 100 households	8.3
Av. no. per household	5.3	Telephone lines per 100 pop.	3.1
Marriages per 1,000 pop.	...	Mobile telephone subscribers	
Divorces per 1,000 pop.	...	per 100 pop.	...
Cost of living, Dec. 1999		Computers per 100 pop.	...
New York = 100	...	Internet hosts per 100 pop.	...

a 1993, estimated.
b 1990
c Trade and balance of payments data for Iraq are estimates based on limited and
   inconsistent information.
d 1997
e 1996

IRELAND

Area	70,282 sq km	Capital	Dublin
Arable as % of total land	13	Currency	Punt (I£)

People

Population	3.7m	Life expectancy: men	74 yrs
Pop. per sq km	53	women	79 yrs
Av. ann. growth		Adult literacy	99.0%
in pop. 1990–2000	0.63%	Fertility rate (per woman)	1.9
Pop. under 15	21.3%	Urban population	59.0%
Pop. over 65	11.3%		per 1,000 pop.
No. of men per 100 women	98.6	Crude birth rate	14.2
Human Development Index	90.0	Crude death rate	8

The economy

GDP	I£59.6bn	GDP per head	$18,710
GDP	$69.3bn	GDP per head in purchasing	
Av. ann. growth in real		power parity (USA=100)	61.5
GDP 1990–98	7.7%	Economic freedom index	1.85

Origins of GDP		**Components of GDP**	
	% of total		% of total
Agriculture	5	Private consumption	51.5
Industry, of which:	39	Public consumption	13.4
manufacturing	...	Investment	23.8
Services	56	Exports	84.4
		Imports	-72.6

Structure of employment

	% of total		% of labour force
Agriculture	14	Unemployed 1998	7.8
Industry	29	Av. ann. rate 1990–98	12.8
Services	57		

Energy

	m TCE		
Total output	5.191	% output exported	26.1
Total consumption	16.450	% consumption imported	81.2
Consumption per head,			
kg coal equivalent	4,629		

Inflation and finance

Consumer price		av. ann. increase 1993–98	
inflation 1999	1.6%	Euro area:	
Av. ann. inflation 1990–99	2.2%	Narrow money (M1)	6.4%
Money market rate, 1999	3.14%	Broad money	4.0%

Exchange rates

	end 1999		December 1999
I£ per $	0.78	Effective rates	1995 = 100
I£ per SDR	1.07	– nominal	92.24
I£ per euro	0.78	– real	...

Principal exports

	$bn fob
Machinery & transport equipment	23.5
Chemicals	20.3
Manufactured goods	7.5
Agric. products & foodstuffs	5.7
Total incl. others	**64.0**

Principal imports

	$bn cif
Machinery & transport equipment	22.5
Manufactured goods	4.9
Chemicals	4.9
Total incl. others	**44.4**

Main export destinations

	% of total
United Kingdom	22.2
Germany	14.6
United States	13.7
France	8.3
Netherlands	6.4
Belgium & Luxembourg	5.5

Main origins of imports

	% of total
United Kingdom	33.6
United States	16.1
Japan	7.1
Germany	6.2
Singapore	5.0
France	3.9

Balance of payments, reserves and aid, $bn

Visible exports fob	65.0	Capital balance	0.7
Visible imports fob	-41.7	Overall balance	2.4
Trade balance	23.4	Change in reserves	2.9
Invisibles inflows	16.7	Level of reserves	
Invisibles outflows	-40.7	end Dec.	9.5
Net transfers	1.5	No. months of import cover	1.4
Current account balance	0.8	Aid given	0.20
– as % of GDP	1.2	– as % of GDP	0.30

Health and education

Health spending, % of GDP	6.3	Education spending, % of GDP	6.0
Doctors per 1,000 pop.	2.1	Enrolment, %: primary	105
Hospital beds per 1,000 pop.	3.7	secondary	118
Safe water access, % of pop.	…	tertiary	41

Society

No. of households	0.9m	Colour TVs per 100 households	99.0
Av. no. per household	4.3	Telephone lines per 100 pop.	43.5
Marriages per 1,000 pop.	4.5	Mobile telephone subscribers	
Divorces per 1,000 pop.	…	per 100 pop.	25.7
Cost of living, Dec. 1999		Computers per 100 pop.	27.2
New York = 100	83	Internet hosts per 100 pop.	16.2

ISRAEL

Area	20,770 sq km	Capital	Jerusalem
Arable as % of total land	21	Currency	New Shekel (NIS)

People

Population	6.0m	Life expectancy: men	76 yrs
Pop. per sq km	295	women	80 yrs
Av. ann. growth		Adult literacy	95.4%
in pop. 1990–2000	2.88%	Fertility rate (per woman)	2.7
Pop. under 15	27.7%	Urban population	91.2%
Pop. over 65	9.8%		*per 1,000 pop.*
No. of men per 100 women	98.5	Crude birth rate	19.8
Human Development Index	88.3	Crude death rate	6

The economy

GDP	NIS376bn	GDP per head	$16,180
GDP	$96.5bn	GDP per head in purchasing	
Av. ann. growth in real		power parity (USA=100)	57.7
GDP 1990–98	5.4%	Economic freedom index	2.75

Origins of GDP[a]

	% of total
Agriculture	4.2
Industry, of which:	36.9
manufacturing	...
Services	58.9

Components of GDP

	% of total
Private consumption	62.4
Public consumption	29.5
Investment	20.7
Exports	31.9
Imports	-43.1

Structure of employment

	% of total		*% of labour force*
Agriculture	2	Unemployed 1998	8.6
Industry	19	Av. ann. rate 1990–98	8.8
Services	79		

Energy

	m TCE		
Total output	0.15	% output exported[b]	1,663.3
Total consumption	21.852	% consumption imported[b]	112.1
Consumption per head,			
kg coal equivalent	3,858		

Inflation and finance

Consumer price			*av. ann. increase 1993–98*
inflation 1999	5.2%	Narrow money (M1)	13.3%
Av. ann. inflation 1990–99	10.5%	Broad money	21.1%
Treasury bill rate, 1999	11.7%		

Exchange rates

	end 1999		*December 1999*
NIS per $	4.15	Effective rates	*1995 = 100*
NIS per SDR	5.70	– nominal	83.03
NIS per euro	4.17	– real	104.30

Principal exports

	$bn fob
Industrial goods	16.0
Diamonds	4.3
Agricultural goods	0.8
Total incl. others	**21.2**

Principal imports

	$bn cif
Raw materials	12.9
Investment goods	4.5
Consumer goods	3.9
Diamonds	3.8
Fuel	1.8
Total incl. others	**27.0**

Main export destinations

	% of total
United States	35.4
United Kingdom	5.7
Germany	4.8
Belgium & Luxembourg	4.7
Netherlands	4.7
Hong Kong	3.4

Main origins of imports

	% of total
United States	19.6
Belgium & Luxembourg	10.5
Germany	8.8
United Kingdom	7.5
Italy	6.7
Switzerland	5.5

Balance of payments, reserves and debt, $bn

Visible exports fob	23.0	Overall balance	-0.1
Visible imports fob	-26.2	Change in reserves	2.3
Trade balance	-3.2	Level of reserves	
Invisibles inflows	12.0	end Dec.	22.7
Invisibles outflows	-15.8	No. months of import cover	6.5
Net transfers	6.1	Foreign debt	35.9
Current account balance	-0.8	– as % of GDP	37
– as % of GDP	-0.7	Debt service	6.9
Capital balance	1.3	Debt service ratio	19

Health and education

Health spending, % of GDP	10.4	Education spending, % of GDP	7.6
Doctors per 1,000 pop.	4.6	Enrolment, %: primary	98
Hospital beds per 1,000 pop.	6.0	secondary	88
Safe water access, % of pop.	…	tertiary	44

Society

No. of households	1.5m	Colour TVs per 100 households	87.5
Av. no. per household	4.0	Telephone lines per 100 pop.	47.1
Marriages per 1,000 pop.	6.1	Mobile telephone subscribers	
Divorces per 1,000 pop.	1.9	per 100 pop.	35.9
Cost of living, Dec. 1999		Computers per 100 pop.	21.7
New York = 100	93	Internet hosts per 100 pop.	23.4

a Estimates.
b Energy trade data are distorted by transitory and oil refining activities.

ITALY

Area	301,245 sq km	Capital	Rome
Arable as % of total land	41	Currency	Lira (L)

People

Population	57.4m	Life expectancy: men	75 yrs
Pop. per sq km	190	women	81 yrs
Av. ann. growth		Adult literacy	98.3%
in pop. 1990–2000	0.05%	Fertility rate (per woman)	1.2
Pop. under 15	14.3%	Urban population	67.0%
Pop. over 65	18.2%	*per 1,000 pop.*	
No. of men per 100 women	94.3	Crude birth rate	9.0
Human Development Index	90.0	Crude death rate	10

The economy

GDP	L2,058trn	GDP per head	$20,090
GDP	$1,157bn	GDP per head in purchasing	
Av. ann. growth in real		power parity (USA=100)	69.6
GDP 1990–98	1.2%	Economic freedom index	2.30

Origins of GDP

Components of GDP

	% of total		*% of total*
Agriculture	2.6	Private consumption	61.9
Industry, of which:	31.6	Public consumption	16.7
manufacturing	...	Investment	18.9
Services	65.8	Exports	24.3
		Imports	-21.7

Structure of employment

	% of total		*% of labour force*
Agriculture	6	Unemployed 1998	11.9
Industry	33	Av. ann. rate 1990–98	10.6
Services	61		

Energy

	m TCE		
Total output	44.288	% output exported	56.8
Total consumption	230.350	% consumption imported	95.3
Consumption per head,			
kg coal equivalent	4,024		

Inflation and finance

Consumer price		*av. ann. increase 1993–98*	
inflation 1999	1.7%	Euro area:	
Av. ann. inflation 1990–99	3.9%	Narrow money (M1)	6.4%
Money market rate, 1999	2.95%	Broad money	4.0%

Exchange rates

	end 1999		*December 1999*
L per $	1,913	Effective rates	*1995 = 100*
L per SDR	2,621	– nominal	106.5
L per euro	1,923	– real	112.5

Principal exports

	$bn fob
Engineering products	85.9
Textiles & clothing	38.4
Transport equipment	26.8
Chemicals	20.7
Food, drink & tobacco	10.0
Total incl. others	**242.4**

Principal imports

	$bn cif
Engineering products	54.0
Chemicals	29.8
Transport equipment	29.0
Minerals	20.0
Energy products	17.1
Total incl. others	**215.9**

Main export destinations

	% of total
Germany	16.5
France	12.7
United States	8.5
United Kingdom	7.2
Spain	5.8
EU15	56.2

Main origins of imports

	% of total
Germany	18.8
France	13.1
United Kingdom	6.4
Netherlands	6.2
United States	5.1
EU15	61.3

Balance of payments, reserves and aid, $bn

Visible exports fob	242.6	Capital balance	-15.7
Visible imports fob	-206.9	Overall balance	-21.5
Trade balance	35.6	Change in reserves	-21.2
Invisibles inflows	118.9	Level of reserves	
Invisibles outflows	-127.0	end Dec.	53.9
Net transfers	-7.5	No. months of import cover	1.9
Current account balance	20.0	Aid given	2.28
– as % of GDP	1.7	– as % of GDP	0.20

Health and education

Health spending, % of GDP	7.6	Education spending, % of GDP	4.9
Doctors per 1,000 pop.	5.5	Enrolment, %: primary	101
Hospital beds per 1,000 pop.	6.5	secondary	95
Safe water access, % of pop.	…	tertiary	47

Society

No. of households	22.9m	Colour TVs per 100 households	94.2
Av. no. per household	2.5	Telephone lines per 100 pop.	45.3
Marriages per 1,000 pop.	4.9	Mobile telephone subscribers	
Divorces per 1,000 pop.	0.6	per 100 pop.	35.7
Cost of living, Dec. 1999		Computers per 100 pop.	17.3
New York = 100	80	Internet hosts per 100 pop.	11.5

JAPAN

Area	377,727 sq km	Capital	Tokyo
Arable as % of total land	12	Currency	Yen (¥)

People

Population	126.3m	Life expectancy: men	77 yrs
Pop. per sq km	335	women	83 yrs
Av. ann. growth		Adult literacy	99.0%
in pop. 1990–2000	0.26%	Fertility rate (per woman)	1.4
Pop. under 15	14.8%	Urban population	78.8%
Pop. over 65	17.1%		per 1,000 pop.
No. of men per 100 women	96.1	Crude birth rate	9.9
Human Development Index	92.4	Crude death rate	8

The economy

GDP	¥495trn	GDP per head	$32,350
GDP	$4,089bn	GDP per head in purchasing	
Av. ann. growth in real		power parity (USA=100)	80.7
GDP 1990–98	1.5%	Economic freedom index	2.15

Origins of GDP		**Components of GDP**	
	% of total		% of total
Agriculture	1.7	Private consumption	58.7
Industry, of which:	36.0	Public consumption	9.5
manufacturing	23.5	Investment	29.2
Services	62.3	Exports	13.7
		Imports	-11.1

Structure of employment

	% of total		% of labour force
Agriculture	5	Unemployed 1998	4.1
Industry	32	Av. ann. rate 1990–98	2.9
Services	63		

Energy

	m TCE		
Total output	137.427	% output exported[a]	10.3
Total consumption	655.219	% consumption imported[a]	87.6
Consumption per head,			
kg coal equivalent	5,277		

Inflation and finance

Consumer price		av. ann. increase 1993–98	
inflation 1999	-0.3%	Narrow money (M1)	8.0%
Av. ann. inflation 1990–99	1.0%	Broad money	3.1%
Money market rate, 1999	0.06%		

Exchange rates

	end 1999		December 1999
¥ per $	102.2	Effective rates	1995 = 100
¥ per SDR	140.3	– nominal	97.8
¥ per euro	102.7	– real	85.9

Principal exports
$bn fob

Motor vehicles	59.5
Integrated circuits	28.3
Office machinery	27.9
Chemicals	27.1
Metals	24.5
Total incl. others	**386.9**

Principal imports
$bn cif

Mineral fuels	42.9
Agric. products & foodstuffs	41.2
Chemicals	20.8
Textiles	18.9
Office machinery	16.3
Total incl. others	**280.0**

Main export destinations
% of total

United States	30.5
Taiwan	6.6
Hong Kong	5.8
China	5.2
Germany	4.9

Main origins of imports
% of total

United States	23.9
China	13.2
Australia	4.6
South Korea	4.3
Indonesia	3.9

Balance of payments, reserves and aid, $bn

Visible exports fob	374.0	Capital balance	-131.2
Visible imports fob	-251.7	Overall balance	-6.2
Trade balance	122.4	Change in reserves	-4.2
Invisibles inflows	272.0	Level of reserves end Dec.	222.4
Invisibles outflows	-264.8		
Net transfers	-8.8	No. months of import cover	5.2
Current account balance	120.7	Aid given	10.64
– as % of GDP	3.0	– as % of GDP	0.28

Health and education

Health spending, % of GDP	7.1	Education spending, % of GDP	3.6
Doctors per 1,000 pop.	1.8	Enrolment, %: primary	101
Hospital beds per 1,000 pop.	16.2	secondary	103
Safe water access, % of pop.	97	tertiary	43

Society

No. of households	41.5m	Colour TVs per 100 households	99.6
Av. no. per household	3.0	Telephone lines per 100 pop.	50.3
Marriages per 1,000 pop.	6.3	Mobile telephone subscribers per 100 pop.	37.4
Divorces per 1,000 pop.	1.7	Computers per 100 pop.	23.7
Cost of living, Dec. 1999 New York = 100	164	Internet hosts per 100 pop.	20.9

a Energy trade data are distorted by transitory and oil refining activities.

KENYA

Area	582,646 sq km	Capital	Nairobi
Arable as % of total land	8	Currency	Kenyan shilling (KSh)

People

Population	29.0m	Life expectancy: men	51 yrs
Pop. per sq km	52	women	53 yrs
Av. ann. growth		Adult literacy	79.3%
in pop. 1990–2000	2.45%	Fertility rate (per woman)	4.5%
Pop. under 15	43.0%	Urban population	33.1%
Pop. over 65	3.0%		per 1,000 pop.
No. of men per 100 women	100.5	Crude birth rate	34.3
Human Development Index	51.9	Crude death rate	12

The economy

GDP	KSh699bn	GDP per head	$350
GDP	$10.2bn	GDP per head in purchasing	
Av. ann. growth in real		power parity (USA=100)	3.3
GDP 1990–98	2.2%	Economic freedom index	3.05

Origins of GDP

Components of GDP

	% of total		% of total
Agriculture	26.0	Private consumption	74.5
Industry, of which:	...	Public consumption	16.1
manufacturing	10.8	Investment	17.2
Other	63.2	Exports	24.6
		Imports	-32.3

Structure of employment[a]

	% of total		% of labour force
Agriculture	80	Unemployed 1998	...
Industry	7	Av. ann. rate 1990–98	...
Services	13		

Energy

	m TCE		
Total output	0.740	% output exported[b]	72.4
Total consumption	3.808	% consumption imported[b]	99.9
Consumption per head,			
kg coal equivalent	137		

Inflation and finance

Consumer price			av. ann. increase 1993–98
inflation 1999	2.6%	Narrow money (M1)	9.7%
Av. ann. inflation 1990–99	16.3%	Broad money	20.2%
Treasury bill rate, 1999	13.87%		

Exchange rates

	end 1999		December 1999
KSh per $	72.9	Effective rates	1995 = 100
KSh per SDR	100.1	– nominal	...
KSh per euro	73.3	– real	...

Principal exports

	$m fob
Tea	546
Horticultural products	247
Coffee	212
Petroleum products	51
Total incl. others	**2,009**

Principal imports

	$m cif
Petroleum & products	519
Industrial machinery	518
Motor vehicles & chassis	243
Iron & steel	131
Total incl. others	**3,198**

Main export destinations

	% of total
Uganda	16.1
United Kingdom	13.4
Tanzania	13.3
Egypt	4.7

Main origins of imports

	% of total
United Kingdom	12.3
United Arab Emirates	9.0
United States	8.4
Japan	7.9

Balance of payments, reserves and debt, $bn

Visible exports fob	2.0	Overall balance	0.1
Visible imports fob	-3.0	Change in reserves	-0.0
Trade balance	-1.0	Level of reserves	
Invisibles inflows	0.9	end Dec.	0.8
Invisibles outflows	-0.9	No. months of import cover	2.4
Net transfers	0.7	Foreign debt	7.0
Current account balance	-0.4	– as % of GDP	62
– as % of GDP	-3.6	Debt service paid	0.4
Capital balance	0.6	Debt service ratio	19

Health and education

Health spending, % of GDP	1.0	Education spending, % of GDP	6.5
Doctors per 1,000 pop.	...	Enrolment, %: primary	85
Hospital beds per 1,000 pop.	1.6	secondary	24
Safe water access, % of pop.	44	tertiary	2

Society

No. of households	5.9m	Colour TVs per 100 households	2.1
Av. no. per household	4.9	Telephone lines per 100 pop.	1.0
Marriages per 1,000 pop.	...	Mobile telephone subscribers	
Divorces per 1,000 pop.	...	per 100 pop.	...
Cost of living, Dec. 1999		Computers per 100 pop.	0.3
New York = 100	55	Internet hosts per 100 pop.	...

a 1990
b Energy trade data are distorted by transitory and oil refining activities.

MALAYSIA

Area	332,665 sq km	Capital	Kuala Lumpur
Arable as % of total land	15	Currency	Malaysian dollar/ringgit (M$)

People

Population	21.4m	Life expectancy: men	70 yrs
Pop. per sq km	67	women	74 yrs
Av. ann. growth		Adult literacy	85.7%
in pop. 1990–2000	2.21%	Fertility rate (per woman)	3.2
Pop. under 15	34.0%	Urban population	57.4%
Pop. over 65	4.1%		*per 1,000 pop.*
No. of men per 100 women	102.8	Crude birth rate	25.0
Human Development Index	76.8	Crude death rate	5

The economy

GDP	M$284bn	GDP per head	$3,670
GDP	$81.3bn	GDP per head in purchasing	
Av. ann. growth in real		power parity (USA=100)	26.3
GDP 1990–98	7.4%	Economic freedom index	2.70

Origins of GDP		**Components of GDP**	
	% of total		*% of total*
Agriculture	11.5	Private consumption	44.7
Industry, of which:	46.1	Public consumption	11.3
manufacturing	32.2	Investment	30.3
Services	42.4	Exports	102.0
		Imports	-88.2

Structure of employment

	% of total		*% of labour force*
Agriculture	26	Unemployed 1997	2.5
Industry	29	Av. ann. rate 1990–97	3.4
Services	45		

Energy

	m TCE		
Total output	97.918	% output exported	53.7
Total consumption	54.146	% consumption imported	29.2
Consumption per head,			
kg coal equivalent	2,631		

Inflation and finance

		av. ann. increase 1993–98	
Consumer price inflation 1999	2.7%	Narrow money (M1)	4.0%
Av. ann. inflation 1990–99	4.0%	Broad money	14.4%
Money market rate, 1999	3.38%		

Exchange rates

	end 1999		*December 1999*
M$ per $	3.80	Effective rates	*1995 = 100*
M$ per SDR	5.22	– nominal	76.9
M$ per euro	3.82	– real	82.2

Principal exports
$bn fob

Electronics & electrical machinery	41.3
Palm oil	4.5
Petroleum & LNG	3.4
Chemicals & products	2.7
Textiles, clothing & footwear	2.4
Transport equipment	2.1
Total incl. others	**73.2**

Principal imports
$bn cif

Manufacturing supplies	27.6
Machinery & transport equipment	8.0
Metal products	2.7
Food	1.7
Consumer durables	1.3
Total incl. others	**58.2**

Main export destinations
% of total

United States	21.6
Singapore	17.9
Japan	10.0
Hong Kong	4.6
Taiwan	4.1
United Kingdom	3.6

Main origins of imports
% of total

Singapore	24.7
Japan	15.9
United States	13.8
South Korea	6.7
Taiwan	5.1
Thailand	4.2

Balance of payments[a], reserves and debt, $bn

Visible exports fob	77.9	Overall balance	-3.9
Visible imports fob	-74.0	Change in reserves	4.8
Trade balance	3.9	Level of reserves	
Invisibles inflows	17.5	end Dec.	26.2
Invisibles outflows	-25.1	No. months of import cover	3.1
Net transfers	-1.1	Foreign debt	44.8
Current account balance	-4.8	as % of GDP	65
– as % of GDP	-4.9	Debt service paid	5.6
Capital balance	2.5	Debt service ratio	9

Health and education

Health spending, % of GDP	2.4	Education spending, % of GDP	4.9
Doctors per 1,000 pop.	0.5	Enrolment, %: primary	101
Hospital beds per 1,000 pop.	2.0	secondary	64
Safe water access, % of pop.	78	tertiary	11

Society

No. of households	4.4m	Colour TVs per 100 households	89.2
Av. no. per household	4.9	Telephone lines per 100 pop.	20.2
Marriages per 1,000 pop.	...	Mobile telephone subscribers	
Divorces per 1,000 pop.	...	per 100 pop.	10.1
Cost of living, Dec. 1999		Computers per 100 pop.	5.7
New York = 100	59	Internet hosts per 100 pop.	2.8

a 1997

MEXICO

Area	1,972,545 sq km	Capital	Mexico City
Arable as % of total land	13	Currency	Mexican peso (PS)

People

Population	95.8m	Life expectancy: men	70 yrs
Pop. per sq km	50	women	75 yrs
Av. ann. growth		Adult literacy	90.1%
in pop. 1990–2000	1.73%	Fertility rate (per woman)	2.8
Pop. under 15	33.2%	Urban population	74.4%
Pop. over 65	4.7%		*per 1,000 pop.*
No. of men per 100 women	98.0	Crude birth rate	24.6
Human Development Index	78.6	Crude death rate	5

The economy

GDP	3,791bn pesos	GDP per head	$3,840
GDP	$368bn	GDP per head in purchasing	
Av. ann. growth in real		power parity (USA=100)	25.5
GDP 1990–98	2.5%	Economic freedom index	3.00

Origins of GDP

Components of GDP

	% of total		*% of total*
Agriculture	5.8	Private consumption	68.5
Industry, of which:	28.9	Public consumption	9.8
manufacturing	21.4	Investment	22.0
Services	68.1	Exports	29.1
		Imports	-29.5

Structure of employment

	% of total		*% of labour force*
Agriculture	17	Unemployed 1998	2.3
Industry	27	Av. ann. rate 1991–98	3.7
Services	56		

Energy

	m TCE		
Total output	292.529	% output exported	41.0
Total consumption	187.106	% consumption imported	7.2
Consumption per head,			
kg coal equivalent	2,018		

Inflation and finance

Consumer price		*av. ann. increase 1993–98*	
inflation 1999	16.6%	Narrow money (M1)	14.9%
Av. ann. inflation 1990–99	19.4%	Broad money	25.8%
Money market rate, 1999	24.10%		

Exchange rates

	end 1999		*December 1999*
PS per $	9.51	Effective rates	*1995 = 100*
PS per SDR	13.06	– nominal	...
PS per euro	9.56	– real	...

Principal exports

	$bn fob
Manufactured products	106.1
Crude oil & products	7.1
Agricultural products	3.8
Total incl. others	**117.5**

Principal imports

	$bn cif
Intermediate goods	96.9
Capital goods	17.3
Consumer goods	11.1
Total	**125.4**

Main export destinations

	% of total
United States	81.9
Canada	4.6
Japan	1.0
Spain	0.8

Main origins of imports

	% of total
United States	73.9
Japan	4.0
Germany	3.7
France	1.2

Balance of payments, reserves and debt, $bn

Visible exports fob	117.5	Overall balance	3.2
Visible imports fob	-125.4	Change in reserves	3.0
Trade balance	-7.9	Level of reserves	
Invisibles inflows	17.0	end Dec.	31.8
Invisibles outflows	-31.1	No. months of import cover	2.4
Net transfers	6.0	Foreign debt	160.0
Current account balance	-16.0	– as % of GDP	42
– as % of gdp	-4.3	Debt service paid	25.7
Capital balance	17.3	Debt service ratio	20

Health and education

Health spending, % of GDP	4.7	Education spending, % of GDP	4.9
Doctors per 1,000 pop.	1.2	Enrolment, %: primary	114
Hospital beds per 1,000 pop.	1.2	secondary	64
Safe water access, % of pop.	85	tertiary	16

Society

No. of households	21.1m	Colour TVs per 100 households	89.8
Av. no. per household	4.6	Telephone lines per 100 pop.	10.4
Marriages per 1,000 pop.	7.1	Mobile telephone subscribers	
Divorces per 1,000 pop.	0.5	per 100 pop.	3.5
Cost of living, Dec. 1999		Computers per 100 pop.	4.7
New York = 100	79	Internet hosts per 100 pop.	4.4

MOROCCO

Area	446,550 sq km	Capital	Rabat
Arable as % of total land	22	Currency	Dirham (Dh)

People

Population	27.4m	Life expectancy: men	65 yrs
Pop. per sq km	63	women	69 yrs
Av. ann. growth		Adult literacy	45.9%
in pop. 1990–2000	1.70%	Fertility rate (per woman)	3.1
Pop. under 15	32.5%	Urban population	56.1%
Pop. over 65	4.4%		per 1,000 pop.
No. of men per 100 women	100.2	Crude birth rate	25.6
Human Development Index	58.2	Crude death rate	7

The economy

GDP	Dh341bn	GDP per head	$1,240
GDP	$34.4bn	GDP per head in purchasing	
Av. ann. growth in real		power parity (USA=100)	10.9
GDP 1990–98	2.2%	Economic freedom index	2.75

Origins of GDP

Components of GDP

	% of total		% of total
Agriculture	16.0	Private consumption	67.2
Industry, of which:	29.7	Public consumption	18.2
manufacturing	17.7	Investment	22.5
Services	54.3	Exports	23.5
		Imports	-27.0

Structure of employment[a]

	% of total		% of labour force
Agriculture	5	Unemployed 1996	17.8
Industry	41	Av. ann. rate 1995–96	20.0
Services	54		

Energy

	m TCE		
Total output	0.631	% output exported	nil
Total consumption	11.497	% consumption imported	101.0
Consumption per head,			
kg coal equivalent	425		

Inflation and finance

Consumer price		*av. ann. increase 1993–98*	
inflation 1999	0.7%	Narrow money (M1)	9.3%
Av. ann. inflation 1990–99	4.2%	Broad money	9.1%
Money market rate, 1999	5.64%		

Exchange rates

	end 1999		December 1999
			1995 = 100
Dh per $	10.09	Effective rates	
Dh per SDR	13.85	– nominal	106.2
Dh per euro	10.14	– real	106.8

Principal exports
	$bn fob
Food, drink & tobacco	1.4
Semi-finished goods	1.1
Finished goods	1.0
Mineral ores	0.6
Raw materials	0.1
Total incl. others	**7.1**

Principal imports
	$bn cif
Machinery & equipment	2.2
Semi-finished goods	2.0
Consumer goods	1.3
Food, drink & tobacco	1.2
Energy & fuels	0.9
Total incl. others	**10.3**

Main export destinations
	% of total
France	26.9
Spain	10.8
India	8.3
Italy	6.4
Japan	5.5

Main origins of imports
	% of total
France	21.8
Spain	9.7
United States	7.3
Germany	6.3
Italy	6.2

Balance of payments, reserves and debt, $bn
Visible exports fob	7.1	Overall balance	-0.7
Visible imports fob	-9.5	Change in reserves	0.4
Trade balance	-2.3	Level of reserves	
Invisibles inflows	3.0	end Dec.	4.6
Invisibles outflows	-3.2	No. months of import cover	4.4
Net transfers	2.3	Foreign debt	20.7
Current account balance	-0.2	– as % of GDP	61
– as % of GDP	-0.7	Debt service paid	2.8
Capital balance	-0.7	Debt service ratio	20

Health and education
Health spending, % of GDP	4.0	Education spending, % of GDP	5.0
Doctors per 1,000 pop.	0.5	Enrolment, %: primary	86
Hospital beds per 1,000 pop.	1.0	secondary	39
Safe water access, % of pop.	65	tertiary	11

Society
No. of households	6.3m	Colour TVs per 100 households	67.0
Av. no. per household	4.4	Telephone lines per 100 pop.	5.5
Marriages per 1,000 pop.	...	Mobile telephone subscribers	
Divorces per 1,000 pop.	...	per 100 pop.	0.4
Cost of living, Dec. 1999		Computers per 100 pop.	0.3
New York = 100	73	Internet hosts per 100 pop.	...

a Urban areas, 1997.

NETHERLANDS

Area[a]	41,526 sq km	Capital	Amsterdam
Arable as % of total land	28	Currency	Guilder (Fl)

People

Population	15.7m	Life expectancy: men	75 yrs
Pop. per sq km	386	women	81 yrs
Av. ann. growth		Adult literacy	99.0%
in pop. 1990–2000	0.55%	Fertility rate (per woman)	1.5
Pop. under 15	18.1%	Urban population	89.4%
Pop. over 65	13.8%		per 1,000 pop.
No. of men per 100 women	98.1	Crude birth rate	11.6
Human Development Index	92.1	Crude death rate	9

The economy

GDP	Fl750bn	GDP per head	$24,780
GDP	$389bn	GDP per head in purchasing	
Av. ann. growth in real		power parity (USA=100)	76.4
GDP 1990–98	2.6%	Economic freedom index	2.05

Origins of GDP

Components of GDP

	% of total		% of total
Agriculture	3.5	Private consumption	59.4
Industry, of which:	26.8	Public consumption	13.6
manufacturing	...	Investment	20.3
Services	69.8	Exports	55.3
		Imports	-48.6

Structure of employment

	% of total		% of labour force
Agriculture	4	Unemployed 1998	4.4
Industry	23	Av. ann. rate 1990–98	6.2
Services	73		

Energy

	m TCE		
Total output	114.260	% output exported[b]	109.0
Total consumption	125.149	% consumption imported[b]	114.4
Consumption per head,			
kg coal equivalent	8,035		

Inflation and finance

Consumer price			av. ann. increase 1993–98
inflation 1999	2.2%	Euro area:	
Av. ann. inflation 1990–99	2.5%	Narrow money (M1)	6.4%
Deposit rate, 1999	2.74%	Broad money	4.0%

Exchange rates

	end 1999		December 1999
Fl per $	2.18	Effective rates	1995 = 100
Fl per SDR	2.99	– nominal	91.0
Fl per euro	2.19	– real	85.5

Principal exports

	$bn fob
Machinery & transport equipment	64.7
Food, drink & tobacco	32.4
Chemicals	31.8
Fuels	10.5
Total incl. others	**198.6**

Principal imports

	$bn cif
Machinery & transport equipment	72.0
Chemicals	22.0
Food, drink & tobacco	18.3
Fuels	9.6
Clothing	6.5
Total incl. others	**184.5**

Main export destinations

	% of total
Germany	26.5
Belgium & Luxembourg	12.6
France	10.7
United Kingdom	10.1
Italy	5.8
EU15	78.2

Main origins of imports

	% of total
Germany	20.1
Belgium & Luxembourg	10.6
United Kingdom	9.7
United States	9.0
France	6.9
EU15	60.6

Balance of payments, reserves and aid, $bn

Visible exports fob	171.1	Capital balance[c]	-21.5
Visible imports fob	-153.1	Overall balance[c]	-2.7
Trade balance	-18.0	Change in reserves	-1.6
Invisibles inflows	99.2	Level of reserves	
Invisibles outflows	-85.9	end Dec.	31.2
Net transfers	-7.2	No. months of import cover	1.6
Current account balance	24.1	Aid given	3.04
– as % of GDP	6.2	– as % of GDP	0.80

Health and education

Health spending, % of GDP	8.5	Education spending, % of GDP	5.1
Doctors per 1,000 pop.	2.6	Enrolment, %: primary	108
Hospital beds per 1,000 pop.	11.3	secondary[d]	132
Safe water access, % of pop.	…	tertiary	47

Society

No. of households	6.7m	Colour TVs per 100 households	98.1
Av. no. per household	2.3	Telephone lines per 100 pop.	59.3
Marriages per 1,000 pop.	5.5	Mobile telephone subscribers	
Divorces per 1,000 pop.	2.1	per 100 pop.	21.3
Cost of living, Dec. 1999		Computers per 100 pop.	31.8
New York = 100	89	Internet hosts per 100 pop.	52.4

a Includes water.
b Energy trade data are distorted due to transitory and oil refining activities.
c 1997
d Includes training for unemployed.

NEW ZEALAND

Area	270,534 sq km	Capital	Wellington
Arable as % of total land	14	Currency New Zealand dollar (NZ$)	

People

Population	3.8m	Life expectancy: men	74 yrs
Pop. per sq km	14	women	80 yrs
Av. ann. growth		Adult literacy	99.0%
in pop. 1990–2000	1.39%	Fertility rate (per woman)	2.0
Pop. under 15	22.7%	Urban population	85.8%
Pop. over 65	11.6%		*per 1,000 pop.*
No. of men per 100 women	97.2	Crude birth rate	15.3
Human Development Index	90.1	Crude death rate	8

The economy

GDP	NZ$99bn	GDP per head	$14,600
GDP	$55.4bn	GDP per head in purchasing	
Av. ann. growth in real		power parity (USA=100)	55.0
GDP 1990–98	3.1%	Economic freedom index	1.70

Origins of GDP		**Components of GDP**	
	% of total		*% of total*
Agriculture	8.3	Private consumption	64.7
Industry, of which:	23.4	Public consumption	15.3
manufacturing	...	Investment	19.3
Services	68.3	Exports	30.3
		Imports	-29.6

Structure of employment

	% of total		*% of labour force*
Agriculture	10	Unemployed 1998	7.5
Industry	23	Av. ann. rate 1990–98	8.1
Services	67		

Energy

	m TCE		
Total output	18.606	% output exported	17.6
Total consumption	21.565	% consumption imported	33.1
Consumption per head,			
kg coal equivalent	5,987		

Inflation and finance

Consumer price		*av. ann. increase 1993–98*	
inflation 1999	-0.1%	Narrow money (M1)	3.2%
Av. ann. inflation 1990–99	1.7%	Broad money	7.9%
Treasury bill rate, 1997	4.58%		

Exchange rates

	end 1999		*December 1999*
NZ$ per $	1.92	Effective rates	*1995 = 100*
NZ$ per SDR	2.64	– nominal	88.9
NZ$ per euro	1.93	– real	87.1

Principal exports

	$bn fob
Dairy produce	2.1
Meat	1.5
Forest products	1.2
Fruit & vegetables	0.6
Wood	1.5
Total incl. others	**12.1**

Principal imports

	$bn cif
Machinery	1.8
Vehicles & aircraft	1.7
Electrical machinery	1.2
Mineral fuels	0.7
Total incl. others	**11.3**

Main export destinations

	% of total
Australia	20.9
Japan	13.1
United States	12.9
United Kingdom	5.9

Main origins of imports

	% of total
Australia	22.3
United States	19.5
Japan	11.2
China	5.2

Balance of payments, reserves and aid, $bn

Visible exports fob	12.2	Capital balance[a]	3.6
Visible imports fob	-11.2	Overall balance[a]	-1.4
Trade balance	0.9	Change in reserves	-0.2
Invisibles inflows	3.7	Level of reserves	
Invisibles outflows	-8.2	end Dec.	4.2
Net transfers	0.3	No. months of import cover	2.6
Current account balance	-3.2	Aid given	0.13
– as % of GDP	-5.8	– as % of GDP	0.27

Health and education

Health spending, % of GDP	7.6	Education spending, % of GDP	7.3
Doctors per 1,000 pop.	2.1	Enrolment, %: primary	101
Hospital beds per 1,000 pop.	6.1	secondary	113
Safe water access, % of pop.	97	tertiary	63

Society

No. of households	1.3m	Colour TVs per 100 households	98.2
Av. no. per household	3.0	Telephone lines per 100 pop.	49.1
Marriages per 1,000 pop.	5.8	Mobile telephone subscribers	
Divorces per 1,000 pop.	3.0	per 100 pop.	20.7
Cost of living, Dec. 1999		Computers per 100 pop.	28.2
New York = 100	72	Internet hosts per 100 pop.	71.4

a 1997

NIGERIA

Area	923,768 sq km	Capital	Abuja
Arable as % of total land	36	Currency	Naira (N)

People

Population	106.4m	Life expectancy: men	49 yrs
Pop. per sq km	121	women	52 yrs
Av. ann. growth		Adult literacy	59.5%
in pop. 1990–2000	2.48%	Fertility rate (per woman)	5.2
Pop. under 15	43.1%	Urban population	44.0%
Pop. over 65	3.0%		per 1,000 pop.
No. of men per 100 women	98.4	Crude birth rate	38.8
Human Development Index	45.6	Crude death rate	15

The economy

GDP[a]	N3,234bn	GDP per head	$300
GDP	$36.4bn	GDP per head in purchasing	
Av. ann. growth in real		power parity (USA=100)	2.5
GDP 1990–98	2.6%	Economic freedom index	3.30

Origins of GDP[a]

Components of GDP[a]

	% of total		% of total
Agriculture	32.8	Private consumption	68.7
Industry, of which:	42.0	Public consumption	5.0
manufacturing	5.5	Investment	15.0
Services	25.2	Exports	38.7
		Imports	-27.4

Structure of employment[b]

	% of total		% of labour force
Agriculture	43	Unemployed 1998	...
Industry	7	Av. ann. rate 1990–98	...
Services	50		

Energy

	m TCE		
Total output	139.367	% output exported	89.4
Total consumption	15.851	% consumption imported	20.2
Consumption per head,			
kg coal equivalent	138		

Inflation and finance

Consumer price		av. ann. increase 1993–98	
inflation 1999	6.6%	Narrow money (M1)	22.6%
Av. ann. inflation 1990–99	31.1%	Broad money	22.3%

Exchange rates

	end 1999		December 1999
N per $	98.15	Effective rates	1995 = 100
N per SDR	134.47	– nominal	50.0
N per euro	98.64	– real	81.3

Principal exports[a]

	$bn fob
Petroleum	14.6
Cocoa beans & products	0.1
Total incl. others	**16.0**

Principal imports[a]

	$bn cif
Manufactured goods	3.0
Machinery & transport equipment	2.4
Chemicals	2.3
Agric products & foodstuffs	1.2
Total incl. others	**10.3**

Main export destinations

	% of total
United States	35.3
Spain	10.5
India	8.7
France	5.7

Main origins of imports[b]

	% of total
United Kingdom	12.7
United States	12.0
Germany	10.1
France	8.8

Balance of payments, reserves[c] and debt, $bn

Visible exports fob	9.0	Overall balance	-2.9
Visible imports fob	-9.2	Change in reserves	2.6
Trade balance	-0.2	Level of reserves	
Invisibles inflows	1.2	end Dec.	4.3
Invisibles outflows	-6.8	No. months of import cover	4.1
Net transfers	1.6	Foreign debt	30.3
Current account balance	-4.2	– as % of GDP	79
– as % of GDP	-11.7	Debt service paid	1.3
Capital balance	1.4	Debt service ratio	10

Health and education

Health spending, % of GDP	0.7	Education spending, % of GDP	0.7
Doctors per 1,000 pop.	0.2	Enrolment, %: primary	98
Hospital beds per 1,000 pop.	1.7	secondary	33
Safe water access, % of pop.	49	tertiary	4

Society

No. of households	23.9m	Colour TVs per 100 households	44.0
Av. no. per household	4.5	Telephone lines per 100 pop.	0.4
Marriages per 1,000 pop.	...	Mobile telephone subscribers	
Divorces per 1,000 pop.	...	per 100 pop.	...
Cost of living, Dec. 1999		Computers per 100 pop.	0.6
New York = 100	81	Internet hosts per 100 pop.	...

a 1997
b 1990
c 1996

NORWAY

Area	323,878 sq km	Capital	Oslo
Arable as % of total land	3	Currency	Norwegian krone (Nkr)

People

Population	4.4m	Life expectancy: men		75 yrs
Pop. per sq km	14		women	81 yrs
Av. ann. growth		Adult literacy		99.0%
in pop. 1990–2000	0.51%	Fertility rate (per woman)		1.9
Pop. under 15	19.6%	Urban population		75.5%
Pop. over 65	15.4%			*per 1,000 pop.*
No. of men per 100 women	98.3	Crude birth rate		13.2
Human Development Index	92.7	Crude death rate		10

The economy

GDP	Nkr1,101bn	GDP per head	$34,310
GDP	$152bn	GDP per head in purchasing	
Av. ann. growth in real		power parity (USA=100)	89.6
GDP 1990–98	3.9%	Economic freedom index	2.30

Origins of GDP		**Components of GDP**	
	% of total		*% of total*
Agriculture	2.2	Private consumption	49.8
Industry, of which:	26.3	Public consumption	21.5
manufacturing	11.7	Investment	28.6
Services	71.5	Exports	37.4
		Imports	-37.2

Structure of employment

	% of total		*% of labour force*
Agriculture	5	Unemployed 1997	4.1
Industry	22	Av. ann. rate 1990–97	5.2
Services	73		

Energy

	m TCE		
Total output	296.267	% output exported	89.0
Total consumption	31.434	% consumption imported	22.6
Consumption per head,			
kg coal equivalent	7,221		

Inflation and finance

Consumer price		*av. ann. increase 1993–98*	
inflation 1999	2.3%	Narrow money (M1)	7.9%
Av. ann. inflation 1990–99	2.3%	Broad money	6.4%
Deposit rate, 1999	5.38%		

Exchange rates

	end 1999		*December 1999*
Nkr per $	8.04	Effective rates	*1995 = 100*
Nkr per SDR	11.03	– nominal	94.9
Nkr per euro	8.08	– real	112.4

Principal exports

	$bn fob
Oil, gas & products	17.5
Machinery & transport equipment	6.3
Metal products	5.1
Food, drink & tobacco	4.0
Total incl. others	**40.4**

Principal imports

	$bn cif
Machinery & transport equipment	13.1
Metal products	3.7
Road vehicles	3.4
Chemicals	3.2
Total incl. others	**37.4**

Main export destinations

	% of total
United Kingdom	16.9
Germany	12.3
Sweden	9.8
Netherlands	9.7
France	8.4
EU15	76.9

Main origins of imports

	% of total
Sweden	14.7
Germany	13.5
United Kingdom	9.9
Denmark	6.7
United States	6.6
EU15	68.8

Balance of payments, reserves and aid, $bn

Visible exports fob	40.6	Capital balance	-0.2
Visible imports fob	-39.1	Overall balance	-6.4
Trade balance	1.6	Change in reserves	-4.8
Invisibles inflows	20.6	Level of reserves	
Invisibles outflows	-22.8	end Dec.	18.9
Net transfers	-1.6	No. months of import cover	3.7
Current account balance	-2.2	Aid given	1.32
– as % of GDP	-1.4	– as % of GDP	0.91

Health and education

Health spending, % of GDP	7.5	Education spending, % of GDP	7.4
Doctors per 1,000 pop.	2.5	Enrolment, %: primary	100
Hospital beds per 1,000 pop.	15.0	secondary	119
Safe water access, % of pop.	…	tertiary	62

Society

No. of households	2.0m	Colour TVs per 100 households	98.0
Av. no. per household	2.3	Telephone lines per 100 pop.	66.0
Marriages per 1,000 pop.	4.8	Mobile telephone subscribers	
Divorces per 1,000 pop.	2.7	per 100 pop.	47.4
Cost of living, Dec. 1999		Computers per 100 pop.	37.3
New York = 100	112	Internet hosts per 100 pop.	90.7

PAKISTAN

Area	803,940 sq km	Capital	Islamabad
Arable as % of total land	28	Currency	Pakistan rupee (PRs)

People

Population	148.2m	Life expectancy: men	63 yrs
Pop. per sq km	197	women	65 yrs
Av. ann. growth		Adult literacy	40.9%
in pop. 1990–2000	2.73%	Fertility rate (per woman)	5.0
Pop. under 15	41.8%	Urban population	37.0%
Pop. over 65	3.2%		per 1,000 pop.
No. of men per 100 women	106.6	Crude birth rate	36.1
Human Development Index	50.8	Crude death rate	8

The economy

GDP[a]	PRs3,026bn	GDP per head	$470
GDP	$61.5bn	GDP per head in purchasing	
Av. ann. growth in real		power parity (USA=100)	5.6
GDP 1990–98	4.2%	Economic freedom index	3.40

Origins of GDP[a]

	% of total
Agriculture	25.4
Industry, of which:	24.8
manufacturing	17.1
Other	49.8

Components of GDP[a]

	% of total
Private consumption	72.5
Public consumption	11.4
Investment	16.0
Exports	15.2
Imports	-15.3

Structure of employment[b]

	% of total[c]		% of labour force
Agriculture	44	Unemployed 1997	6.1
Industry	18	Av. ann. rate 1990–95	5.0
Services	38		

Energy

	m TCE		
Total output	30.967	% output exported	1.3
Total consumption	50.659	% consumption imported	42.6
Consumption per head,			
kg coal equivalent	362		

Inflation and finance

Consumer price		av. ann. increase 1993–98	
inflation 1999	4.1%	Narrow money (M1)	14.1%
Av. ann. inflation 1990–99	9.8%	Broad money	15.7%
Money market rate, 1999	9.04%		

Exchange rates

	end 1999		December 1999
PRs per $	51.79	Effective rates	1995 = 100
PRs per SDR	71.08	– nominal	70.65
PRs per euro	52.05	– real	90.72

Principal exports

	$bn fob
Textile yarn & fabrics	2.1
Apparel & clothing accessories	1.4
Rice	0.6
Total incl. others	**8.1**

Main export destinations[d]

	% of total
United States	20.5
Hong Kong	7.1
United Kingdom	6.9
Germany	6.3

Principal imports

	$bn cif
Machinery	2.0
Petroleum & products	1.3
Palm oil	0.6
Wheat	0.4
Total incl. others	**9.0**

Main origins of imports[d]

	% of total
United States	11.2
Japan	7.8
Malaysia	7.1
Saudi Arabia	6.7

Balance of payments[e], reserves and debt, $bn

Visible exports fob	8.4	Overall balance	0.5
Visible imports fob	-10.8	Change in reserves	-0.2
Trade balance	-2.4	Level of reserves	
Invisibles inflows	1.8	end Dec.	1.6
Invisibles outflows	-5.0	No. months of import cover	1.2
Net transfers	3.9	Foreign debt	32.2
Current account balance	-1.7	– as % of GDP	50
– as % of GDP	-2.8	Debt service paid	2.4
Capital balance	2.3	Debt service ratio	21

Health and education

Health spending, % of GDP	3.9	Education spending, % of GDP	2.7
Doctors per 1,000 pop.	0.6	Enrolment, %: primary	…
Hospital beds per 1,000 pop.	0.7	secondary	…
Safe water access, % of pop.	79	tertiary	4

Society

No. of households	21.0m	Colour TVs per 100 households	30.6
Av. no. per household	7.1	Telephone lines per 100 pop.	1.9
Marriages per 1,000 pop.	…	Mobile telephone subscribers	
Divorces per 1,000 pop.	…	per 100 pop.	0.1
Cost of living, Dec. 1999		Computers per 100 pop.	0.4
New York = 100	48	Internet hosts per 100 pop.	…

a Fiscal year ending June 30, 1999.
b Fiscal year ending June 30, 1995.
c Employed labour force.
d Fiscal year ending June 30, 1998.
e 1997

PERU

Area	1,285,216 sq km	Capital	Lima
Arable as % of total land	3	Currency	Nuevo Sol (New Sol)

People

Population	24.8m	Life expectancy: men	66 yrs
Pop. per sq km	20	women	71 yrs
Av. ann. growth		Adult literacy[a]	88.7%
in pop. 1990–2000	1.74%	Fertility rate (per woman)	3.0
Pop. under 15	33.4%	Urban population	72.8%
Pop. over 65	4.8%		*per 1,000 pop.*
No. of men per 100 women	98.4	Crude birth rate	24.9
Human Development Index	73.9	Crude death rate	6

The economy

GDP	New Soles 183.8bn	GDP per head	$2,440
GDP	$60.5bn	GDP per head in purchasing	
Av. ann. growth in real		power parity (USA=100)	14.3
GDP 1990–98	5.7%	Economic freedom index	2.45

Origins of GDP

	% of total
Agriculture	13.2
Industry, of which:	41.8
manufacturing	21.1
Services	45.0

Components of GDP

	% of total
Private consumption	58.3
Public consumption	7.7
Investment	26.0
Exports	29.6
Imports	-21.6

Structure of employment

	% of total		% of labour force
Agriculture	7	Unemployed 1998[b]	7.7
Industry	21	Av. ann. rate 1996–97[b]	7.5
Services	72		

Energy

	m TCE		
Total output	11.261	% output exported	46.4
Total consumption	11.731	% consumption imported	55.9
Consumption per head,			
kg coal equivalent	490		

Inflation and finance

Consumer price		*av. ann. increase 1993–98*	
inflation 1999	3.5%	Narrow money (M1)	34.6%
Av. ann. inflation 1990–99	42.5%	Broad money	30.2%
Deposit rate, 1999	16.3%		

Exchange rates

	end 1999		December 1999
New Soles per $	3.51	Effective rates	1995 = 100
New Soles per SDR	4.82	– nominal	...
New Soles per Ecu	3.53	– real	...

Principal exports

	$bn fob
Gold	0.9
Copper	0.8
Fish & fish products	0.6
Textiles	0.5
Zinc	0.4
Total incl. others	**5.7**

Principal imports

	$bn fob
Industrial supplies	3.4
Capital goods	2.6
Consumer goods	1.9
Total incl. others	**8.2**

Main export destinations

	% of total
United States	32.0
China	4.1
Germany	4.0
Japan	3.8
Brazil	3.1

Main origins of imports

	% of total
United States	26.2
Chile	4.5
Brazil	3.4
Venezuela	2.7
Colombia	2.6

Balance of payments, reserves and debt, $bn

Visible exports fob	5.7	Overall balance	-2.2
Visible imports fob	-8.2	Change in reserves	-1.4
Trade balance	-2.5	Level of reserves	
Invisibles inflows	2.5	end Dec.	9.9
Invisibles outflows	-4.6	No. months of import cover	9.3
Net transfers	0.7	Foreign debt	32.4
Current account balance	-3.8	– as % of GDP	53
– as % of GDP	-6.3	Debt service paid	1.9
Capital balance	1.2	Debt service ratio	27

Health and education

Health spending, % of GDP	5.6	Education spending, % of GDP	2.9
Doctors per 1,000 pop.	0.9	Enrolment, %: primary	123
Hospital beds per 1,000 pop.	1.5	secondary	73
Safe water access, % of pop.	67	tertiary	26

Society

No. of households	5.4m	Colour TVs per 100 households	63.2
Av. no. per household	4.6	Telephone lines per 100 pop.	6.3
Marriages per 1,000 pop.	4.0	Mobile telephone subscribers	
Divorces per 1,000 pop.	...	per 100 pop.	3.0
Cost of living, Dec. 1999		Computers per 100 pop.	1.8
New York = 100	65	Internet hosts per 100 pop.	0.4

a Excluding indigenous jungle population.
b Urban areas.

PHILIPPINES

Area	300,000 sq km	Capital	Manila
Arable as % of total land	31	Currency	Philippine peso (P)

People

Population	72.9m	Life expectancy: men	67 yrs
Pop. per sq km	253	women	70 yrs
Av. ann. growth		Adult literacy	94.6%
in pop. 1990–2000	2.25%	Fertility rate (per woman)	3.6
Pop. under 15	36.7%	Urban population	58.6%
Pop. over 65	3.6%		*per 1,000 pop.*
No. of men per 100 women	101.8	Crude birth rate	28.6
Human Development Index	74.0	Crude death rate	6

The economy

GDP	P2,667bn	GDP per head	$1,050
GDP	$78.9bn	GDP per head in purchasing	
Av. ann. growth in real		power parity (USA=100)	12.7
GDP 1990–98	3.3%	Economic freedom index	2.85

Origins of GDP

Components of GDP

	% of total		*% of total*
Agriculture	19.4	Private consumption	79.7
Industry, of which:	35.4	Public consumption	7.9
manufacturing	24.9	Investment	21.6
Services	45.2	Exports	44.9
		Imports	-54.8

Structure of employment

	% of total		*% of labour force*
Agriculture	40	Unemployed 1998	9.6
Industry	16	Av. ann. rate 1990–98	8.5
Services	44		

Energy

	m TCE		
Total output	9.120	% output exported	4.5
Total consumption	30.270	% consumption imported	97.4
Consumption per head,			
kg coal equivalent	437		

Inflation and finance

Consumer price		*av. ann. increase 1993–98*	
inflation 1999	6.7%	Narrow money (M1)	14.8%
Av. ann. inflation 1990–99	9.0%	Broad money	21.1%
Treasury bill rate, 1999	10.00%		

Exchange rates

	end 1999		*December 1999*
P per $	40.31	Effective rates	*1995 = 100*
P per SDR	55.33	– nominal	73.3
P per euro	40.51	– real	93.0

Principal exports

	$bn fob
Electrical & electronic equipment	17.2
Machinery & transport equipment	3.3
Clothing	2.4
Coconut products	0.8
Total incl. others	**29.5**

Principal imports

	$bn cif
Semi-processed raw materials	10.4
Telecom & electrical machinery	6.9
Electrical equipment parts	4.6
Semi-processed manufactures	2.8
Power equipment & specialised machines	2.6
Total incl. others	**29.5**

Main export destinations

	% of total
United States	34.2
Japan	14.3
Netherlands	7.9
Singapore	6.2
United Kingdom	6.0
Hong Kong	4.5

Main origins of imports

	% of total
United States	21.8
Japan	20.4
South Korea	7.4
Singapore	5.9
Taiwan	4.8
Hong Kong	4.4

Balance of payments, reserves and debt, $bn

Visible exports fob	29.5	Overall balance	1.3
Visible imports fob	-29.5	Change in reserves	2.1
Trade balance	0.0	Level of reserves end Dec.	10.8
Invisibles inflows	13.9		
Invisibles outflows	-13.0	No. months of import cover	3.0
Net transfers	0.4	Foreign debt	47.8
Current account balance	1.3	– as % of GDP	70
– as % of GDP	1.6	Debt service paid	4.8
Capital balance	1.0	Debt service ratio	12

Health and education

Health spending, % of GDP	3.7	Education spending, % of GDP	3.4
Doctors per 1,000 pop.	0.1	Enrolment, %: primary	117
Hospital beds per 1,000 pop.	1.1	secondary	78
Safe water access, % of pop.	85	tertiary	35

Society

No. of households	13.8m	Colour TVs per 100 households	37.5
Av. no. per household	5.3	Telephone lines per 100 pop.	3.7
Marriages per 1,000 pop.	6.9	Mobile telephone subscribers per 100 pop.	2.4
Divorces per 1,000 pop.	...		
Cost of living, Dec. 1999 New York = 100	49	Computers per 100 pop.	1.5
		Internet hosts per 100 pop.	0.2

POLAND

Area	312,683 sq km	Capital	Warsaw
Arable as % of total land	48	Currency	Zloty (Zl)

People

Population	38.7m	Life expectancy: men	68 yrs
Pop. per sq km	120	women	77 yrs
Av. ann. growth		Adult literacy	99.0%
in pop. 1990–2000	0.17%	Fertility rate (per woman)	1.5
Pop. under 15	19.4%	Urban population	65.6%
Pop. over 65	12.0%		per 1,000 pop.
No. of men per 100 women	94.5	Crude birth rate	11.0
Human Development Index	80.2	Crude death rate	10

The economy

GDP[a]	Zl469bn	GDP per head	$3,910
GDP	$151.3bn	GDP per head in purchasing	
Av. ann. growth in real		power parity (USA=100)	25.8
GDP 1990–98	4.6%	Economic freedom index	2.80

Origins of GDP		**Components of GDP**	
	% of total		% of total
Agriculture	5.0	Private consumption	63.5
Industry, of which:	32.9	Public consumption	15.6
manufacturing	...	Investment	25.6
Services	62.1	Exports	27.2
		Imports	-33.5

Structure of employment

	% of total		% of labour force
Agriculture	19	Unemployed 1998	10.5
Industry	32	Av. ann. rate 1992–97	12.7
Services	49		

Energy

	m TCE		
Total output	135.716	% output exported	20.8
Total consumption	144.291	% consumption imported	27.3
Consumption per head,			
kg coal equivalent	3,738		

Inflation and finance

Consumer price		av. ann. increase 1993–98	
inflation 1999	7.3%	Narrow money (M1)	29.5%
Av. ann. inflation 1990–99	29.0%	Broad money	31.6%
Money market rate, 1999	14.0%		

Exchange rates

	end 1999		December 1999
Zl per $	4.15	Effective rates	1995 = 100
Zl per SDR	5.69	– nominal	73.0
Zl per euro	4.17	– real	110.4

Principal exports

	$bn fob
Machinery & transport equipment	8.1
Semi-manufactured goods	7.2
Other manufactured goods	5.9
Agric. products & foodstuffs	3.0
Chemicals	1.9
Total incl. others	**27.3**

Principal imports

	$bn fob
Machinery & transport equipment	18.0
Semi-manufactured goods	9.8
Chemicals	6.4
Other manufactured goods	4.4
Agric. products & foodstuffs	3.3
Total incl. others	**46.9**

Main export destinations

	% of total
Germany	36.0
Italy	5.8
Russia	5.6
Netherlands	4.7
France	4.6
Ukraine	3.8
United Kingdom	3.8

Main origins of imports

	% of total
Germany	19.5
Italy	7.9
France	6.5
Russia	5.4
United Kingdom	4.7
Netherlands	3.8
United States	3.8

Balance of payments, reserves and debt, $bn

Visible exports fob	32.5	Overall balance	5.7
Visible imports fob	-45.3	Change in reserves	6.7
Trade balance	-12.8	Level of reserves	
Invisibles inflows	13.1	end Dec.	27.4
Invisibles outflows	-10.1	No. months of import cover	5.9
Net transfers	2.9	Foreign debt	47.7
Current account balance	-6.9	– as % of GDP	31
– as % of GDP	-4.6	Debt service paid	4.3
Capital balance	13.1	Debt service ratio	10

Health and education

Health spending, % of GDP	5.9	Education spending, % of GDP	7.5
Doctors per 1,000 pop.	2.3	Enrolment, %: primary	96
Hospital beds per 1,000 pop.	5.4	secondary	98
Safe water access, % of pop.	…	tertiary	24

Society

No. of households	11.8m	Colour TVs per 100 households	97.0
Av. no. per household	3.9	Telephone lines per 100 pop.	22.8
Marriages per 1,000 pop.	5.4	Mobile telephone subscribers	
Divorces per 1,000 pop.	1.2	per 100 pop.	5.0
Cost of living, Dec. 1999		Computers per 100 pop.	4.4
New York = 100	59	Internet hosts per 100 pop.	5.1

a 1997

PORTUGAL

Area	88,940 sq km	Capital	Lisbon
Arable as % of total land	35	Currency	Escudo (Esc)

People

Population	9.9m	Life expectancy: men	72 yrs
Pop. per sq km	107	women	79 yrs
Av. ann. growth		Adult literacy	90.8%
in pop. 1990–2000	0.01%	Fertility rate (per woman)	1.4
Pop. under 15	16.3%	Urban population	64.4%
Pop. over 65	15.7%		per 1,000 pop.
No. of men per 100 women	92.7	Crude birth rate	10.6
Human Development Index	85.8	Crude death rate	11

The economy

GDP	Esc19,246bn	GDP per head	$10,670
GDP	$106.4bn	GDP per head in purchasing	
Av. ann. growth in real		power parity (USA=100)	49.8
GDP 1990–98	2.3%	Economic freedom index	2.30

Origins of GDP		**Components of GDP**	
	% of total		% of total
Agriculture	3.6	Private consumption	65.7
Industry, of which:	35.5	Public consumption	20.2
manufacturing	...	Investment	26.5
Services	60.9	Exports	27.5
		Imports	-40.0

Structure of employment

	% of total		% of labour force
Agriculture	13	Unemployed 1998	5.0
Industry	36	Av. ann. rate 1990–98	5.9
Services	51		

Energy

	m TCE		
Total output	1.962	% output exported[a]	168.5
Total consumption	22.561	% consumption imported[a]	115.7
Consumption per head,			
kg coal equivalent	2,300		

Inflation and finance

Consumer price		av. ann. increase 1993–98	
inflation 1999	2.3%	Euro area:	
Av. ann. inflation 1990–99	5.1%	Narrow money (M1)	6.4%
Money market rate, 1999	2.71%	Broad money	4.0%

Exchange rates

	end 1999		December 1999
			1995 = 100
Esc per $	198.1	Effective rates	
Esc per SDR	271.0	– nominal	94.6
Esc per euro	199.1	– real	98.0

Principal exports

	$bn fob
Consumer goods	9.9
Raw materials & semi-manufactures	7.1
Capital goods	6.8
Energy products	0.3
Total incl. others	**24.2**

Principal imports

	$bn cif
Capital goods	13.8
Raw materials & semi-manufactures	12.7
Consumer goods	8.5
Energy products	2.0
Total incl. others	**37.0**

Main export destinations

	% of total
Germany	19.8
Spain	15.5
France	14.4
United Kingdom	12.1
United States	4.9
EU15	81.5

Main origins of imports

	% of total
Spain	24.0
Germany	14.9
France	11.2
Italy	7.9
United Kingdom	6.6
EU15	77.2

Balance of payments, reserves and debt, $bn

Visible exports fob	26.0	Overall balance	0.5
Visible imports fob	-38.3	Change in reserves	1.3
Trade balance	-12.3	Level of reserves	
Invisibles inflows	13.2	end Dec.	21.6
Invisibles outflows	-12.2	No. months of import cover	5.1
Net transfers	4.0	Aid given	0.26
Current account balance	-7.3	– as % of GDP	0.24
– as % of GDP	-6.8		
Capital balance	9.1		

Health and education

Health spending, % of GDP	7.9	Education spending, % of GDP	5.8
Doctors per 1,000 pop.	3.0	Enrolment, %: primary	128
Hospital beds per 1,000 pop.	4.1	secondary[a]	111
Safe water access, % of pop.	…	tertiary	38

Society

No. of households	3.7m	Colour TVs per 100 households	96.4
Av. no. per household	2.7	Telephone lines per 100 pop.	41.4
Marriages per 1,000 pop.	6.7	Mobile telephone subscribers	
Divorces per 1,000 pop.	1.5	per 100 pop.	30.9
Cost of living, Dec. 1999		Computers per 100 pop.	8.1
New York = 100	77	Internet hosts per 100 pop.	9.6

a Includes training for unemployed.

ROMANIA

Area	237,500 sq km	Capital	Bucharest
Arable as % of total land	44	Currency	Leu (L)

People

Population	22.5m	Life expectancy: men	66 yrs
Pop. per sq km	94	women	74 yrs
Av. ann. growth		Adult literacy	97.8%
in pop. 1990–2000	-0.39%	Fertility rate (per woman)	1.2
Pop. under 15	17.8%	Urban population	56.2%
Pop. over 65	13.3%		per 1,000 pop.
No. of men per 100 women	96.4	Crude birth rate	9.2
Human Development Index	75.2	Crude death rate	11

The economy

GDP	L368,260bn	GDP per head	$1,360
GDP	$30.6bn	GDP per head in purchasing	
Av. ann. growth in real		power parity (USA=100)	19.1
GDP 1990–98	-0.7%	Economic freedom index	3.30

Origins of GDP[a]		Components of GDP	
	% of total		% of total
Agriculture	23.0	Private consumption	72.7
Industry, of which:	50.5	Public consumption	14.0
manufacturing	...	Investment	21.4
Services	26.5	Exports	23.7
		Imports	-31.8

Structure of employment[a]

	% of total		% of labour force
Agriculture	39	Unemployed 1998	6.3
Industry	31	Av. ann. rate 1991–98	7.4
Services	30		

Energy

	m TCE		
Total output	42.791	% output exported	12.7
Total consumption	60.820	% consumption imported	44.8
Consumption per head,			
kg coal equivalent	2,685		

Inflation and finance

Consumer price			av. ann. increase 1993–98
inflation 1999	45.8%	Narrow money (M1)	59.2%
Av. ann. inflation 1990–99	114%	Broad money	57.0%
Treasury bill rate, 1999	74.2%		

Exchange rates

	end 1999		December 1999
L per $	18,255	Effective rates	1995 = 100
L per SDR	25,055	– nominal	...
L per euro	18,346	– real	...

Principal exports

	$bn fob
Textiles & footwear	2.8
Basic metals & products	1.6
Machinery & equipment	0.8
Minerals & fuels	0.5
Total incl. others	**8.3**

Principal imports

	$bn cif
Machinery & equipment	2.7
Textiles & footwear	2.0
Fuels & minerals	1.7
Chemicals	1.0
Total incl. others	**11.8**

Main export destinations

	% of total
Italy	22.0
Germany	19.6
France	5.9
United States	3.8
EU15	64.5

Main origins of imports

	% of total
Italy	17.5
Germany	17.4
Russia	9.0
France	6.9
EU15	57.7

Balance of payments, reserves and debt, $bn

Visible exports fob	8.3	Overall balance	-0.6
Visible imports fob	-10.9	Change in reserves	-0.9
Trade balance	-2.6	Level of reserves	
Invisibles inflows	1.5	end Dec.	3.8
Invisibles outflows	-2.6	No. months of import cover	3.4
Net transfers	0.8	Foreign debt	9.5
Current account balance	-2.9	– as % of GDP	25
– as % of GDP	-9.5	Debt service paid	2.1
Capital balance	2.1	Debt service ratio	23

Health and education

Health spending, % of GDP	4.2	Education spending, % of GDP	3.6
Doctors per 1,000 pop.	1.8	Enrolment, %: primary	104
Hospital beds per 1,000 pop.	7.6	secondary	78
Safe water access, % of pop.	...	tertiary	23

Society

No. of households	7.6m	Colour TVs per 100 households	67.0
Av. no. per household	3.0	Telephone lines per 100 pop.	16.2
Marriages per 1,000 pop.	6.4	Mobile telephone subscribers	
Divorces per 1,000 pop.	1.5	per 100 pop.	2.9
Cost of living, Dec. 1999		Computers per 100 pop.	1.0
New York = 100	49	Internet hosts per 100 pop.	1.5

a 1997

RUSSIA

Area	17,075,400 sq km	Capital	Moscow
Arable as % of total land	8	Currency	Rouble (Rb)

People

Population	147.4m	Life expectancy: men	61 yrs
Pop. per sq km	9	women	73 yrs
Av. ann. growth		Adult literacy	99.0%
in pop. 1990–2000	-0.10%	Fertility rate (per woman)	1.4
Pop. under 15	18.2%	Urban population	77.7%
Pop. over 65	12.5%		per 1,000 pop.
No. of men per 100 women	87.8	Crude birth rate	9.6
Human Development Index	74.7	Crude death rate	14

The economy

GDP	Rb2,696bn	GDP per head	$2,260
GDP	$331.8bn	GDP per head in purchasing	
Av. ann. growth in real		power parity (USA=100)	21.1
GDP 1990–98	-7.0%	Economic freedom index	3.70

Origins of GDP		**Components of GDP**	
	% of total		% of total
Agriculture	6.5	Private consumption	58.9
Industry, of which:	35.3	Public consumption	19.5
manufacturing	...	Investment	15.7
Services	58.2	Exports	31.1
		Imports	-23.6

Structure of employment

	% of total		% of labour force
Agriculture	18	Unemployed 1998	13.3
Industry	31	Av. ann. rate 1992–98	8.6
Services	51		

Energy

	m TCE		
Total output	1,430.169	% output exported	37.7
Total consumption	896.226	% consumption imported	4.4
Consumption per head,			
kg coal equivalent	6,050		

Inflation and finance

Consumer price		av. ann. increase 1993–98	
inflation 1999	85.7%	Narrow money (M1)	70.4%
Av. ann. inflation 1991–98	191%	Broad money	72.6%
Money market rate, 1999	14.8%		

Exchange rates

	end 1999		December 1999
Rb per $	27.00	Effective rates	1995 = 100
Rb per SDR	37.06	– nominal	32.40
Rb per euro	27.14	– real	84.42

Principal exports

	$bn
Fuels & energy	29.7
Metals	11.6
Machinery & equipment	7.8
Timber	2.5
Total incl. others	**74.2**

Principal imports

	$bn
Machinery & equipment	20.9
Food products	5.8
Industrial goods	3.5
Clothing & household items	3.2
Total incl. others	**59.0**

Main export destinations

	% of total
Ukraine	9.1
Germany	9.0
Belarus	7.9
United States	6.8
Netherlands	6.2
China	5.3

Main origins of imports

	% of total
Germany	11.7
Belarus	10.9
Ukraine	6.9
United States	6.2
Kazakhstan	4.8
Italy	4.5

Balance of payments, reserves and debt, $bn

Visible exports fob	74.8	Overall balance	-19.8
Visible imports fob	-57.4	Change in reserves	-5.6
Trade balance	17.4	Level of reserves	
Invisibles inflows	17.1	end Dec.	12.0
Invisibles outflows	-32.0	No. months of import cover	1.6
Net transfers	-0.4	Foreign debt	183.6
Current account balance	2.1	– as % of GDP	69
– as % of GDP	0.5	Debt service paid	9.1
Capital balance	-12.4	Debt service ratio	12

Health and education

Health spending, % of GDP	5.7	Education spending, % of GDP	3.5
Doctors per 1,000 pop.	4.6	Enrolment, %: primary	107
Hospital beds per 1,000 pop.	12.1	secondary	...
Safe water access, % of pop.	...	tertiary	41

Society

No. of households	51.9m	Colour TVs per 100 households	79.0
Av. no. per household	2.8	Telephone lines per 100 pop.	19.7
Marriages per 1,000 pop.	6.5	Mobile telephone subscribers	
Divorces per 1,000 pop.	3.9	per 100 pop.	0.5
Cost of living, Dec. 1999		Computers per 100 pop.	4.1
New York = 100	87	Internet hosts per 100 pop.	1.5

SAUDI ARABIA

Area	2,200,000 sq km	Capital	Riyadh
Arable as % of total land	2	Currency	Riyal (SR)

People

Population	20.2m	Life expectancy: men	70 yrs
Pop. per sq km	10	women	73 yrs
Av. ann. growth		Adult literacy	73.4%
in pop. 1990–2000	2.98%	Fertility rate (per woman)	5.8
Pop. under 15	40.5%	Urban population	85.7%
Pop. over 65	2.9%		per 1,000 pop.
No. of men per 100 women	123.3	Crude birth rate	33.8
Human Development Index	74.0	Crude death rate	4

The economy

GDP	SR483bn	GDP per head	$6,910
GDP	$143.4bn	GDP per head in purchasing	
Av. ann. growth in real		power parity (USA=100)	35.9
GDP 1990–98	1.6%	Economic freedom index	2.95

Origins of GDP		Components of GDP	
	% of total		% of total
Agriculture	7.0	Private consumption	41.3
Industry, of which:	46.8	Public consumption	32.5
manufacturing	9.7	Investment	21.0
Services	46.2	Exports	35.9
		Imports	-30.7

Structure of employment[a]

	% of total		% of labour force
Agriculture	5	Unemployed 1998	...
Industry	26	Av. ann. rate 1990–98	...
Services	69		

Energy

	m TCE		
Total output	668.145	% output exported	73.8
Total consumption	121.844	% consumption imported	0.2
Consumption per head,			
kg coal equivalent	6,469		

Inflation and finance

Consumer price		av. ann. increase 1993–98	
inflation 1999	-1.6%	Narrow money (M1)	2.9%
Av. ann. inflation 1990–99	1.2%	Broad money	4.5%
Deposit rate, 1999	6.14%		

Exchange rates

	end 1999		December 1999
SR per $	3.75	Effective rates	1995 = 100
SR per SDR	5.14	– nominal	115.1
SR per euro	3.77	– real	104.9

Principal exports[b]

	$bn fob
Crude oil & refined petroleum	52.3
Petrochemicals	2.6
Total incl. others	**59.7**

Principal imports

	$bn cif
Machinery	6.0
Transport equipment	5.5
Chemical products	2.5
Textiles & clothing	2.0
Total incl. others	**30.0**

Main export destinations[b]

	% of total
Japan	17.0
United States	14.8
South Korea	11.0
Singapore	8.0
India	3.8
France	3.8

Main origins of imports

	% of total
United States	21.4
Japan	8.6
United Kingdom	8.5
Germany	6.3
France	5.2
Italy	4.2

Balance of payments, reserves and aid, $bn

Visible exports fob	38.8	Overall balance	0.1
Visible imports fob	-27.5	Change in reserves	-0.7
Trade balance	11.3	Level of reserves	
Invisibles inflows	10.5	end Dec.	15.5
Invisibles outflows	-19.9	No. months of import cover	3.9
Net transfers	-15.1	Aid given	0.29
Current account balance	-13.2	– as % of GDP	0.20
– as % of GDP	-9.0		
Capital balance	13.3		

Health and education

Health spending, % of GDP	8.0	Education spending, % of GDP	7.5
Doctors per 1,000 pop.	1.7	Enrolment, %: primary	76
Hospital beds per 1,000 pop.	2.3	secondary	61
Safe water access, % of pop.	95	tertiary	16

Society

No. of households	3.2m	Colour TVs per 100 households	97.0
Av. no. per household	6.3	Telephone lines per 100 pop.	14.3
Marriages per 1,000 pop.	3.1	Mobile telephone subscribers	
Divorces per 1,000 pop.	...	per 100 pop.	3.1
Cost of living, Dec. 1999		Computers per 100 pop.	5.0
New York = 100	72	Internet hosts per 100 pop.	0.2

a % of workers, 1994.
b 1997

SINGAPORE

Area	639 sq km	Capital	Singapore
Arable as % of total land	8	Currency	Singapore dollar (S$)

People

Population	3.5m	Life expectancy: men		75 yrs
Pop. per sq km	5,771		women	79 yrs
Av. ann. growth		Adult literacy		91.4%
in pop. 1990–2000	1.68%	Fertility rate (per woman)		1.7
Pop. under 15	22.1%	Urban population		100.0%
Pop. over 65	7.2%			*per 1,000 pop.*
No. of men per 100 women	101.5	Crude birth rate		14.8
Human Development Index	88.8	Crude death rate		5

The economy

GDP	S$141bn	GDP per head	$30,170
GDP	$95.5bn	GDP per head in purchasing	
Av. ann. growth in real		power parity (USA=100)	86.5
GDP 1990–98	8.5%	Economic freedom index	1.45

Origins of GDP		**Components of GDP**	
	% of total		*% of total*
Agriculture	0.2	Private consumption	40.1
Industry, of which:	34.7	Public consumption	10.0
manufacturing	23.4	Investment	33.5
Services	65.1	Exports less imports	17.8

Structure of employment

	% of total		*% of labour force*
Agriculture	0	Unemployed 1998	3.2
Industry	29	Av. ann. rate 1990–98	2.5
Services	71		

Energy

	m TCE		
Total output	...	% output exported	...
Total consumption	29.895	% consumption imported[a]	357.3
Consumption per head,			
kg coal equivalent	8,834		

Inflation and finance

Consumer price		*av. ann. increase 1993–98*	
inflation 1999	0.4%	Narrow money (M1)	3.5%
Av. ann. inflation 1990–99	1.8%	Broad money	14.4%
Money market rate, 1999	2.04%		

Exchange rates

	end 1999		*December 1999*
S$ per $	1.67	Effective rates	*1995 = 100*
S$ per SDR	2.29	– nominal	101.0
S$ per euro	1.68	– real	95.3

Principal exports

	$bn fob
Machinery & equipment	69.4
Mineral fuels	9.5
Chemicals	6.7
Manufactured products	4.7
Agric. products & foodstuffs	1.7
Crude materials	1.0
Total incl. others	**110.0**

Principal imports

	$bn cif
Machinery & equipment	58.3
Manufactured products	8.6
Mineral fuels	7.8
Chemicals	5.8
Agric. products & foodstuffs	2.6
Crude minerals	0.8
Total incl. others	**101.7**

Main export destinations

	% of total
United States	19.8
Malaysia	15.2
Hong Kong	8.4
Japan	6.6
Taiwan	4.3
Thailand	3.8
China	3.7

Main origins of imports

	% of total
United States	18.4
Japan	16.7
Malaysia	15.5
China	4.8
Thailand	4.8
Taiwan	3.8
Germany	3.4
Saudi Arabia	3.2

Balance of payments, reserves and debt[b], $bn

Visible exports fob	110.4	Overall balance	3.0
Visible imports fob	-95.7	Change in reserves	3.6
Trade balance	14.7	Level of reserves	
Invisibles inflows	32.0	end Dec.	74.9
Invisibles outflows	-27.9	No. months of import cover	7.3
Net transfers	-1.2	Foreign debt	12.5
Current account balance	17.6	– as % of GDP	13
– as % of GDP	18.4	Debt service	2.9
Capital balance	-17.9	Debt service ratio	2

Health and education

Health spending, % of GDP	3.2	Education spending, % of GDP	3.0
Doctors per 1,000 pop.	1.4	Enrolment, %: primary	94
Hospital beds per 1,000 pop.	3.6	secondary	74
Safe water access, % of pop.	100	tertiary	39

Society

No. of households	0.9m	Colour TVs per 100 households	99.1
Av. no. per household	4.1	Telephone lines per 100 pop.	56.2
Marriages per 1,000 pop.	6.7	Mobile telephone subscribers	
Divorces per 1,000 pop.	1.6	per 100 pop.	34.6
Cost of living, Dec. 1999		Computers per 100 pop.	45.8
New York = 100	96	Internet hosts per 100 pop.	42.7

a Energy trade data are distorted by transitory and oil refining activities.
b 1997

SLOVAKIA

Area	49,035 sq km	Capital	Bratislava
Arable as % of total land	34	Currency	Koruna (Kc)

People

Population	5.4m	Life expectancy: men	69 yrs
Pop. per sq km	110	women	77 yrs
Av. ann. growth		Adult literacy	99.0%
in pop. 1990–2000	0.25%	Fertility rate (per woman)	1.4
Pop. under 15	19.6%	Urban population	57.4%
Pop. over 65	11.4%		per 1,000 pop.
No. of men per 100 women	95.0	Crude birth rate	10.8
Human Development Index	81.3	Crude death rate	10

The economy

GDP	Kc714bn	GDP per head	$3,700
GDP	$19.9bn	GDP per head in purchasing	
Av. ann. growth in real		power parity (USA=100)	32.9
GDP 1990–98	1.5%	Economic freedom index	3.00

Origins of GDP

	% of total
Agriculture	5.2
Industry, of which:	36.1
manufacturing	...
Services	58.7

Components of GDP

	% of total
Private consumption	49.2
Public consumption	21.2
Investment	36.7
Exports	67.1
Imports	-74.3

Structure of employment

	% of total		% of labour force
Agriculture	9	Unemployed 1998	11.9
Industry	39	Av. ann. rate 1991–98	10.4
Services	52		

Energy

	m TCE		
Total output	6.824	% output exported	42.6
Total consumption	23.148	% consumption imported	93.1
Consumption per head,			
kg coal equivalent	4,329		

Inflation and finance

			av. ann. increase 1993–98
Consumer price			
inflation 1999	10.6%	Narrow money (M1)	4.7%
Av. ann. inflation 1991–98	15.3%	Broad money	23.2%
Deposit rate, 1999	14.37%		

Exchange rates

	end 1999		December 1999
Kc per $	42.27	Effective rates	1995 = 100
Kc per SDR	58.01	– nominal	94.53
Kc per euro	42.49	– real	105.03

Principal exports

	$bn fob
Machinery & transport equipment	4.0
Manufactured goods	3.2
Other manufactured goods	1.3
Chemicals	0.9
Raw materials	0.4
Total incl. others	**10.7**

Principal imports

	$bn fob
Machinery & transport equipment	5.2
Intermediate manufactured goods	2.4
Chemicals	1.4
Fuels	1.4
Total incl. others	**13.0**

Main export destinations

	% of total
Germany	28.9
Czech Republic	20.3
Austria	7.4
Poland	7.1
EU15	55.8

Main origins of imports

	% of total
Germany	25.9
Czech Republic	18.5
Russia	9.9
Italy	6.5
EU15	50.4

Balance of payments, reserves and debt, $bn

Visible exports fob	10.7	Overall balance	-0.5
Visible imports fob	-13.1	Change in reserves	-0.4
Trade balance	-2.4	Level of reserves	
Invisibles inflows	2.7	end Dec.	3.2
Invisibles outflows	-2.9	No. months of import cover	2.4
Net transfers	0.4	Foreign debt	9.9
Current account balance	-2.1	– as % of GDP	49
– as % of GDP	-10.7	Debt service paid	2.0
Capital balance	2.0	Debt service ratio	16

Health and education

Health spending, % of GDP	6.8	Education spending, % of GDP	5.0
Doctors per 1,000 pop.	3.0	Enrolment, %: primary	102
Hospital beds per 1,000 pop.	7.5	secondary	94
Safe water access, % of pop.	…	tertiary	22

Society

No. of households	1.4m	Colour TVs per 100 households	92.0
Av. no. per household	3.9	Telephone lines per 100 pop.	28.6
Marriages per 1,000 pop.	5.2	Mobile telephone subscribers	
Divorces per 1,000 pop.	1.7	per 100 pop.	8.7
Cost of living, Dec. 1999		Computers per 100 pop.	6.5
New York = 100	…	Internet hosts per 100 pop.	5.0

SLOVENIA

Area	20,253 sq km	Capital	Ljubljana
Arable as % of total land	15	Currency	Tolars (SIT)

People

Population	2.0m	Life expectancy: men	71 yrs
Pop. per sq km	98	women	78 yrs
Av. ann. growth		Adult literacy	%
in pop. 1990–2000	0.35%	Fertility rate (per woman)	1.26
Pop. under 15	15.9%	Urban population	50.4%
Pop. over 65	13.8%		*per 1,000 pop.*
No. of men per 100 women	94.5	Crude birth rate	9.2
Human Development Index	84.5	Crude death rate	10

The economy

GDP	SIT3,244bn	GDP per head	$9,780
GDP	$19.4bn	GDP per head in purchasing	
Av. ann. growth in real		power parity (USA=100)	49.2
GDP 1990–98	2.0%	Economic freedom index	3.00

Origins of GDP		**Components of GDP**	
	% of total		*% of total*
Agriculture	4.0	Private consumption	67.3
Industry, of which:	38.6	Public consumption	9.0
manufacturing	28.0	Investment	25.2
Services	57.4	Exports	56.7
		Imports	-58.1

Structure of employment

	% of total		*% of labour force*
Agriculture	12	Unemployed 1998	7.7
Industry	40	Av. ann. rate 1990–98	8.0
Services	48		

Energy

	m TCE		
Total output	3.158	% output exported	10.1
Total consumption	7.986	% consumption imported	65.8
Consumption per head,			
kg coal equivalent	4,151		

Inflation and finance

Consumer price		*av. ann. increase 1993–98*	
inflation 1999	6.6%	Narrow money (M1)	24.2%
Av. ann. inflation 1990–99	36.2%	Broad money	27.8%
Money market rate, 1999	6.87%		

Exchange rates

	end 1999		*December 1999*
SIT per $	270.1	Effective rates	*1995 = 100*
SIT per SDR	196.8	– nominal	...
SIT per euro	271.5	– real	...

Principal exports

	$bn fob
Manufactures	4.2
Machinery & transport equipment	3.3
Chemicals	0.9
Food & live animals	0.2
Total incl. others	**9.1**

Principal imports

	$bn cif
Machinery & transport equipment	3.7
Manufactures	3.5
Chemicals	1.2
Food & live animals	0.6
Total incl. others	**10.1**

Main export destinations

	% of total
Germany	28.4
Italy	13.9
Croatia	9.0
France	8.3
Austria	6.9

Main origins of imports

	% of total
Germany	20.7
Italy	16.8
France	12.4
Austria	7.9
Croatia	4.3

Balance of payments, reserves and debt[a], $bn

Visible exports fob	9.1	Overall balance	0.2
Visible imports fob	-9.9	Change in reserves	0.3
Trade balance	-0.8	Level of reserves end Dec.	3.6
Invisibles inflows	2.5	No. months of import cover	3.7
Invisibles outflows	-1.8	Foreign debt	4.0
Net transfers	0.1	– as % of GDP	22
Current account balance	-0.0	Debt service paid	1.0
– as % of GDP	-0.0	Debt service ratio	0.9
Capital balance	-0.0		

Health and education

Health spending, % of GDP	7.8	Education spending, % of GDP	5.7
Doctors per 1,000 pop.	2.1	Enrolment, %: primary	98
Hospital beds per 1,000 pop.	5.7	secondary	92
Safe water access, % of pop.	…	tertiary	36

Society

No. of households	0.5m	Colour TVs per 100 households	91.0
Av. no. per household	3.8	Telephone lines per 100 pop.	38.0
Marriages per 1,000 pop.	3.7	Mobile telephone subscribers per 100 pop.	8.1
Divorces per 1,000 pop.	1.1	Computers per 100 pop.	25.1
Cost of living, Dec. 1999 New York = 100	…	Internet hosts per 100 pop.	10.6

a 1996

SOUTH AFRICA

Area	1,225,815 sq km	Capital	Pretoria
Arable as % of total land	11	Currency	Rand (R)

People

Population	39.4m	Life expectancy: men	52 yrs
Pop. per sq km	33	women	58 yrs
Av. ann. growth		Adult literacy	84.0%
in pop. 1990–2000	1.72%	Fertility rate (per woman)	3.3
Pop. under 15	35.0%	Urban population	50.4%
Pop. over 65	3.6%		*per 1,000 pop.*
No. of men per 100 women	96.5	Crude birth rate	27.1
Human Development Index	69.5	Crude death rate	12

The economy

GDP	R741bn	GDP per head	$3,310
GDP	$136.9bn	GDP per head in purchasing	
Av. ann. growth in real		power parity (USA=100)	28.4
GDP 1990–98	1.9%	Economic freedom index	2.90

Origins of GDP		**Components of GDP**	
	% of total		*% of total*
Agriculture	3.9	Private consumption	63.0
Industry, of which:	28.6	Public consumption	20.2
manufacturing	18.9	Investment	15.6
Services	67.5	Exports	25.8
		Imports	-24.5

Structure of employment

	% of total		*% of labour force*
Agriculture	9	Unemployed 1996	5.1
Industry	25	Av. ann. rate 1994–96	4.7
Services	66		

Energy

	m TCE		
Total output	174.895	% output exported	41.1
Total consumption	115.994	% consumption imported	18.0
Consumption per head,			
kg coal equivalent	2,396		

Inflation and finance

Consumer price		*av. ann. increase 1993–98*	
inflation 1999	5.2%	Narrow money (M1)	23.1%
Av. ann. inflation 1990–99	9.4%	Broad money	16.0%
Money market rate, 1999	13.06%		

Exchange rates

	end 1999		*December 1999*
R per $	6.15	Effective rates	*1995 = 100*
R per SDR	8.45	– nominal	68.8
R per euro	6.18	– real	83.8

Principal exports[a]

	$bn fob
Metals & metal products	6.3
Gold	6.0
Diamonds	2.9
Machinery & transport equipment	2.6
Total incl. others	**23.5**

Principal imports[b]

	$bn cif
Machinery & appliances	8.9
Mineral products	3.7
Chemicals	3.4
Transport & equipment	1.7
Total incl. others	**28.4**

Main export destinations

	% of total
United States	8.1
Japan	5.9
Germany	6.1
United Kingdom	6.0
Italy	5.8

Main origins of imports

	% of total
United States	13.1
Germany	13.0
United Kingdom	9.2
Japan	6.5

Balance of payments, reserves and debt, $bn

Visible exports fob	29.2	Overall balance	0.9
Visible imports fob	-27.2	Change in reserves	-0.4
Trade balance	2.0	Level of reserves	
Invisibles inflows	6.6	end Dec.	5.5
Invisibles outflows	-9.8	No. months of import cover	1.8
Net transfers	-0.7	Foreign debt	24.7
Current account balance	-1.9	– as % of GDP	19
– as % of GDP	-1.4	Debt service	3.3
Capital balance	4.8	Debt service ratio	12

Health and education

Health spending, % of GDP	7.1	Education spending, % of GDP	7.9
Doctors per 1,000 pop.	0.6	Enrolment, %: primary	133
Hospital beds per 1,000 pop.	…	secondary	95
Safe water access, % of pop.	87	tertiary	17

Society

No. of households	8.5m	Colour TVs per 100 households	37.0
Av. no. per household	5.6	Telephone lines per 100 pop.	12.5
Marriages per 1,000 pop.	3.9	Mobile telephone subscribers	
Divorces per 1,000 pop.	0.8	per 100 pop.	6.1
Cost of living, Dec. 1999		Computers per 100 pop.	4.7
New York = 100	54	Internet hosts per 100 pop.	6.1

a 1996
b 1997

SOUTH KOREA

Area	99,274 sq km	Capital	Seoul
Arable as % of total land	21	Currency	Won (W)

People

Population	46.1m	Life expectancy: men	69 yrs
Pop. per sq km	473	women	76 yrs
Av. ann. growth		Adult literacy	97.2%
in pop. 1990–2000	0.89%	Fertility rate (per woman)	1.7
Pop. under 15	21.5%	Urban population	81.9%
Pop. over 65	6.7%		per 1,000 pop.
No. of men per 100 women	101.7	Crude birth rate	14.9
Human Development Index	85.2	Crude death rate	6

The economy

GDP	W449,509bn	GDP per head	$8,600
GDP	$398.8bn	GDP per head in purchasing	
Av. ann. growth in real		power parity (USA=100)	45.4
GDP 1990–98	6.1%	Economic freedom index	2.40

Origins of GDP

Components of GDP

	% of total		% of total
Agriculture	4.9	Private consumption	55.7
Industry, of which:	43.5	Public consumption	10.9
manufacturing	30.7	Investment	20.8
Services	51.6	Exports	48.7
		Imports	-35.8

Structure of employment

	% of total		% of labour force
Agriculture	12	Unemployed 1998	6.8
Industry	27	Av. ann. rate 1990–98	2.9
Services	61		

Energy

	m TCE		
Total output	31.322	% output exported	80.7
Total consumption	201.478	% consumption imported	112.4
Consumption per head,			
kg coal equivalent	4,446		

Inflation and finance

Consumer price		*av. ann. increase 1993–98*	
inflation 1999	0.8%	Narrow money (M1)	4.1%
Av. ann. inflation 1990–99	5.4%	Broad money	18.2%
Money market rate, 1999	5.0%		

Exchange rates

	end 1999		December 1999
W per $	1,138	Effective rates	1995 = 100
W per SDR	1,562	– nominal	...
W per euro	1,144	– real	...

Principal exports

	$bn fob
Electronic products	25.7
Textiles	15.8
Machinery & equipment	14.8
Vehicles	11.2
Ships	8.0
Total incl. others	**132.3**

Principal imports

	$bn cif
Electrical machinery	18.9
Mineral fuels & lubricants	11.2
Other machinery & equipment	9.5
Chemicals	6.1
Total incl. others	**93.3**

Main export destinations

	% of total
United States	17.2
Japan	9.2
China	9.0
Hong Kong	7.0
Taiwan	3.9

Main origins of imports

	% of total
United States	21.9
Japan	18.1
China	7.0
Australia	5.0
Saudi Arabia	4.7

Balance of payments, reserves and debt, $bn

Visible exports fob	132.1	Overall balance	25.9
Visible imports fob	-90.5	Change in reserves	31.6
Trade balance	41.6	Level of reserves	
Invisibles inflows	27.9	end Dec.	52.1
Invisibles outflows	-32.3	No. months of import cover	5.1
Net transfers	3.3	Foreign debt	139.1
Current account balance	40.6	– as % of GDP	44
– as % of GDP	10.2	Debt service paid	14.6
Capital balance	-8.3	Debt service ratio	13

Health and education

Health spending, % of GDP	5.6	Education spending, % of GDP	3.7
Doctors per 1,000 pop.	1.1	Enrolment, %: primary	94
Hospital beds per 1,000 pop.	4.6	secondary	102
Safe water access, % of pop.	93	tertiary	68

Society

No. of households	13.9m	Colour TVs per 100 households	98.2
Av. no. per household	3.3	Telephone lines per 100 pop.	43.3
Marriages per 1,000 pop.	7.0	Mobile telephone subscribers	
Divorces per 1,000 pop.	1.4	per 100 pop.	30.2
Cost of living, Dec. 1999		Computers per 100 pop.	15.3
New York = 100	92	Internet hosts per 100 pop.	6.3

a 1995

SPAIN

Area	504,782 sq km	Capital	Madrid
Arable as % of total land	39	Currency	Peseta (Pta)

People

Population	39.6m	Life expectancy: men	75 yrs
Pop. per sq km	79	women	82 yrs
Av. ann. growth		Adult literacy	97.2%
in pop. 1990–2000	0.08%	Fertility rate (per woman)	1.2
Pop. under 15	14.5%	Urban population	77.6%
Pop. over 65	17.0%		*per 1,000 pop.*
No. of men per 100 women	95.7	Crude birth rate	9.2
Human Development Index	89.4	Crude death rate	9

The economy

GDP	Pta82,650bn	GDP per head	$14,100
GDP	$555.2bn	GDP per head in purchasing	
Av. ann. growth in real		power parity (USA=100)	54.6
GDP 1990–98	1.9%	Economic freedom index	2.40

Origins of GDP

	% of total
Agriculture	4.4
Industry, of which:	30.7
manufacturing	...
Services	64.9

Components of GDP

	% of total
Private consumption	59.4
Public consumption	17.1
Investment	23.4
Exports	27.4
Imports	-27.3

Structure of employment

	% of total		*% of labour force*
Agriculture	7	Unemployed 1998	18.8
Industry	31	Av. ann. rate 1990–98	20.1
Services	62		

Energy

	m TCE		
Total output	41.409	% output exported[a]	19.0
Total consumption	127.041	% consumption imported[a]	89.4
Consumption per head,			
kg coal equivalent	3,202		

Inflation and finance

Consumer price		*av. ann. increase 1993–98*	
inflation 1999	2.3%	Euro area:	
Av. ann. inflation 1990–99	3.9%	Narrow money (M1)	6.4%
Money market rate, 1999	2.72%	Broad money	4.0%

Exchange rates

	end 1999		*December 1999*
Pta per $	164.4	Effective rates	*1995 = 100*
Pta per SDR	225.2	– nominal	93.5
Pta per euro	165.2	– real	107.9

Principal exports

	$bn fob
Raw materials & intermediate products	47.0
Consumer goods	44.5
Capital goods	15.7
Energy products	2.5
Total incl. others	**107.1**

Principal imports

	$bn cif
Raw materials & intermediate products (excl. fuels)	66.9
Consumer goods	34.7
Capital goods	23.3
Energy products	8.7
Total incl. others	**130.9**

Main export destinations

	% of total
France	19.6
Germany	13.6
Italy	9.3
Portugal	9.3
United Kingdom	8.4
EU15	71.6

Main origins of imports

	% of total
France	18.2
Germany	15.4
Italy	9.7
United Kingdom	7.5
United States	5.5
EU15	67.0

Balance of payments, reserves and aid, $bn

Visible exports fob	109.8	Capital balance	-9.0
Visible imports fob	-128.5	Overall balance	-14.3
Trade balance	-18.7	Change in reserves	-12.1
Invisibles inflows	63.6	Level of reserves	
Invisibles outflows	-49.9	end Dec.	60.9
Net transfers	3.4	No. months of import cover	4.1
Current account balance	-1.6	Aid given	1.38
– as % of GDP	0.3	– as % of GDP	0.24

Health and education

Health spending, % of GDP	7.4	Education spending, % of GDP	5.0
Doctors per 1,000 pop.	4.2	Enrolment, %: primary	107
Hospital beds per 1,000 pop.	3.9	secondary	120
Safe water access, % of pop.	…	tertiary	53

Society

No. of households	14.8m	Colour TVs per 100 households	87.0
Av. no. per household	2.7	Telephone lines per 100 pop.	41.4
Marriages per 1,000 pop.	5.1	Mobile telephone subscribers	
Divorces per 1,000 pop.	0.9	per 100 pop.	17.9
Cost of living, Dec. 1999		Computers per 100 pop.	14.5
New York = 100	80	Internet hosts per 100 pop.	10.8

a Energy trade data are distorted by transitory and oil refining activities.

SWEDEN

Area	449,964 sq km	Capital	Stockholm
Arable as % of total land	7	Currency	Swedish krona (Skr)

People

Population	8.9m	Life expectancy: men	76 yrs
Pop. per sq km	20	women	81 yrs
Av. ann. growth		Adult literacy	99.0%
in pop. 1990–2000	0.41%	Fertility rate (per woman)	1.6
Pop. under 15	18.2%	Urban population	83.3%
Pop. over 65	17.4%		*per 1,000 pop.*
No. of men per 100 women	98.4	Crude birth rate	10.2
Human Development Index	92.3	Crude death rate	11

The economy

GDP	Skr1,890bn	GDP per head	$25,580
GDP	$226.5bn	GDP per head in purchasing	
Av. ann. growth in real		power parity (USA=100)	67.9
GDP 1990–98	1.2%	Economic freedom index	2.35

Origins of GDP

	% of total
Agriculture	2.2
Industry, of which:	28.0
manufacturing	...
Services	69.9

Components of GDP

	% of total
Private consumption	50.0
Public consumption	25.3
Investment	17.1
Exports	47.9
Imports	-40.3

Structure of employment

	% of total		*% of labour force*
Agriculture	2	Unemployed 1998	6.5
Industry	26	Av. ann. rate 1990–98	6.2
Services	72		

Energy

	m TCE		
Total output	34.016	% output exported	41.8
Total consumption	60.196	% consumption imported	72.9
Consumption per head,			
kg coal equivalent	6,826		

Inflation and finance

Consumer price			*av. ann. increase 1993–98*
inflation 1999	0.5%	Narrow money (M1)	...
Av. ann. inflation 1990–99	2.4%	Broad money	2.5%
Money market rate, 1999	3.14%		

Exchange rates

	end 1999		*December 1999*
Skr per $	8.53	Effective rates	*1995 = 100*
Skr per SDR	11.70	– nominal	102.3
Skr per euro	8.57	– real	97.5

Principal exports

	$bn fob
Machinery incl. electricals	29.6
Manufactures	24.6
Transport equipment	12.1
Chemicals	7.6
Total incl. others	**82.5**

Principal imports

	$bn cif
Machinery incl. electricals	21.5
Transport equipment	7.3
Chemicals	6.8
Food, beverages & tobacco	4.4
Mineral fuels	3.5
Total incl. others	**64.2**

Main export destinations

	% of total
Germany	11.2
United Kingdom	9.1
Norway	8.8
United States	8.8
Denmark	6.0
EU15	56.8

Main origins of imports

	% of total
Germany	19.0
United Kingdom	10.2
Norway	7.6
Denmark	6.5
France	6.3
EU15	68.3

Balance of payments, reserves and aid, $bn

Visible exports fob	85.2	Capital balance	6.8
Visible imports fob	-67.5	Overall balance	3.3
Trade balance	17.6	Change in reserves	3.3
Invisibles inflows	34.5	Level of reserves	
Invisibles outflows	-44.1	end Dec.	15.5
Net transfers	-3.4	No. months of import cover	1.7
Current account balance	4.6	Aid given	1.57
– as % of GDP	2.0	– as % of GDP	0.72

Health and education

Health spending, % of GDP	8.6	Education spending, % of GDP	8.3
Doctors per 1,000 pop.	3.1	Enrolment, %: primary	107
Hospital beds per 1,000 pop.	5.6	secondary[a]	140
Safe water access, % of pop.	…	tertiary	50

Society

No. of households	4.0m	Colour TVs per 100 households	97.0
Av. no. per household	2.2	Telephone lines per 100 pop.	67.4
Marriages per 1,000 pop.	3.6	Mobile telephone subscribers	
Divorces per 1,000 pop.	2.3	per 100 pop.	46.4
Cost of living, Dec. 1999		Computers per 100 pop.	36.1
New York = 100	99	Internet hosts per 100 pop.	67

a Includes training for unemployed.

SWITZERLAND

Area	41,293 sq km	Capital	Berne
Arable as % of total land	12	Currency	Swiss franc (SFr)

People

Population	7.3m	Life expectancy: men	75 yrs
Pop. per sq km	179	women	82 yrs
Av. ann. growth		Adult literacy	99.0%
in pop. 1990–2000	0.78%	Fertility rate (per woman)	1.5
Pop. under 15	17.4%	Urban population	67.7%
Pop. over 65	14.7%		*per 1,000 pop.*
No. of men per 100 women	97.8	Crude birth rate	11.1
Human Development Index	91.4	Crude death rate	9

The economy

GDP	SFr380bn	GDP per head	$39,980
GDP	$284.1bn	GDP per head in purchasing	
Av. ann. growth in real		power parity (USA=100)	91.9
GDP 1990–98	0.4%	Economic freedom index	1.90

Origins of GDPa		**Components of GDP**	
	% of total		*% of total*
Agriculture	2.6	Private consumption	59.6
Industry, of which:	32.1	Public consumption	14.7
manufacturing	...	Investment	22.1
Services	65.3	Exports	39.8
		Imports	-36.2

Structure of employment

	% of total		*% of labour force*
Agriculture	5	Unemployed 1998	3.6
Industry	26	Av. ann. rate 1990–98	3.0
Services	69		

Energy

	m TCE		
Total output	13.002	% output exported	16.9
Total consumption	34.039	% consumption imported	73.8
Consumption per head,			
kg coal equivalent	4,692		

Inflation and finance

Consumer price		*av. ann. increase 1996–98*	
inflation 1999	0.8%	Narrow money (M1)	7.9%
Av. ann. inflation 1990–99	2.0%	Broad money	5.9%
Money market rate, 1999	0.93%		

Exchange rates

	end 1999		*December 1999*
SFr per $	1.60	Effective rates	*1995 = 100*
SFr per SDR	2.20	– nominal	92.3
SFr per euro	1.61	– real	99.9

Principal exports

	$bn fob
Machinery	22.0
Chemicals	21.6
Precision instruments, watches & jewellery	11.5
Metals & metal manufactures	6.6
Textiles & clothing	2.7
Total incl. others	**75.3**

Principal imports

	$bn cif
Machinery	17.0
Chemicals	12.3
Motor vehicles	8.5
Metals & metals manufactures	6.6
Agricultural products	6.4
Total incl. others	**73.7**

Main export destinations

	% of total
Germany	23.6
United States	10.2
France	9.6
Italy	7.8
United Kingdom	5.7
Japan	3.5
EU15	63.3

Main origins of imports

	% of total
Germany	32.7
France	11.6
Italy	10.4
United States	6.3
Netherlands	5.4
United Kingdom	4.6
EU15	79.9

Balance of payments, reserves and aid, $bn

Visible exports fob	93.9	Capital balance	-30.0
Visible imports fob	-92.9	Overall balance	0.9
Trade balance	1.0	Change in reserves	2.0
Invisibles inflows	70.4	Level of reserves	
Invisibles outflows	-43.1	end Dec.	65.2
Net transfers	-3.7	No. months of import cover	5.8
Current account balance	24.5	Aid given	0.90
– as % of GDP	8.6	– as % of GDP	0.32

Health and education

Health spending, % of GDP	10.0	Education spending, % of GDP	5.4
Doctors per 1,000 pop.	3.2	Enrolment, %: primary	97
Hospital beds per 1,000 pop.	20.8	secondary	100
Safe water access, % of pop.	…	tertiary	34

Society

No. of households	3.0m	Colour TVs per 100 households	96.7
Av. no. per household	2.5	Telephone lines per 100 pop.	67.4
Marriages per 1,000 pop.	5.4	Mobile telephone subscribers	
Divorces per 1,000 pop.	2.5	per 100 pop.	23.5
Cost of living, Dec. 1999		Computers per 100 pop.	42.2
New York = 100	112	Internet hosts per 100 pop.	41.9

a 1994

TAIWAN

Area	36,179 sq km	Capital	Taipei
Arable as % of total land	25	Currency	Taiwan dollar (T$)

People

Population	21.9m	Life expectancy: men		...
Pop. per sq km	607	women		...
Av. ann. growth		Adult literacy		...
in pop. 1985–95	1.14%	Fertility rate (per woman)		1.8
Pop. under 15	22.0%	Urban population		...
Pop. over 65	8.2%			*per 1,000 pop.*
No. of men per 100 women	105.2	Crude birth rate		1.5
Human Development Index	...	Crude death rate[a]		6

The economy

GDP	T$8,747bn	GDP per head	$12,040
GDP	$262.3bn	GDP per head in purchasing	
Av. ann. growth in real		power parity (USA=100)	61.6
GDP 1988–97	6.3%	Economic freedom index	2.00

Origins of GDP		Components of GDP	
	% of total		*% of total*
Agriculture	2.9	Private consumption	61.4
Industry, of which:	34.0	Public consumption	14.2
manufacturing	27.0	Investment	22.4
Services	63.1	Exports	48.9
		Imports	-46.9

Structure of employment

	% of total		*% of labour force*
Agriculture	8	Unemployed 1997	2.7
Industry	37	Av. ann. rate 1990–97	1.9
Services	55		

Energy

	m TCE		
Total output	...	% output exported	3.3
Total consumption	...	% consumption imported	76.7
Consumption per head, kg coal equivalent	...		

Inflation and finance

Consumer price		*av. ann. increase 1993–98*	
inflation 1999	0.2%	Narrow money (M1)	6.6%
Av. ann. inflation 1990–99	2.7%	Broad money	10.0%

Exchange rates

	end 1999		*December 1999*
T$ per $	31.55	Effective rates	*1995 = 100*
T$ per SDR	43.22	– nominal	...
T$ per euro	31.71	– real	...

Principal exports

	$bn fob
Machinery & electrical equipment	55.3
Textiles & clothing	14.6
Base metals & manufactures	10.9
Chemicals	8.8
Vehicles, aircraft & ships	5.2
Total incl. others	**110.6**

Principal imports

	$bn cif
Machinery & electrical equipment	43.0
Chemicals	12.7
Metals	9.5
Transport equipment	5.6
Precision instruments, clocks & watches	5.2
Crude petroleum	3.5
Total incl. others	**104.7**

Main export destinations

	% of total
United States	26.6
Hong Kong	22.5
Japan	8.4
Netherlands	3.8
Germany	3.7
United Kingdom	3.0
Singapore	2.9
Malaysia	2.1

Main origins of imports

	% of total
Japan	25.8
United States	18.8
South Korea	5.4
France	5.1
Germany	4.9
Malaysia	3.5
Australia	2.8
Singapore	2.6

Balance of payments, reserves and debt[b], $bn

Visible exports fob	110.2	Overall balance	4.8
Visible imports fob	-99.9	Change in reserves	6.8
Trade balance	10.3	Level of reserves	
Invisibles inflows	23.3	end Dec.	90.3
Invisibles outflows	-28.6	No. months of import cover	8.3
Net transfers	-1.6	Foreign debt	33.5
Current account balance	3.4	– as % of GDP	12
– as % of GDP	1.4	Debt service paid	2.9
Capital balance	1.6	Debt service ratio	2

Health and education

Health spending, % of GDP	6.2	Education spending, % of GDP	...
Doctors per 1,000 pop.	0.4	Enrolment, %: primary	89
Hospital beds per 1,000 pop.	2.0	secondary	59
Safe water access, % of pop.	...	tertiary	21

Society

No. of households	6.2m	Colour TVs per 100 households	99.5
Av. no. per household	3.5	Telephone lines per 100 pop.	52.4
Marriages per 1,000 pop.	7.8	Mobile telephone subscribers	
Divorces per 1,000 pop.	1.8	per 100 pop.	21.6
Cost of living, Dec. 1999		Computers per 100 pop.	17.3
New York = 100	100	Internet hosts per 100 pop.	27.3

a 1995–2000.
b 1997

THAILAND

Area	513,115 sq km	Capital	Bangkok
Arable as % of total land	40	Currency	Baht (Bt)

People

Population	60.3m	Life expectancy: men		66 yrs
Pop. per sq km	120	women		72 yrs
Av. ann. growth		Adult literacy		94.7%
in pop. 1990–2000	1.0%	Fertility rate (per woman)		1.7
Pop. under 15	25.3%	Urban population		21.6%
Pop. over 65	5.8%			*per 1,000 pop.*
No. of men per 100 women	99.5	Crude birth rate		16.7
Human Development Index	75.3	Crude death rate		7

The economy

GDP	Bt4,604bn	GDP per head	$2,160
GDP	$131.9bn	GDP per head in purchasing	
Av. ann. growth in real		power parity (USA=100)	18.9
GDP 1990–98	5.7%	Economic freedom index	2.70

Origins of GDP		**Components of GDP**	
	% of total		*% of total*
Agriculture	11.2	Private consumption	55.2
Industry, of which:	49.1	Public consumption	9.6
manufacturing	32.1	Investment	23.4
Services	39.7	Exports	53.8
		Imports	-34.9

Structure of employment

	% of total		*% of labour force*
Agriculture	49	Unemployed 1998	3.4
Industry	18	Av. ann. rate 1990–98	1.7
Services	33		

Energy

	m TCE		
Total output	38.603	% output exported	16.1
Total consumption	86.953	% consumption imported	68.5
Consumption per head,			
kg coal equivalent	1,481		

Inflation and finance

			av. ann. increase 1993–98
Consumer price			
inflation 1999	0.3%	Narrow money (M1)	8.8%
Av. ann. inflation 1990–99	4.8%	Broad money	13.7%
Money market rate, 1999	1.77%		

Exchange rates

	end 1999		*December 1999*
Bt per $	37.52	Effective rates	*1995 = 100*
Bt per SDR	51.50	– nominal	...
Bt per euro	37.71	– real	...

Principal exports

	$bn fob
Computers & parts	7.6
Textiles & clothing	4.4
Integrated circuits	2.2
Rice	2.1
Total incl. others	**54.3**

Principal imports

	$bn cif
Capital goods	21.6
Raw materials & intermediates	11.7
Consumer goods	4.9
Petroleum & products	3.2
Total incl. others	**42.9**

Main export destinations

	% of total
United States	22.3
Japan	13.7
Singapore	8.7
Hong Kong	5.1
Malaysia	3.3

Main origins of imports

	% of total
Japan	23.7
United States	14.1
Singapore	5.6
Malaysia	5.2
Germany	5.1

Balance of payments, reserves and debt, $bn

Visible exports fob	52.7	Overall balance	1.3
Visible imports fob	-36.7	Change in reserves	2.6
Trade balance	16.0	Level of reserves	
Invisibles inflows	16.5	end Dec.	29.5
Invisibles outflows	-18.9	No. months of import cover	6.4
Net transfers	0.4	Foreign debt	86.2
Current account balance	14.0	– as % of GDP	76
– as % of GDP	10.8	Debt service paid	11.6
Capital balance	-9.4	Debt service ratio	19

Health and education

Health spending, % of GDP	6.2	Education spending, % of GDP	4.8
Doctors per 1,000 pop.	0.4	Enrolment, %: primary	89
Hospital beds per 1,000 pop.	2.0	secondary	59
Safe water access, % of pop.	81	tertiary	21

Society

No. of households	13.4m	Colour TVs per 100 households	78.2
Av. no. per household	4.5	Telephone lines per 100 pop.	8.4
Marriages per 1,000 pop.	7.0	Mobile telephone subscribers	
Divorces per 1,000 pop.	0.9	per 100 pop.	3.3
Cost of living, Dec. 1999		Computers per 100 pop.	2.2
New York = 100	57	Internet hosts per 100 pop.	0.7

TURKEY

Area	779,452 sq km	Capital	Ankara
Arable as % of total land	36	Currency	Turkish Lira (L)

People

Population	64.5m	Life expectancy: men	67 yrs
Pop. per sq km	85	women	72 yrs
Av. ann. growth		Adult literacy	83.2%
in pop. 1990–2000	1.72%	Fertility rate (per woman)	2.5
Pop. under 15	28.3%	Urban population	75.3%
Pop. over 65	5.8%		*per 1,000 pop.*
No. of men per 100 women	102.0	Crude birth rate	22.1
Human Development Index	72.8	Crude death rate	6

The economy

GDP	L51,625trn	GDP per head	$3,160
GDP	$200.5bn	GDP per head in purchasing	
Av. ann. growth in real		power parity (USA=100)	22.6
GDP 1990–98	4.2%	Economic freedom index	2.75

Origins of GDP		**Components of GDP**	
	% of total		*% of total*
Agriculture	17.5	Private consumption	67.5
Industry, of which:	28.9	Public consumption	12.4
manufacturing	...	Investment	23.6
Services	53.6	Exports	23.8
		Imports	-27.2

Structure of employment

	% of total		*% of labour force*
Agriculture	43	Unemployed 1998	6.2
Industry	23	Av. ann. rate 1990–98	7.3
Services	34		

Energy

	m TCE		
Total output	28.406	% output exported	6.3
Total consumption	78.566	% consumption imported	73.8
Consumption per head,			
kg coal equivalent	1,271		

Inflation and finance

Consumer price		*av. ann. increase 1989–98*	
inflation 1999	64.9%	Narrow money (M1)	80.8%
Av. ann. inflation 1990–99	78.7%	Broad money	109.8%
Money market rate, 1999	73.53%		

Exchange rates

	end 1999		*December 1999*
L per $	541,400	Effective rates	*1995 = 100*
L per SDR	743,077	– nominal	...
L per euro	544,107	– real	...

Principal exports		Principal imports	
	$bn fob		*$bn cif*
Clothing & textiles	10.6	Machinery	5.8
Vegetables, fruit & nuts	2.3	Vehicles	3.7
Iron & steel	1.8	Electrical machinery	2.8
Electrical machinery	1.0	Petroleum & products	2.6
Total incl. others	**25.9**	Total incl. others	**45.4**

Main export destinations		Main origins of imports	
	% of total		*% of total*
Germany	20.3	Germany	15.9
United States	8.3	Italy	9.3
United Kingdom	6.4	United States	8.8
Italy	5.8	France	6.6
Russia	5.0	United Kingdom	5.8
EU15	50.0	EU15	52.5

Balance of payments, reserves and debt, $bn

Visible exports fob	31.2	Overall balance	0.4
Visible imports fob	-45.6	Change in reserves	0.8
Trade balance	-14.3	Level of reserves	
Invisibles inflows	25.8	end Dec.	20.6
Invisibles outflows	-15.3	No. months of import cover	4.1
Net transfers	5.7	Foreign debt	102.1
Current account balance	1.9	– as % of GDP	50
– as % of GDP	0.9	Debt service paid	11.5
Capital balance	0.8	Debt service ratio	19

Health and education

Health spending, % of GDP	5.8	Education spending, % of GDP	2.2
Doctors per 1,000 pop.	1.1	Enrolment, %: primary	107
Hospital beds per 1,000 pop.	2.5	secondary	58
Safe water access, % of pop.	49	tertiary	21

Society

No. of households	14.9m	Colour TVs per 100 households	67.8
Av. no. per household	4.3	Telephone lines per 100 pop.	25.4
Marriages per 1,000 pop.	7.8	Mobile telephone subscribers	
Divorces per 1,000 pop.	0.5	per 100 pop.	5.3
Cost of living, Dec. 1999		Computers per 100 pop.	2.3
New York = 100	67	Internet hosts per 100 pop.	1.4

UKRAINE

Area	603,700 sq km	Capital	Kiev
Arable as % of total land	60	Currency	Hryvnya (UAH)

People

Population	50.9m	Life expectancy: men	64 yrs
Pop. per sq km	84	women	74 yrs
Av. ann. growth		Adult literacy	98.0%
in pop. 1990–2000	-0.28%	Fertility rate (per woman)	1.4
Pop. under 15	17.8%	Urban population	68.0%
Pop. over 65	14.1%		*per 1,000 pop.*
No. of men per 100 women	87.2	Crude birth rate	9.7
Human Development Index	72.1	Crude death rate	14

The economy

GDP	UAH92.5bn	GDP per head	$980
GDP	$49.2bn	GDP per head in purchasing	
Av. ann. growth in real		power parity (USA=100)	10.7
GDP 1990–98	-11.9%	Economic freedom index	3.60

Origins of GDP		**Components of GDP**	
	% of total		*% of total*
Agriculture	12	Private consumption	74.6
Industry, of which:	31	Public consumption	9.1
manufacturing	...	Investment	20.1
Services	57	Net exports	-3.8

Structure of employment[a]

	% of total		*% of labour force*
Agriculture	22.0	Unemployed 1998	11.3
Industry	22.8	Av. ann. rate 1995–98	8.3
Services	55.6		

Energy

	m TCE		
Total output	111.301	% output exported	3.35
Total consumption	223.229	% consumption imported	53.16
Consumption per head,			
kg coal equivalent	4,325		

Inflation and finance

Consumer price		*av. ann. increase 1993–98*	
inflation 1997	15.9%	Narrow money (M1)	97.7%
Av. ann. inflation 1990–97	431%	Broad money	99.8%
Money market rate, 1999	44.98%		

Exchange rates

	end 1999		*December 1999*
UAH per $	5.22	Effective rates	*1995 = 100*
UAH per SDR	7.16	– nominal	124.5
UAH per euro	5.25	– real	115.1

Principal exports

	$bn fob
Metals	5.3
Chemicals	1.7
Machinery & transport equipment	1.7
Food & agricultural produce	1.4
Total incl. others	**13.7**

Principal imports

	$bn fob
Fuels, mineral products	6.2
Machinery & transport equipment	3.2
Chemicals	1.8
Food & agricultural produce	1.1
Total incl. others	**16.3**

Main export destinations

	% of total
Russia	23.0
China	5.8
Turkey	5.5
Germany	5.1
Italy	4.4
Belarus	4.3

Main origins of imports

	% of total
Russia	48.1
Germany	8.6
United States	4.0
Poland	3.3
Italy	2.8
Belarus	2.4

Balance of payments, reserves and debt, $bn

Visible exports fob	13.7	Overall balance	-3.5
Visible imports fob	-16.3	Change in reserves	-1.6
Trade balance	-2.6	Level of reserves	
Invisibles inflows	4.0	end Dec.	0.8
Invisibles outflows	-3.5	No. months of import cover	0.5
Net transfers	0.8	Foreign debt	12.7
Current account balance	-1.3	– as % of GDP	30
– as % of GDP	-2.6	Debt service paid	1.8
Capital balance	-1.3	Debt service ratio	11

Health and education

Health spending, % of GDP	5.4	Education spending, % of GDP	7.3
Doctors per 1,000 pop.	4.5	Enrolment, %: primary	…
Hospital beds per 1,000 pop.	11.8	secondary	…
Safe water access, % of pop.	…	tertiary	42

Society

No. of households	9.0m	Colour TVs per 100 households	49.0
Av. no. per household	7.2	Telephone lines per 100 pop.	19.1
Marriages per 1,000 pop.	6.1	Mobile telephone subscribers	
Divorces per 1,000 pop.	3.9	per 100 pop.	0.2
Cost of living, Dec. 1999		Computers per 100 pop.	1.4
New York = 100	…	Internet hosts per 100 pop.	0.7

a 1996

UNITED KINGDOM

Area	242,534 sq km	Capital	London
Arable as % of total land	25	Currency	Pound (£)

People

Population	58.7m	Life expectancy: men	75 yrs
Pop. per sq km	241	women	80 yrs
Av. ann. growth		Adult literacy	99.0%
in pop. 1990–2000	0.22%	Fertility rate (per woman)	1.7
Pop. under 15	18.8%	Urban population	89.5%
Pop. over 65	16.0%		per 1,000 pop.
No. of men per 100 women	96.5	Crude birth rate	11.9
Human Development Index	91.8	Crude death rate	11

The economy

GDP	£847bn	GDP per head	$21,410
GDP	$1,264bn	GDP per head in purchasing	
Av. ann. growth in real		power parity (USA=100)	69.5
GDP 1990–98	2.2%	Economic freedom index	1.90

Origins of GDP		Components of GDP	
	% of total		% of total
Agriculture	1.7	Private consumption	64.7
Industry, of which:	25.3	Public consumption	18.2
manufacturing	20.2	Investment	18.1
Services	73.0	Exports	26.9
		Imports	-27.9

Structure of employment

	% of total		% of labour force
Agriculture	2	Unemployed 1998	6.1
Industry	26	Av. ann. rate 1990–98	8.3
Services	72		

Energy

	m TCE		
Total output	382.455	% output exported	38.1
Total consumption	328.043	% consumption imported	31.6
Consumption per head,			
kg coal equivalent	5,620		

Inflation and finance

Consumer price			av. ann. increase 1993–98
inflation 1999	1.6%	Narrow money (M0)	6.2%
Av. ann. inflation 1990–99	3.1%	Broad money	7.5%
Money market rate, 1999	5.11%		

Exchange rates

	end 1999		December 1999
£ per $	0.62	Effective rates	1995 = 100
£ per SDR	0.85	– nominal	124.9
£ per euro	0.62	– real	148.0

Principal exports
$bn fob

Finished manufactured products	163.1
Semi-manufactured products	71.9
Food, beverages & tobacco	17.0
Fuels	12.4
Basic materials	4.2
Total incl. others	**271.7**

Principal imports
$bn cif

Finished manufactured products	183.8
Semi-manufactured products	74.7
Food, beverages & tobacco	27.0
Basic materials	9.3
Fuels	8.0
Total incl. others	**305.9**

Main export destinations
% of total

United States	13.3
Germany	12.4
France	9.9
Netherlands	7.8
Ireland	5.7
EU15	57.5

Main origins of imports
% of total

Germany	13.5
United States	13.3
France	9.3
Netherlands	7.1
Italy	5.1
EU15	53.3

Balance of payments, reserves and aid, $bn

Visible exports fob	271.8	Capital balance	-4.2
Visible imports fob	-305.8	Overall balance	-0.3
Trade balance	-34.0	Change in reserves	1.2
Invisibles inflows	281.7	Level of reserves	
Invisibles outflows	-237.7	end Dec.	38.8
Net transfers	-10.8	No. months of import cover	0.9
Current account balance	-0.8	Aid given	3.86
– as % of GDP	-0.1	– as % of GDP	0.27

Health and education

Health spending, % of GDP	6.8	Education spending, % of GDP	5.3
Doctors per 1,000 pop.	1.6	Enrolment, %: primary	116
Hospital beds per 1,000 pop.	4.5	secondary[a]	129
Safe water access, % of pop.	…	tertiary	52

Society

No. of households	22.0m	Colour TVs per 100 households	98.3
Av. no. per household	2.7	Telephone lines per 100 pop.	55.7
Marriages per 1,000 pop.	10.8	Mobile telephone subscribers	
Divorces per 1,000 pop.	3.3	per 100 pop.	25.2
Cost of living, Dec. 1999		Computers per 100 pop.	26.3
New York = 100	109	Internet hosts per 100 pop.	32.4

a Includes training for unemployed.

UNITED STATES

Area	9,372,610 sq km	Capital	Washington DC
Arable as % of total land	19	Currency	US dollar ($)

People

Population	274.0m	Life expectancy: men	73 yrs
Pop. per sq km	30	women	80 yrs
Av. ann. growth		Adult literacy	99.0%
in pop. 1990–2000	0.91%	Fertility rate (per woman)	2.0
Pop. under 15	21.5%	Urban population	77.2%
Pop. over 65	12.5%		per 1,000 pop.
No. of men per 100 women	97.2	Crude birth rate	14.0
Human Development Index	92.7	Crude death rate	8

The economy

GDP	$7,903bn	GDP per head	$29,240
Av. ann. growth in real		GDP per head in purchasing	
GDP 1990–98	3.2%	power parity (USA=100)	100
		Economic freedom index	1.80

Origins of GDP[a]		**Components of GDP**	
	% of total		% of total
Agriculture	1.6	Private consumption	66.7
Industry, of which:	22.6	Public consumption	17.4
manufacturing	17.0	Investment	17.4
Services[b]	75.8	Exports	11.0
		Imports	-12.7

Structure of employment

	% of total		% of labour force
Agriculture	3	Unemployed 1998	4.5
Industry	23	Av. ann. rate 1990–98	5.9
Services	74		

Energy

	m TCE		
Total output	2,494.292	% output exported	5.1
Total consumption	3,095.167	% consumption imported	26.0
Consumption per head,			
kg coal equivalent	11,487		

Inflation and finance

Consumer price		*av. ann. increase 1993–98*	
inflation 1999	2.2%	Narrow money (M1)	-0.6%
Av. ann. inflation 1990–99	2.7%	Broad money	7.0%
Treasury bill rate, 1999	4.66%		

Exchange rates

	end 1999		December 1999
$ per SDR	1.37	Effective rates	1995 = 100
$ per euro	1.00	– nominal	114.1
		– real	123.7

Principal exports

	$bn fob
Capital goods, excl. vehicles	299.6
Industrial supplies	148.3
Consumer goods, excl. vehicles	79.3
Vehicles & products	73.2
Food & beverages	46.4
Total incl. others	**682.1**

Principal imports

	$bn fob
Capital goods, excl. vehicles	269.6
Consumer goods, excl. vehicles	216.5
Industrial supplies	200.1
Vehicles & products	149.1
Food & beverages	41.2
Total incl. others	**911.9**

Main export destinations

	% of total
Canada	23.3
Mexico	11.7
Japan	8.4
United Kingdom	5.6
Germany	3.9
EU15	21.8

Main origins of imports

	% of total
Canada	19.3
Japan	13.3
Mexico	10.4
China	7.7
Germany	5.4
United Kingdom	3.7
EU15	19.2

Balance of payments, reserves and aid, $bn

Visible exports fob	672.2	Capital balance	217.2
Visible imports fob	-917.2	Overall balance	6.73
Trade balance	-245.0	Change in reserves	11.1
Invisibles inflows	520.0	Level of reserves	
Invisibles outflows	-451.5	end Dec.	146.0
Net transfers	-44.1	No. months of import cover	1.3
Current account balance	-220.6	Aid given	8.79
– as % of GDP	-2.8	– as % of GDP	0.10

Health and education

Health spending, % of GDP	13.9	Education spending, % of GDP	5.4
Doctors per 1,000 pop.	2.6	Enrolment, %: primary	102
Hospital beds per 1,000 pop.	4.0	secondary	97
Safe water access, % of pop.	…	tertiary	81

Society

No. of households	101.0m	Colour TVs per 100 households	98.1
Av. no. per household	2.7	Telephone lines per 100 pop.	66.1
Marriages per 1,000 pop.	8.1	Mobile telephone subscribers	
Divorces per 1,000 pop.	4.5	per 100 pop.	31.3
Cost of living, Dec. 1999		Computers per 100 pop.	45.9
New York = 100	100	Internet hosts per 100 pop.	168.9

a 1997
b Including utilities.

VENEZUELA

Area	912,050 sq km	Capital	Caracas
Arable as % of total land	5	Currency	Bolivar (Bs)

People

Population	23.2m	Life expectancy: men		70 yrs
Pop. per sq km	27		women	76 yrs
Av. ann. growth		Adult literacy		92.0%
in pop. 1990–2000	2.15%	Fertility rate (per woman)		3.0
Pop. under 15	34.1%	Urban population		86.9%
Pop. over 65	4.4%			per 1,000 pop.
No. of men per 100 women	101.3	Crude birth rate		24.9
Human Development Index	79.2	Crude death rate		5

The economy

GDP	Bs52,030bn	GDP per head	$3,530
GDP	$82.1bn	GDP per head in purchasing	
Av. ann. growth in real		power parity (USA=100)	19.5
GDP 1990–98	2.2%	Economic freedom index	3.30

Origins of GDP		Components of GDP	
	% of total		% of total
Agriculture	4.8	Private consumption	72.9
Industry, of which:	37.5	Public consumption	7.5
manufacturing	26.5	Investment	18.2
Services	57.7	Exports	20.0
		Imports	-20.1

Structure of employment

	% of total		% of labour force
Agriculture	14	Unemployed 1997	11.4
Industry	16	Av. ann. rate 1990–95	8.8
Services	70		

Energy

	m TCE		
Total output	287.716	% output exported	65.7
Total consumption	101.322	% consumption imported	0.4
Consumption per head,			
kg coal equivalent	4,541		

Inflation and finance

Consumer price		av. ann. increase 1993–98	
inflation 1999	23.6%	Narrow money (M1)	66.2%
Av. ann. inflation 1990–99	46.7%	Broad money	45.9%
Money market rate, 1999	7.48%		

Exchange rates

	end 1999		December 1999
Bs per $	890	Effective rates	1995 = 100
Bs per SDR	648	– nominal	32.0
Bs per euro	894	– real	153.7

Principal exports

	$bn fob
Petroleum & products	12.0
Metals	1.6
Total incl. others	**17.2**

Main export destinations

	% of total
United States	44.3
Colombia	7.3
Brazil	3.8
Canada	2.8

Principal imports

	$bn fob
Machinery & transport equipment	6.0
Chemicals	1.8
Agricultural products	1.3
Total incl. others	**13.2**

Main origins of imports

	% of total
United States	42.4
Colombia	6.2
Italy	4.8
Germany	4.5

Balance of payments, reserves and debt, $bn

Visible exports fob	17.6	Overall balance	-2.9
Visible imports fob	-14.8	Change in reserves	-3.0
Trade balance	2.7	Level of reserves	
Invisibles inflows	3.9	end Dec.	14.7
Invisibles outflows	-9.0	No. months of import cover	7.4
Net transfers	-0.2	Foreign debt	37.0
Current account balance	-2.6	– as % of GDP	40
– as % of GDP	-3.1	Debt service paid	5.2
Capital balance	0.8	Debt service ratio	27

Health and education

Health spending, % of GDP	7.5	Education spending, % of GDP	5.2
Doctors per 1,000 pop.	2.4	Enrolment, %: primary	91
Hospital beds per 1,000 pop.	1.5	secondary	40
Safe water access, % of pop.	79	tertiary	25

Society

No. of households	4.1m	Colour TVs per 100 households	87.5
Av. no. per household	5.6	Telephone lines per 100 pop.	11.7
Marriages per 1,000 pop.	3.7	Mobile telephone subscribers	
Divorces per 1,000 pop.	0.9	per 100 pop.	8.7
Cost of living, Dec. 1999		Computers per 100 pop.	4.3
New York = 100	76	Internet hosts per 100 pop.	0.6

VIETNAM

Area	331,114 sq km	Capital	Hanoi
Arable as % of total land	21	Currency	Dong (D)

People

Population	77.6m	Life expectancy: men		65 yrs
Pop. per sq km	241	women		70 yrs
Av. ann. growth		Adult literacy		91.9%
in pop. 1990–2000	1.8%	Fertility rate (per woman)		2.6
Pop. under 15	33.2%	Urban population		19.7%
Pop. over 65	5.3%			*per 1,000 pop.*
No. of men per 100 women	97.6	Crude birth rate		22.4
Human Development Index	66.4	Crude death rate		7

The economy

GDP		GDP per head	$350
GDP	$26.5bn	GDP per head in purchasing	
Av. ann. growth in real		power parity (USA=100)	5.8
GDP 1990–98	8.4%	Economic freedom index	4.30

Origins of GDP		**Components of GDP**[a]	
	% of total		*% of total*
Agriculture	23.7	Private consumption	70.3
Industry, of which:	33.5	Public consumption	13.7
manufacturing	...	Investment	27.9
Services	42.8	Exports	42.9
		Imports	-56.5

Structure of employment

	% of total		*% of labour force*
Agriculture	...	Unemployed 1998	...
Industry	...	Av. ann. rate 1990–98	...
Services	...		

Energy

	m TCE		
Total output	24.822	% output exported	64.8
Total consumption	15.969	% consumption imported	49.8
Consumption per head,			
kg coal equivalent	212		

Inflation and finance

Consumer price		*av. ann. increase 1993–99*	
inflation 1998	8.7%	Narrow money (M1)	...
Av. ann. inflation 1990–98	8.6%	Broad money	...

Exchange rates

	end 1999		*December 1999*
D per $	14,026	Effective rates	*1995 = 100*
D per SDR	19,216	– nominal	...
D per euro	14,096	– real	...

Principal exports

	$bn fob
Textiles & garments	1.3
Crude oil	1.2
Rice	1.1
Footwear	1.0
Total incl. others	**9.4**

Principal imports

	$bn cif
Machinery & parts	2.1
Textiles & garments	1.3
Petroleum products	0.8
Steel	0.5
Total incl. others	**11.6**

Main export destinations

	% of total
Japan	15.8
Singapore	11.5
Taiwan	7.1
Germany	6.3
United States	5.9
China	5.1

Main origins of imports

	% of total
Singapore	19.9
Japan	12.8
South Korea	12.4
Taiwan	11.9
Sweden	6.8
Thailand	5.9

Balance of payments, reserves and debt, $bn

Visible exports fob	9.4	Overall balance	...
Visible imports fob	-10.4	Change in reserves	-0.8
Trade balance	-1.0	Level of reserves	
Invisibles inflows	2.7	end Dec.	1.1
Invisibles outflows	-4.0	No. months of import cover	1.0
Net transfers[a]	1.2	Foreign debt	22.4
Current account balance[a]	-2.4	– as % of GDP	82
– as % of GDP	-9.2	Debt service paid	1.0
Capital balance	...	Debt service ratio	9

Health and education

Health spending, % of GDP	4.3	Education spending, % of GDP	3.0
Doctors per 1,000 pop.	0.4	Enrolment, %: primary	114
Hospital beds per 1,000 pop.	3.8	secondary	57
Safe water access, % of pop.	45	tertiary	7

Society

No. of households	16.8m	Colour TVs per 100 households	28.3
Av. no. per household	4.6	Telephone lines per 100 pop.	2.6
Marriages per 1,000 pop.	...	Mobile telephone subscribers	
Divorces per 1,000 pop.	...	per 100 pop.	0.2
Cost of living, Dec. 1999		Computers per 100 pop.	0.6
New York = 100	70	Internet hosts per 100 pop.	...

a 1996

ZIMBABWE

Area	390,759 sq km	Capital	Harare
Arable as % of total land	7	Currency	Zimbabwe dollar (Z$)

People

Population	11.4m	Life expectancy: men	44 yrs
Pop. per sq km	30	women	45 yrs
Av. ann. growth		Adult literacy	90.9%
in pop. 1990–2000	1.7%	Fertility rate (per woman)	3.8
Pop. under 15	41.3%	Urban population	35.3%
Pop. over 65	2.8%		*per 1,000 pop.*
No. of men per 100 women	98.7	Crude birth rate	31.5
Human Development Index	56.0	Crude death rate	18

The economy

GDP	Z$131bn	GDP per head	$620
GDP	$7.2bn	GDP per head in purchasing	
Av. ann. growth in real		power parity (USA=100)	8.5
GDP 1990–98	2.3%	Economic freedom index	3.90

Origins of GDP[a]		Components of GDP[a]	
	% of total		*% of total*
Agriculture	18.6	Private consumption	69.5
Industry, of which:	19.3	Public consumption	17.8
manufacturing	...	Investment	19.8
Services	62.1	Exports	38.5
		Imports	-45.7

Structure of employment[b]

	% of total		*% of labour force*
Agriculture	68	Unemployed 1998	...
Industry	8	Av. ann. rate 1990–98	...
Services	24		

Energy

	m TCE		
Total output	5.514	% output exported	2.2
Total consumption	7.811	% consumption imported	32.1
Consumption per head,			
kg coal equivalent	683		

Inflation and finance

Consumer price		*av. ann. increase 1993–98*	
inflation 1998	31.8%	Narrow money (M1)	33.3%
Av. ann. inflation 1990–98	26.0%	Broad money	28.9%
Money market rate, 1999	72.50%		

Exchange rates

	end 1999		*December 1999*
Z$ per $	38.17	Effective rates	*1995 = 100*
Z$ per SDR	52.36	– nominal	...
Z$ per euro	38.36	– real	...

Principal exports

	$m fob
Tobacco	493
Gold	154
Ferro-alloys	141
Cotton	131
Total incl. others	**2,047**

Principal imports

	$m fob
Machinery & transport equipment	712
Manufactured products	340
Chemicals	311
Petroleum products & electricity	238
Total incl. others	**1,968**

Main export destinations[c]

	% of total
South Africa	13.8
United Kingdom	7.6
Botswana	7.5
Malawi	5.9
Japan	5.8

Main origins of imports

	% of total
South Africa	52.3
United Kingdom	4.8
China	3.8
Japan	3.5
United States	3.4

Balance of payments[d], reserves and debt, $bn

Visible exports fob	2.4	Overall balance[e]	-0.1
Visible imports fob	-2.2	Change in reserves	-0.1
Trade balance	0.2	Level of reserves	
Invisibles inflows	0.7	end Dec.	0.3
Invisibles outflows	-1.2	No. months of import cover[a]	1.3
Net transfers	0.2	Foreign debt	4.7
Current account balance	-0.1	– as % of GDP	80
– as % of GDP	-1.5	Debt service paid	0.9
Capital balance[e]	0.3	Debt service ratio	38

Health and education

Health spending, % of GDP	6.4	Education spending, % of GDP	9.0
Doctors per 1,000 pop.	0.1	Enrolment, %: primary	112
Hospital beds per 1,000 pop.	0.5	secondary	50
Safe water access, % of pop.	79	tertiary	7

Society

No. of households	3.0m	Colour TVs per 100 households	3.0
Av. no. per household	3.8	Telephone lines per 100 pop.[a]	1.9
Marriages per 1,000 pop.	...	Mobile telephone subscribers	
Divorces per 1,000 pop.	...	per 100 pop.	0.5
Cost of living, Dec. 1999		Computers per 100 pop.	0.9
New York = 100	42	Internet hosts per 100 pop.	0.2

a 1997
b 1990
c Excluding gold.
d 1996
e 1994

Glossary

Balance of payments The record of a country's transactions with the rest of the world. The **current account** of the balance of payments consists of: visible trade (goods); "invisible" trade (services and income); private transfer payments (eg, remittances from those working abroad); official transfers (eg, payments to international organisations, famine relief). Visible imports and exports are normally compiled on rather different definitions to those used in the trade statistics (shown in principal imports and exports) and therefore the statistics do not match. The **capital account** consists of long- and short-term transactions relating to a country's assets and liabilities (eg, loans and borrowings). Adding the current to the capital account gives the **overall balance**. This is compensated by net monetary movements and changes in reserves. In practice methods of statistical recording are neither complete nor accurate and an errors and omissions item, sometimes quite large, will appear. In the country pages of this book this item is included in the overall balance. **Changes in reserves** exclude revaluation effects and are shown without the practice often followed in balance of payments presentations of reversing the sign.

CFA Communauté Financière Africaine. Its members, most of the francophone African nations, share a common currency, the CFA franc, which is maintained at a fixed rate of 1FFr = 100 CFAfr by the French treasury.

Cif/fob Measures of the value of merchandise trade. Imports include the cost of "carriage, insurance and freight" (cif) from the exporting country to the importing. The value of exports des not include these elements and is recorded 'free on board' (fob). Balance of payments statistics are generally adjusted so that both exports and imports are shown fob; the cif elements are included in invisibles.

Commonwealth of Independent States All former Soviet Union Republics, excluding Estonia, Latvia and Lithuania. It was established January 1 1992; Azerbaijan joined in September 1993 and Georgia in December 1993.

Crude birth rate The number of live births in a year per 1,000 population. The crude rate will automatically be relatively high if a large proportion of the population is of childbearing age.

Crude death rate The number of deaths in a year per 1,000 population. Also affected by the population's age structure.

Debt, foreign Financial obligations owed by a country to the rest of the world and repayable in foreign currency. **Debt service paid** is the sum of principal repayments and interest payments actually made. **The debt service ratio** is debt service expressed as a percentage of the country's earnings from exports of goods and services.

EU European Union. Members are: Belgium, Denmark, France, Germany, Greece, Ireland, Italy, Luxembourg, Netherlands, Portugal, Spain and the United Kingdom and, since January 1 1995, Austria, Finland and Sweden.

Ecu European currency unit. An accounting measure used within the EU and composed of a weighted basket of the currencies of 12 EU members, replaced by the euro on January 1 1999.

Effective exchange rate This measures a currency's depreciation (figures below 100) or appreciation (figures over 100) from a base date against a trade weighted basket of the currencies of the country's main trading partners.

Euro Replaced the ecu, on a one-to-one basis on January 1 1999. The currencies of the 11 euro area members have irrevocably fixed conversion rates for the euro. Notes and coins will begin circulation on January 1 2002.

Euro area (EU11) Members are those of the EU except Denmark, Greece, Sweden and the United Kingdom.

Fertility rate The average number of children born to a woman who completes her childbearing years.

GDP Gross domestic product. The sum of all output produced by economic activity within a country. GNP (gross national product) includes net income from abroad eg, rent, profits.

Import cover The number of months of imports covered by reserves, ie reserves $\div \frac{1}{12}$ annual imports (visibles and invisibles).

Inflation The annual rate at which prices are increasing. The most common measure and the one shown here is the increase in the consumer price index.

Internet hosts Websites and other computers that sit permanently on the Internet.

Life expectancy The average length of time a baby born today can expect to live.

Literacy is defined by UNESCO as the ability to read and write a simple sentence, but definitions can vary from country to country.

Money supply A measure of the "money" available to buy goods and services. Various definitions exist. The measures shown here are based on definitions used by the IMF and may differ from measures used nationally. Narrow money (M1) consists of cash in circulation and demand deposits (bank deposits that can be withdrawn on demand). "Quasi-money" (time, savings and foreign currency deposits) is added to this to create broad money.

OECD Organisation for Economic Co-operation and Development. The "rich countries" club was established in 1961 to promote economic growth and the expansion of world trade. It is based in Paris and now has 29 members.

Opec Organisation of Petroleum Exporting Countries. Set up in 1960 and based in Vienna, Opec is mainly concerned with oil pricing and production issues. Members are; Algeria, Indonesia, Iran, Iraq, Kuwait, Libya, Nigeria, Qatar, Saudi Arabia, United Arab Emirates and Venezuela.

PPP Purchasing power parity. PPP statistics adjust for cost of living differences by replacing normal exchange rates with rates designed to equalise the prices of a standard "basket"of goods and services. These are used to obtain PPP estimates of GDP per head. PPP estimates are normally shown on a scale of 1 to 100, taking the United States as 100.

Real terms Figures adjusted to exclude the effect of inflation.

Reserves The stock of gold and foreign currency held by a country to finance any calls that may be made for the settlement of foreign debt.

SDR Special drawing right. The reserve currency, introduced by the IMF in 1970, was intended to replace gold and national currencies in settling international transactions. The IMF uses SDRs for book-keeping purposes and issues them to member countries. Their value is based on a basket of the US dollar (with a weight of 39%), the euro (32%), the Japanese yen (18%) and the pound sterling (11%).

List of countries

Whenever data is available, the world rankings consider 171 countries: all those which had, in 1998, a population of at least 1m or a GDP/GNP of at least $1bn. Here is a list of them.

	Population	GDP	GDP per head	Area	Median age
	m	$bn	$	'000 sq km	years
Afghanistan	21.4	20.0[a]	937	652	18.5
Albania	3.1	2.7	810	29	26.7
Algeria	30.1	46.4	1,550	2,382	21.1
Angola	12.1	4.6	380	1,247	16.2
Argentina	36.1	290.3	8,030	2,767	27.8
Armenia	3.5	1.7	460	30	30.4
Australia	18.5	387.0	20,640	7,682	35.3
Austria	8.1	216.7	26,830	84	37.8
Azerbaijan	7.7	3.8	480	87	27.0
Bahamas	0.3	4.9	16,554	14	26.4
Bahrain	0.6	6.2	7,640	1	28.6
Bangladesh	124.8	44.2	350	144	20.9
Barbados	0.3	2.3	8,582	0.4	32.5
Belarus	10.3	22.3	2,180	208	36.4
Belgium	10.1	259.0	25,380	31	39.3
Benin	5.8	2.3	380	113	16.8
Bermuda	0.1	2.5	39,063	1	…
Bhutan	2.0	354.0	470	47	18.7
Bolivia	8.0	8.0	1,010	1,099	20.0
Bosnia	3.7	4.1[a]	1,116	51	35.1
Botswana	1.6	4.8	3,070	581	18.3
Brazil	165.9	767.6	4,630	8,512	25.7
Brunei	0.3	5.4[b]	17,532[b]	6	25.4
Bulgaria	8.3	10.1	1,220	111	38.8
Burkina Faso	11.3	2.6	240	274	16.2
Burundi	6.5	0.9	140	28	16.7
Cambodia	10.7	2.9	260	181	19.3
Cameroon	14.3	8.7	610	475	18.0
Canada	30.6	580.9	19,170	9,971	36.8
Central African Rep	3.5	1.1	300	622	18.5
Chad	7.3	1.7	230	1,284	17.1
Chile	14.8	73.9	4,990	757	28.3
China	1,255.7	923.6	750	9,561	30.0
Colombia	40.8	100.7	2,470	1,142	24.0
Congo	49.1	5.4	110	342	15.8
Congo-Brazzaville	2.8	1.9	680	2,345	16.7
Costa Rica	3.8	9.8	2,770	51	24.2
Côte d'Ivoire	14.3	10.2	700	322	17.7
Croatia	4.5	20.8	4,620	57	38.8
Cuba	11.1	20.3[a]	1,826	111	32.9
Cyprus	0.8	9.0	11,920	9	33.3
Czech Republic	10.3	53.0	5,150	79	37.5
Denmark	5.3	175.2	33,040	43	39.0
Dominican Republic	8.2	14.6	1,770	48	23.9
Ecuador	12.2	18.4	1,520	272	22.9
Egypt	66.0	79.2	1,290	1,000	22.0

	Population	GDP	GDP per head	Area	Median age
	m	*$bn*	*$*	*'000 sq km*	*years*
El Salvador	6.0	11.2	1,850	21	21.8
Eritrea	3.6	0.8	200	117	17.8
Estonia	1.4	4.9	3,360	45	37.5
Ethiopia	59.6	6.2	100	1,134	16.9
Fiji	0.8	1.7	2,210	18	23.6
Finland	5.2	125.1	24,280	338	39.4
France	58.7	1,465.4c	24,210	544	37.6
Gabon	1.2	4.9	4,170	268	20.4
Gambia, The	1.2	0.4	340	11	20.1
Georgia	5.1	5.3	970	70	34.1
Germany	82.1	2,179.8	26,570	358	40.0
Ghana	19.2	7.3	390	239	18.1
Greece	10.6	123.4	11,740	132	39.4
Guadeloupe	0.4	3.7d	8,352	2	30.0
Guatemala	10.8	17.8	1,640	109	17.8
Guinea	7.3	3.8	530	246	17.7
Guinea-Bissau	1.2	0.2	160	36	18.6
Haiti	8.0	3.2	410	28	18.9
Honduras	6.1	4.6	740	112	18.8
Hong Kong	6.7	158.2	23,660	1	35.9
Hungary	10.1	45.7	4,510	93	38.1
Iceland	0.3	7.6	27,830	103	32.9
India	982.2	427.4	440	3,287	23.8
Indonesia	206.3	130.6	640	1,904	24.8
Iran	65.8	102.2	1,650	1,648	20.7
Iraq	21.8	11.5a	528	438	19.0
Ireland	3.7	69.3	18,710	70	32.3
Israel	6.0	96.5	16,180	21	28.4
Italy	57.4	1,157.0	20,090	301	40.6
Jamaica	2.5	4.5	1,740	11	25.0
Japan	126.3	4,089.1	32,350	378	41.2
Jordan	6.3	5.3	1,150	89	18.8
Kazakhstan	16.3	20.9	1,340	2,717	27.9
Kenya	29.0	10.2	350	583	17.9
Kirgizstan	4.6	1.8	380	583	22.7
Kuwait	1.8	25.2	13,915	18	22.8
Laos	5.2	1.6	320	237	18.0
Latvia	2.4	5.9	2,420	64	37.7
Lebanon	3.2	15.0	3,560	10	24.4
Lesotho	2.1	1.2	570	30	19.9
Liberia	2.7	19.7a	7,389	111	18.1
Libya	5.3	38.0a	7,117	1,760	20.0
Lithuania	3.7	9.4	2,540	65	36.0
Luxembourg	0.4	19.2	45,100	3	37.8
Macau	0.5	6.8	14,815	0.02	33.5
Macedonia	2.0	2.6	1,290	26	32.2
Madagascar	15.1	3.7	260	587	17.9
Malawi	10.3	2.2	210	118	16.3

	Population	GDP	GDP per head	Area	Median age
	m	$bn	$	'000 sq km	years
Malaysia	21.4	81.3	3,670	333	23.3
Mali	10.7	2.6	250	1,240	16.6
Malta	0.4	3.8	10,100	0.3	36.1
Martinique	0.4	4.6[d]	11,825	1	32.3
Mauritania	2.5	1.1	410	1,031	18.0
Mauritius	1.1	4.3	3,730	2	29.1
Mexico	95.8	368.1	3,840	1,973	23.3
Moldova	4.4	1.7	380	34	31.6
Mongolia	2.6	1.0	380	1,565	22.1
Morocco	27.4	34.4	1,240	447	23.2
Mozambique	18.9	3.5	210	799	17.4
Myanmar	44.5	4.6[a]	103	677	25.5
Namibia	1.7	3.2	1,940	824	19.0
Nepal	22.8	4.9	210	147	19.1
Netherlands	15.7	389.1	24,780	42	37.8
Netherlands Antilles	0.2	2.4[a]	11,268	1	31.8
New Zealand	3.8	55.4	14,600	271	34.0
Nicaragua	4.8	1.8	370	130	18.1
Niger	10.1	2.0	200	1,267	15.9
Nigeria	106.4	36.4	300	924	18.1
North Korea	23.3	21.8[a]	930	121	28.8
Norway	4.4	152.0	34,310	324	37.4
Oman	2.4	14.2	5,961	310	17.7
Pakistan	148.2	61.5	470	804	19.0
Panama	2.8	8.3	2,990	77	25.2
Papua New Guinea	4.6	4.1	890	463	20.5
Paraguay	5.2	9.2	1,760	407	19.8
Peru	24.8	60.5	2,440	1,285	23.1
Philippines	72.9	78.9	1,050	300	21.5
Poland	38.7	151.3	3,910	313	35.1
Portugal	9.9	106.4	10,670	89	37.3
Puerto Rico	3.8	34.7	9,108	9	30.4
Qatar	0.6	11.3[b]	19,516	11	35.0
Réunion	0.7	6.6[d]	9,677	3	27.9
Romania	22.5	30.6	1,360	238	34.9
Russia	147.4	331.8	2,260	17,075	36.7
Rwanda	6.6	1.9	230	26	17.0
Saudi Arabia	20.2	143.4	6,910	2,200	19.7
Senegal	9.0	4.7	520	197	17.5
Serbia & Montenegro	10.6	25.4[a]	2,388	102	35.6
Sierra Leone	4.6	0.7	140	72	17.9
Singapore	3.5	95.5	30,170	1	34.4
Slovakia	5.4	19.9	3,700	49	34.0
Slovenia	2.0	19.4	9,780	20	38.1
Somalia	9.2	4.0[a]	433	638	16.0
South Africa	39.4	136.9	3,310	1,226	22.5
South Korea	46.1	398.8	8,600	99	31.4
Spain	39.6	555.2	14,100	505	37.9

	Population	GDP	GDP per head	Area	Median age
	m	$bn	$	'000 sq km	years
Sri Lanka	18.5	16.2	810	66	27.5
Sudan	28.3	8.2	290	2,506	19.5
Suriname	0.4	0.7	1,660	164	24.0
Swaziland	1.0	1.4	1,400	17	18.3
Sweden	8.9	226.5	25,580	450	39.9
Switzerland	7.3	284.1	39,980	41	38.3
Syria	15.3	15.5	1,020	185	18.8
Taiwan	21.9	262.3	12,040	36	30.1a
Tajikistan	6.0	2.3	370	143	19.5
Tanzania	32.1	7.2	220	945	17.1
Thailand	60.3	131.9	2,160	513	28.0
Togo	4.4	1.5	330	57	16.9
Trinidad & Tobago	1.3	5.8	4,520	5	27.7
Tunisia	9.3	19.2	2,060	164	24.4
Turkey	64.5	200.5	3,160	779	25.6
Turkmenistan	4.3	2.0a	464	488	21.1
Uganda	20.6	6.6	310	241	30.5
Ukraine	50.9	49.2	980	604	15.0
United Arab Emirates	2.4	48.7	17,870	84	37.6
United Kingdom	58.6	1,264.3	21,410	243	38.2
United States	274.0	7,903.0	29,240	9,373	35.8
Uruguay	3.3	20.0	6,070	176	31.4
Uzbekistan	23.6	22.9	950	447	21.0
Venezuela	23.2	82.1	3,530	912	23.1
Vietnam	77.6	26.5	350	331	23.1
West Bank and Gaza	1.0	4.3	1,560	6	14.4
Yemen	16.9	4.6	280	528	15.8
Zambia	8.8	3.2	330	753	16.1
Zimbabwe	11.4	7.2	620	391	18.6
Euro area	291.6	6,542.0	22,350	2,365	38.0

a Estimate.
b 1997
c Including French Guiana, Guadeloupe, Martinique and Réunion.
d 1995–97

Sources

Airports Council International,
Worldwide Airport Traffic Report

Alan Guttmacher Institute

BP, *Statistical Review of World Energy*

British Mountaineering Council

Corporate Resources Group,
Quality of Living Report

Council of Europe

The Economist Intelligence Unit,
*Cost of Living Survey; Country
Forecasts; Country Reports; Country
Risk Service; Global Outlook –
Business Environment Rankings;
Motor Business International*

ERC Statistics International, *World
Cigarette Report*

Euromonitor, *International Marketing
Data and Statistics; European
Marketing Data and Statistics; World
Consumer Markets 1997–98 on CD-
ROM*

Europa Publications, *The Europa World
Yearbook*

European Bank for Reconstruction and
Development, *Transition Report*

Eurostat, *Statistics in Focus*

FAO, *Production Yearbook*

Financial Times Business Information,
The Banker

Gold Fields Mineral Services Ltd.

The Heritage Foundation, *The 2000 Index
of Economic Freedom*

ILO, *Year Book of Labour Statistics*

IMD, *World Competitiveness Yearbook*

IMF, *Direction of Trade; International
Financial Statistics; World Economic
Outlook*

International Cocoa Organisation,
Quarterly Bulletin of Cocoa Statistics

International Civil Aviation Organisation,
Civil Aviation Statistics of the World

International Coffee Organisation

International Cotton Advisory Committee,
Bulletin

International Criminal Police
Organisation (Interpol), *International
Crime Statistics*

International Finance Corporation,
Emerging Stock Markets Factbook

International Road Federation, *World
Road Statistics*

International Rubber Study Group,
Rubber Statistical Bulletin

International Federation of the
Phonographic Industry

International Grains Council, *The Grain
Market Report*

International Sugar Organisation, *Sugar
Yearbook*

International Tea Committee, *Annual
Bulletin of Statistics*

International Wool Textile Organisation

ISTA Mielke, *Oil World*

Lloyd's Register, *Statistical Tables*

Network Wizards

Nobel Foundation

OECD, *Development Assistance
Committee Report; Environmental Data*

Swiss Re, *sigma*

Taiwan Statistical Data Book

The Times, *Atlas of the World*

Time Inc Magazines, *Fortune International*

UK Home Office

UN, *Energy Statistics Yearbook; State of
World Population Report; Statistical
Chart on World Families; Urban
Agglomerations; World Population;
World Population Prospects*

UN Development Programme, *Human
Development Report*

UNESCO, website: unescostat.
unesco.org

UNICEF, *The State of the World's
Children Report*

Union International des Chemins de Fer,
*Statistiques Internationales des
Chemins de Fer*

US Department of Agriculture, *Rice
Report*

University of Michigan, Windows to the
Universe website

WHO, *Weekly Epidemiological Record;
World Health Report; World Health
Statistics Annual*

World Bank, *Global Development
Finance; World Development
Indicators; World Development Report*

World Bureau of Metal Statistics, *World
Metal Statistics*

World Drink Trends in association with
NTC Publications

World Resources Institute, *World
Resources*

World Tourist Organisation, *Yearbook of
Tourism Statistics*

World Trade Organisation, *Annual Report*

ICELAND

NORWAY
SWEDEN
ESTONIA
FINLA
LATV
LITHUANIA

IRELAND
DENMARK
U. K.
NETH
BELG
LUX.
GERMANY
POLAND
CZECH
SLOV
FRANCE
SWITZ
AUSTRIA
HUNGARY
SLOV
CRO
BOS
SER
R
PORTUGAL
ITALY
MON
MA
SPAIN
ALB
G

CANADA

UNITED STATES

BERMUDA

MOROCCO

BAHAMAS

MEXICO
CUBA
DOM. REP.
WESTERN
SAHARA
ALGER

BEL
JAM
HAITI
P. RICO

GUATEMALA
HOND
BARBADOS
MAURITANIA
MALI

EL SALVADOR
NICARAGUA
SENEGAL

COSTA RICA
TRINIDAD & TOBAGO
GAMBIA
GUINEA
BURK. F.

PANAMA
VENEZUELA
SURINAME
GUINEA-BISSAU
GHANA

COLOMBIA
GUY
FRENCH GUIANA
SIERRA LEONE
LIBERIA
TOGO

ECUADOR
CÔTE D'IVOIRE
BENIN

PERU
BRAZIL

BOLIVIA

CHILE
PARAGUAY

URUGUAY

ARGENTINA